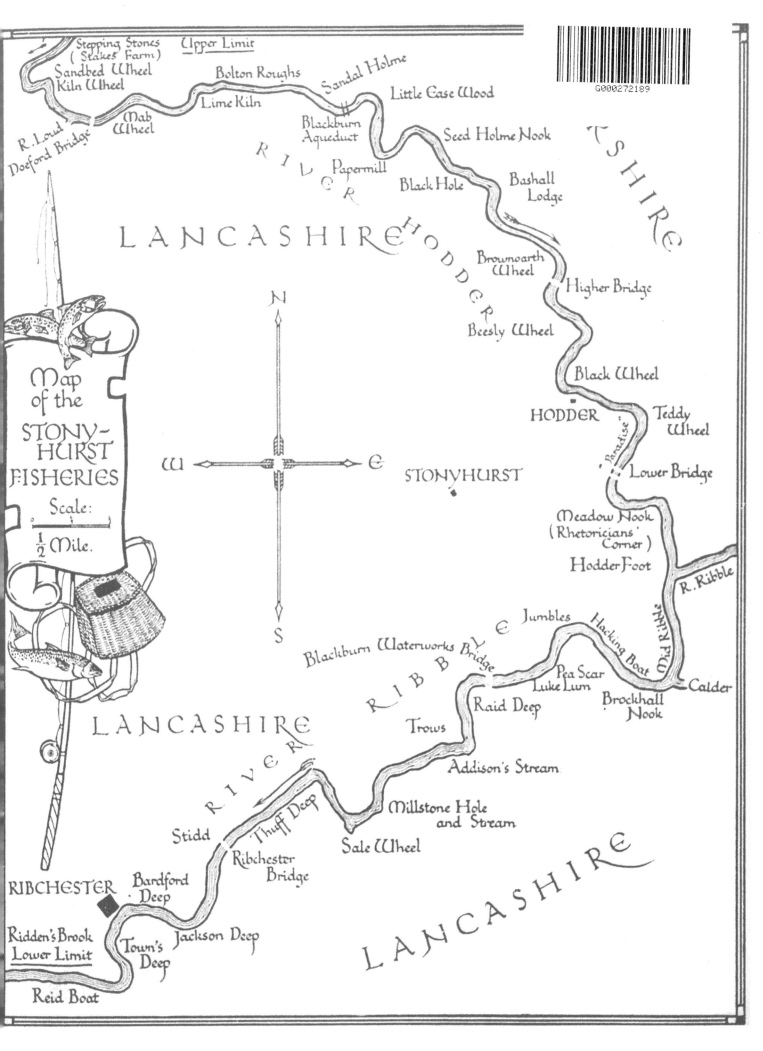

Map
of the
STONY-
HURST
FISHERIES

Scale:

½ Mile.

N

W ◄———► E

S

LANCASHIRE

LANCASHIRE

LANCASHIRE

...TSHIRE

RIVER HODDER

RIVER RIBBLE

River Ribble

STONYHURST

HODDER

RIBCHESTER

Stepping Stones
(Stakes Farm)
Upper Limit
Sandbed Wheel
Kiln Wheel
Bolton Roughs
Sandal Holme
Little Ease Wood
Lime Kiln
Mab Wheel
R. Loud
Doeford Bridge
Blackburn Aqueduct
Papermill
Seed Holme Nook
Black Hole
Bashall Lodge
Brownoarth Wheel
Higher Bridge
Beesly Wheel
Black Wheel
Teddy Wheel
Paradise
Lower Bridge
Meadow Nook
(Rhetoricians' Corner)
Hodder Foot
R. Ribble
Jumbles
Hacking Boat
Pea Scar
Luke Lum
Brockhall Nook
Calder
Blackburn Waterworks Bridge
Raid Deep
Trows
Addison's Stream
Millstone Hole and Stream
Sale Wheel
Stidd
Thuff Deep
Ribchester Bridge
Bardford Deep
Jackson Deep
Ridden's Brook
Lower Limit
Town's Deep
Reid Boat

STONYHURST

AMDG

STONYHURST

T E MUIR

ST OMERS PRESS

First published 1992 under the title *Stonyhurst College 1593–1993*
This revised edition published 2006
© 2006 Stonyhurst College

ISBN 0-9553592-0-1

CIP data for this title are available from the British Library.

The reference in Chapter 1 to 'The English Deborah' comes from C Haigh's *Elizabeth I*
(Longmans 1988). *Protestant Island* is the title of a work by A Bryant (Collins 1967) and
the term 'Sterile Interlude' was used by G R Elton to sum up the reign of
Mary Tudor in *England under the Tudors* (Methuen 1955).
Other works directly referred to or quoted from are listed in the Select Bibliography at the end.

Endpapers: The River Ribble and Stonyhurst fisheries, and a ground plan of Stonyhurst, *c*.1900,
drawn by Raymund L Binns OS for the endpapers of *Stonyhurst*, by Joseph Keating SJ (1909).

Frontispiece: *View of Stonyhurst from Dog Kennel Field, c.1840*. Artist unknown.

The publishers are grateful to the following for permission to reproduce illustrations:
L'Osservatore Romano (p. 172); National Portrait Gallery (p. 191).

Printed in Singapore by Imago Publishing Ltd.

Published by
St Omers Press
3–9 Cripps Road, Cirencester, Gloucestershire GL7 1HN

CONTENTS

FOREWORD

WHEN 'TOM MUIR'S BOOK', as it has come to be known, was first published in 1992, it not surprisingly created a great deal of interest. The limited edition rapidly sold out and in recent years the second-hand book market as a source has all but dried up. I am delighted that this long awaited second edition provides the opportunity to bring the story of Stonyhurst up to date.

The second edition includes revisions, corrections and new material by Tom Muir, together with a new chapter by David Knight and Mark Leslie, which covers the years since Stonyhurst celebrated its 400th anniversary. 'Into the Millennium' gives an account of how Stonyhurst has addressed the challenges of the last decade, transforming itself into a school well placed to meet the demands of an increasingly competitive education market, while staying true to the firmly held Jesuit ethos on which it was founded.

It is most appropriate that this publication is in the year in which we celebrate three great Jesuit anniversaries: the 500th anniversary of the birth of St Francis Xavier; the 450th anniversary of the death of St Ignatius Loyola; and the 500th anniversary of the birth of Blessed Peter Favre. At Easter these were marked by a Stonyhurst family pilgrimage to Rome including a walking pilgrimage from Orvieto, in which more than 200 OS, parents, staff and pupils took part and some 90 walked. It was a great honour for them all to have been present at the Papal audience in St Peter's Basilica when Stonyhurst was given a special mention by Pope Benedict, a moment that will be remembered for many years to come.

Adrian Aylward
June 2006

Foreword to the First Edition

The history of the College, at Stonyhurst since 1794 and on the Continent from 1593, is naturally of interest to all those associated with it, but this history will appeal also to a wider readership: to those involved in Jesuit education in any part of the world, since Stonyhurst is only part of a universal network; to those who wish to explore an important avenue in the development of the Catholic community in this country; to those concerned with the history of education. For all these and for others who simply want a good book to read Mr Tom Muir has provided a stimulating service.

Most Jesuit colleges were founded in or near city centres – Glasgow, New York, Madrid, Sydney – and are primarily day schools. Stonyhurst's origins in urban St Omer partly follow that tradition but circumstances required that it be a boarding school. The move to Stonyhurst came at the beginning of more tolerant times but the rural location suited well the Catholic families who in penal times had had to concentrate religious and educational resources in a few centres in an unobtrusive way. The College, though thoroughly English, began in detachment from the mainstream of national life, almost as a counter force to it, and then gradually over centuries found itself able to open out to the wider society. The history of Stonyhurst is in this respect a microcosm of the post-Reformation history of the Catholic Church in England and Wales.

Are there characteristics which remain essentially the same over 400 years in the College? There are persistent ideals demanding implementation; that nothing can be taught in an ethical vacuum; that education is an apostolate serving families; that the school should foster a strong sense of community; that pupils must always be valued and treated as individuals and every teacher should be a mentor in and out of the classroom; that those who are educated in the College should be taught how to think, not simply what to think, and they should, beginning at school and then through later life, think, judge and act for the good of others and, as the Jesuit motto has it, 'for the greater glory of God'. These ideals are brought out well in this book. So too is Jesuit detachment or basic flexibility; with regard to seizing new educational ideas and using them to serve time-honoured ideals, with regard to recruitment, internal arrangements and even, most fundamentally, with regard to moving location. Such flexibility and openness to the signs of the times are as necessary now as ever.

It is hoped that the natural and artistic beauty which is a distinctive mark of Stonyhurst is brought out in the photographs.

Stonyhurst is most fortunate in having as its Centenaries historian Mr Tom Muir. I warmly commend his work to all readers.

Giles Mercer
June 1992

ACKNOWLEDGEMENTS

THIS BOOK would not have been possible without the help of my many friends and colleagues. In particular I would like to thank the Headmaster and Governing Body for giving me the chance to write the book and for the constant support and encouragement they gave at every stage of its progress. Next it is only right to recognise the contribution made by Fr Frederick Turner SJ and Fr Geoffrey Holt SJ. Without their unstinting kindness and understanding I would never have mastered the archival material here or at Farm Street. I am also grateful for the meticulous attention to detail and the many helpful suggestions made by Fr Michael O'Halloran SJ, Dr Giles Mercer and John Trappes-Lomax in the course of reading through the whole text. In addition Fr George Earle SJ, Fr Michael Bossy SJ, Fr Edward Ennis SJ and Laurence Muskett played a key role in identifying the principal themes delineated in the final chapter. Similarly, in the section dealing with the Observatory I depended heavily on assistance given by Fintan O'Reilly. Many others generously supplied me with data, hints and advice about notable Old Boys. I cannot say I have always followed their counsel, for the drafting of such a list inevitably involves making some rather subjective judgements; but the end product, whatever its deficiencies, would have been poorer without it.

The illustrations and artwork, which constitute an integral part of this book, admirably reflect the vision of Hamish MacGibbon. Alex Ramsay worked with amazing speed and energy to produce the splendid set of new photographs as well as copy dozens of older pictures scrounged from various parts of the school. Here I am indebted to Peter Hardwick for letting me rummage freely through *The Stonyhurst Magazine* office and to David Knight for putting aside time to draw the map in Chapter V. To them and countless others I cannot say anything except 'Thank You'. Any mistakes that remain are mine.

T E Muir

Acknowledgements for the Second Edition

First, I would like to thank the Governors, Headmaster and Bursar for giving me the opportunity to revise and update this volume. Next, it is only right that I acknowledge the enthusiastic and unstinting contribution made by Mark Leslie, the Development Director, in collaboration with Anthony Eyre OS of the St Omers Press and Andrew

Mather. Together they have seen the project through all its various stages dealing with such mundane but vital matters as proofreading, the index, general layout, graphics and photographic illustrations. In this context I am grateful for the help given by my friend David Knight, the College archivist and editor of *The Stonyhurst Magazine*. It is he who, with assistance from Adrian Aylward, John Hartley OS and Mark Leslie, has been the author and guiding spirit behind the new final chapter 'Into the Millennium'; he has rooted out many largely forgotten photographs and illustrations from the archives, picked me up on countless points of editorial detail and coped with my periodic incursions into the House Libraries. Indeed, it has been largely through his efforts and those of Jan Graffius, Curator of the College Collections, that so much detailed knowledge has been added to our understanding of Stonyhurst history over the last ten years. This applies not just to the written record, but to the wealth of additional artifacts and pictures that have been recovered, restored and copied. For access to materials in the Music Department I am indebted to Robin Highcock, Gregory Mann and Kevin Morgan. I also benefited greatly from the information and insights given to me by Anthony John. In addition many OS sent me snippets of information and corrections after the first publication of this book. To them and countless others, once again, I cannot say anything except 'Thank You'.

T E Muir

INTRODUCTION

WHEN FR PERSONS founded his College at St Omer, now in north-eastern France, he produced something exciting and new. From the start this foundation, the ancestor of Stonyhurst, quickly became one of the most prestigious (or notorious) English Catholic schools in Europe. Its powers of survival proved quite remarkable – bouncing back from the effects of wars, two fires, penal legislation, and no less than three migrations. In 1762, threatened with sequestration, the College escaped to Bruges; in 1773 it was violently suppressed, only to reappear as the Academy at Liège; finally, menaced by French invasion, it fled to England. There, contrary to all expectations, it struck root and prospered. Continental in origin, English in character, tenacious in purpose but innovative in method, Stonyhurst presents a startling tension of opposites. Add to that a bewildering diversity of personalities – no wonder you get a school whose influence has been out of all proportion to its size.

The history of the College is closely entwined with that of the Society of Jesus. Traditionally, prejudice against Jesuits was strong, phrases like 'the end justifies the means' springing readily to mind; but whatever we may now think of them, one cannot deny their role in the preservation of English Catholicism, often in the teeth of vicious persecution. In penal times the College educated a large proportion of the Catholic nobility and gentry; they in turn provided the safe houses from which priests, often themselves recruited from St Omers, could work. During the nineteenth century the emphasis shifted. From 1773 to 1829 the College had been the main link between the suppression and restoration of the English Jesuits; then, from its re-establishment at Stonyhurst until the opening of Farm Street in 1849, it was the *de facto* headquarters of the English Province. Here, and for long after, new generations of Jesuits were recruited, trained and sent out to found schools, parishes and missions all over Victoria's empire. Their labours helped create what is the largest single denomination in the country.

Naturally, these activities did not pass unnoticed by the Protestant establishment. In penal times, fired by the spirit of 'No Popery', the tendency was to panic. In the seventeenth century especially, waves of religious hysteria periodically swept the country – often with serious political effects. The Popish Plot, in which St Omers became embroiled, is one example. No matter how implausible the evidence, staunch Protestants could be stampeded all too easily into believing the most fantastic claims. Jesuits were 'known' to be fanatical, cunning, untrustworthy and cruel. Were they not the agents of the Antichrist, accustomed at 'divers times in these their vaults underground, to make the Devil very fine sport,' as James Wadsworth, himself a St

Omers renegade, quaintly put it? With such an atmosphere it is not surprising that the College, along with all other Catholics, was 'sent to Coventry'. This isolation, symbolised by its Continental location, produced some curious effects. Like primitive organisms trapped in a lost world, many Tudor sports and customs survived at Stonyhurst right into the twentieth century.

But with toleration everything changed. Hitherto a frightened introverted minority, Catholics became more flexible and outward looking as they rejoined the social mainstream. The College illustrates this transformation in microcosm. The crowning glory of St Omers had been its fifteen martyrs; twentieth-century Stonyhurst is celebrated for its seven VCs, symbolically uniting the Jesuit and Public School ideals of service.

Of course this created problems. How do you advance without jettisoning something from the past? Jesuit educational methods arouse ambivalent feelings – not least among Jesuits themselves. For example Fr Turner, Stonyhurst's first officially designated headmaster, simply declared: 'Jesuit education is education by Jesuits'. In other words Ignatian spirituality, not pedagogic technique, is what matters. Yet they were great educationalists, with results that can still be seen today. The 'Ratio Studiorum' synthesised all that was best in medieval and Renaissance education. A comprehensive programme of tests, examinations, Concertatios and Academies – the Jesuits are said to have invented marks – kept 'Mr Average' up to scratch. More radical still was their approach to free time. Until the 1870s most teachers just did not accept the modern principle that boys should be supervised 24 hours a day. St Omers confronted that problem head on. The Playroom system, developed from first principles, is therefore a real alternative to the 'traditional' but in fact younger House system.

This is most effectively expressed by the building – a marvellous agglomeration of different structures. House systems produce a 'scatter' of medium-sized buildings, conjuring up the atmosphere of a village or small suburb. The Playroom system requires every facility to be concentrated under one roof; so Stonyhurst is one enormous pile. This left many practical difficulties; but in solving them the Jesuits carved a niche for themselves in the history of technology. The 1811 gas plant, for instance, was one of the first in the country.

No history of Stonyhurst, then, can be a mere catalogue of events; its impact on Catholic society and education has been too great for that. But, despite pioneer work by Frs Gerard and Chadwick, these themes have scarcely been touched. This was not for lack of resources. Jesuits are great record-keepers, and the archives are stuffed with documentation of every kind, showing us what really made the school 'tick'. However, they do have their limitations. *The Stonyhurst Magazine*, an excellent source, is first and foremost a celebration of the school's achievements; the Minister's Journal and First Prefect's Log may help us get behind the façade, but their primary purpose was to register the duties, routines and privileges negotiated between the Rector and his subordinates. Interpreting school numbers presents real problems; for until the 1950s the College included pupils from the Preparatory school at Hodder and Gentlemen Philosophers, who were of university age, in the general total. There was also a tendency to move up boys from Hodder to the main building as and when vacancies became available. Yet such sources do reveal one great truth. People often imagine that a school's history revolves around its headmasters. At Stonyhurst this was not so. Certainly there has been leadership; but it was always exercised in a context defined by the Society, parents, teachers and pupils; and it is the interplay between these forces, shaping the mental, physical and organisational imperatives within which they operate, that gives dynamism to the whole.

FOUNDATION

The Political and Religious Background

TRADITIONALLY, it has been argued that the English Reformation began when Henry VIII decided to take a new wife. He needed a son; but despite repeated pregnancies, Catherine of Aragon had only produced a daughter; and waiting in the wings was the beautiful, sophisticated and masterful Anne Boleyn – far too great a temptation for that 'proud and ill-disciplined monarch', as Fr Henry More, a later Rector of St Omers, called him. Frustrated by Rome Henry unleashed the pent-up anticlericalism of Parliament. Before the onslaught the English Church proved unexpectedly weak; so it was not difficult for Henry, guided by the political craft of Thomas Cromwell, to break with Rome, declare himself head of the Church, and take the first steps towards a Protestant Reformation.

During the minority of his son Edward VI the work continued; the Dissolution of the Monasteries carried out under Henry being complemented by the seizure of chantry properties and a general despoliation of episcopal lands. More positively the liturgical genius of Thomas Cranmer produced the First and Second Prayer Books. By contrast the reign of Mary Tudor has been described as a 'sterile interlude': a short pause in the steady march towards a fully-fledged Anglican Church. She was half-Spanish, unimaginatively reactionary, and the burning of 300 heretics thoroughly alienated the public. Her death in 1558 left the way clear for the triumphant completion of the work under an 'English Deborah' – Elizabeth I. The Acts of Supremacy and Uniformity re-imposed the Royal Supremacy, restored – with minor modifications – the Second Prayer Book, and laid the foundations of a moderate broad-based Anglican Church. Nearly 30 years later the defeat of the Spanish Armada seemed to affirm England's manifest destiny as a 'Protestant Island'.

Such is the tale, told and retold down the ages to generations of schoolchildren; and until recently its pervasive power silenced the doubters. But it is flawed; not least because it was produced by the victors. To understand fully why St Omers was founded the background needs to be re-examined in detail and important modifications made.

First, the assumption that the medieval Church was weak, that it was rotten to the core, can no longer be sustained. Certainly it had its faults; but you simply cannot uproot a thousand years of accumulated tradition overnight. Besides, in the half-century before the Reformation it showed plenty of vigour. We should never forget that many of the critics came from its own ranks; and if monasticism

The Assertio Septem Sacramentorum *by Henry VIII. First edition printed by Pynson, London, 1521.*

Relic of the Holy Thorn, brought back to France by St Louis and later the property of Mary Queen of Scots. She gave it to Thomas Percy, Earl of Northumberland, who was executed for his part in the Rising of the North. In turn his daughter Elizabeth handed it over to Fr John Gerard who sent it overseas for safekeeping. From St Omers it went to Bruges and there, at the time of the Suppression, it fell into the hands of the local authorities. However Thomas Weld persuaded them to part with it and in 1803 it was restored to the College.

was in decline (itself a somewhat dubious proposition) this was more than compensated by the spread of chantry chapels and a spate of church building, especially at parish level. 'Where your wealth is, there will your heart be also' aptly sums up the argument. Contrary to popular legend the quality of the parish clergy was actually improving; and the same is true with Church Courts. Of course they could be an irritant, but many of the attacks against them were just sour grapes from jealous common lawyers. Often their services were cheaper and more efficient. And even if we do accept that many clergy were ignorant and superstitious, long ago Professor A. G. Dickens showed that they were well attuned to the spiritual needs of a semi-literate peasantry. It is not surprising then to find them in the forefront of a deep-seated protest against change. The Pilgrimage of Grace came within an ace of toppling Henry VIII; and the Prayer Book Rebellion of 1549, when combined with other rather different risings elsewhere, proved highly dangerous. At the centre of power there is a similar picture. Thomas More and John Fisher were not alone. Convocation put up strong resistance to Henry's demands in 1531; there was a strong 'Catholic' party in both Houses of Parliament; while at Court groups led by Carew, Gardiner, Courtenay and the Duke of Norfolk overthrew Anne Boleyn, engineered the execution of Thomas Cromwell, and came near to reversing the political tide in the 1540s. Given these facts it is unlikely that Henry's Reformation would have succeeded had people understood at the start the full implications of his actions.

Second, at long last it is now coming to be recognised that Mary's counterattack, far from being doomed to failure, stood a good chance of success. In 1553, when she came to the throne, Protestantism was utterly discredited. It was associated with greed, vandalism, rebellion and social anarchy. Even its most notable spokesmen felt betrayed by the way monastic and chantry property, which should have been put to new religious, educational and social purposes, had gone instead into the pockets of the Council, nobility and gentry or else been frittered away in futile wars against France and Scotland. It is significant that Wyatt's rebellion of 1554 only took off in Kent and was fuelled not by Protestant fervour but by a xenophobic reaction against Mary's marriage to Philip II. Despite tough resistance within Parliament – mainly caused by court faction squabbles and fears that monastic lands would have to be restored – all the Henrician and Edwardian legislation was reversed and the clock put back to 1529. Alongside the negative policy of persecution, which might have succeeded given more time and greater skill, stood a positive programme of renewal. For instance, in 1555 Cardinal Pole's Synod at Westminster commissioned a Catholic translation of the New Testament, a book of homilies and a catechism. Seminaries supported by 'feeder' schools were planned for every diocese, and there was a drive to raise the value of Church endowments. In this way the causes of clerical inefficiency and corruption would be rooted out. At the other end efforts were made to improve the universities. For instance, Thomas Pope and Thomas White founded Trinity College and St John's College in Oxford; and many of the most notable early English Jesuits, including Frs Persons and Campion, received their first theological training at Oxford. When Elizabeth tried to purge them there was a massive 'brain drain' of some 3,000 academics to the Continent.

Similarly, despite considerable lay apathy, a good start was made to the restoration of monastic and religious life. People often say that the response here was apathetic. Now it is true that Pole rejected the Society's offer of help; but the Jesuits were so overstretched that they probably did not have enough manpower

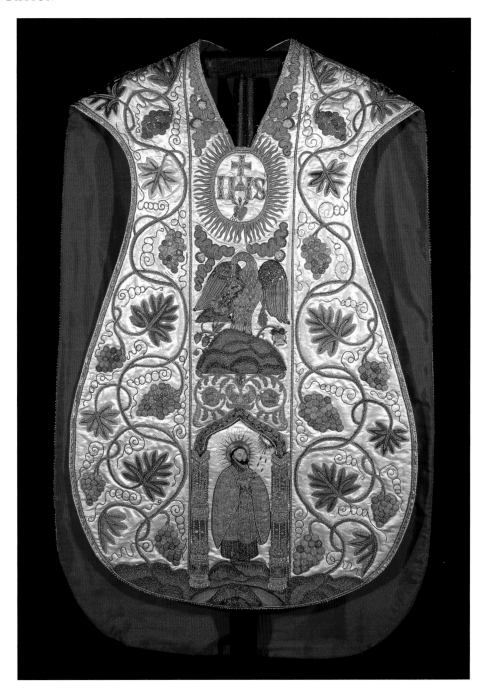

Right: *the St Ignatius Vestments, purchased by Fr Norris SJ in 1835 when he was Provincial.*

Above: *Our Lady with the Holy Child in a detail from the back of the vestments.*

anyway. The real problem was lack of time. Mary reigned for only five years while Pole was Archbishop of Canterbury for just three. Time and money are needed to found monasteries. In this, as in other respects, what is remarkable is not how little but how much was achieved.

The result was that Elizabeth faced stiff religious resistance. Almost to a man the surviving Catholic bishops preferred to be deprived rather than co-operate; in his book *Faith by Statute* Dr Norman Jones has shown that the Acts of Supremacy and Uniformity met substantial opposition in Parliament; and further afield we can see the tremendous power wielded by the conservative nobility in the regions. In the North the Percy, Darcy, Dacre and Stanley families formed a powerful block;

The Henry VII Cope, sole survivor of a set of 29 produced in Florence and left to Westminster Abbey in that King's will. In 1520 his son borrowed them to enhance his 'Field of the Cloth of Gold'. The cope, along with other vestments, was lovingly restored by the master tailor, Brother James Houghton, between 1826 and 1876.

in East Anglia and Sussex Catholics could look to the nominally Protestant fourth Duke of Norfolk; while in Hampshire Elizabeth's first Treasurer, Lord Paulet, exerted substantial influence. This group had power at Court; and under their umbrella Marian priests, whose importance as a link with recusant times has only recently been appreciated, could continue to operate. Elizabeth's moderation and the hope that Catholicism would wither away were not the only reasons why the Government trod cautiously in the 1560s; it was simply too dangerous. It was only after 1569, when the power of the conservatives had been broken after the Rising of the North, that a determined effort could be made to make Catholics conform.

For the truth is that the Elizabethan Reformation was the work of a small committed clique of radicals led by William Cecil, Lord Burghley. Although Elizabeth herself may not have wanted 'to open windows into men's souls' they could and did try to force her hand. Now Cecil has often been seen as the epitome of moderation; but this depends on how the term is used. In comparison with Protestant independents like Brownists and Barrowists he does indeed seem to be no more than a convinced Protestant; but, when set against a spectrum that includes Catholics, he looks much more extreme. Although cautious in stating his views, during Edward's reign he was associated with those calling for a Zwinglian prayer book and denying the doctrine of the Real Presence. Under Elizabeth many of his friends and clients had a Calvinist turn of mind. Such people automatically assumed that the Pope was the Antichrist, that Jesuits were his devilish agents and that most Catholics were predestined to be damned. And if Cecil really was a moderate who subordinated religion to politics then it is difficult to explain his actions at the beginning of the reign. In 1559 the vast majority of people were at least nominally Catholic; even by 1603 Catholics probably still counted for about a third of the population. Surely the obvious move was to make a moderately Catholic settlement? Instead Cecil was the prime mover in the campaign to force the Acts of Supremacy and Uniformity through Parliament; and we know that in subsequent assemblies the 'Puritan Choir', who pushed for yet more radical legislation, were his men of business.

The result was a policy that alienated Catholics and encouraged opposition. In 1568, to replace the ageing Marian priests, William, later Cardinal Allen, founded a seminary at Douai. In 1577 a hospice in Rome dating from Anglo-Saxon times was converted into the English College and from 1579 run under Jesuit management. Finally, 1581 saw Frs Persons and Campion initiate the first Jesuit

Above: *The Pentecost Chasuble, One of the Wintour Vestments, sewn by Helen Wintour (d. 1671). Another, 'Alleluia', dates to 1655. In 1853 they were presented by Fr Henry Campbell SJ to Stonyhurst.*

Above left: *Detail from the back of the vestments.*

mission to England. In these circumstances, as persecution steadily mounted, more and more Catholics had to choose, though some like Sir Richard Shireburn at Stonyhurst managed to postpone the day of reckoning till the early 1590s. In effect government action, instead of fudging the issue, simply uncovered more recusants, or Catholics who refused to attend Protestant services. This gave the frightening impression that, thanks to the efforts of Jesuits and Seminary Priests, their number was actually rising. Moreover, Councillors could use the data to frighten Elizabeth into yet sterner measures. Thus Catholicism was converted from a religious into a political problem and presented as such in official propaganda. Especially alarming was the possibility that Catholics, fortified by the bull *Regnans in Excelsis* of 1570, might become a dangerous fifth column. Yet, in a way the government had only itself to blame. For most of the century Spain had been England's main ally against France and Scotland. Despite the Reformation this could have been maintained. Absorbed in a war with the Turk Philip needed a friendly England to maintain communications with his isolated and increasingly restive subjects in The Netherlands; he was terrified by the prospect that a Guise-controlled Mary Stuart might successfully assert her claim to the English throne and bring the whole of the British Isles under French domination. He therefore pressurised the Pope to refrain from issuing a bull of excommunication. But England responded with a series of highly provocative acts. In 1568 Cecil organised the seizure of four Spanish ships loaded with pay for Alva's army in The Netherlands; Drake raided the Spanish Main; and in 1585, after years of covert aid, Elizabeth deployed a whole army in support of the Dutch rebels. This could not be ignored. Under the influence of Catholic zealots Philip had already participated in at least four plots against Elizabeth. All of them involved that most dangerous combination – English recusants, Spanish troops and the French Catholic League behind the figurehead of Mary Stuart. Now Spain resolved on open war.

The picture then is not of a strong broad-based regime that could count on the support of most of the nation; instead we must substitute the image of a government precariously presiding over a highly unstable domestic situation confronted by war with a mighty superpower. No wonder that, even after the defeat of the Armada, the response could only be more persecution. On 29 November

These relics, closely associated with St Thomas More, were left by his Jesuit name-sake, the last of the family, and his sister, a Mrs Dalton. The 'Sodality' Crucifix, pre-sented to the St Omers Sodality in 1755, once contained a relic of St Thomas the Apostle.

1591 the first broadside of a new campaign was fired. A royal proclamation declared that another Spanish invasion was being planned at the instigation of Cardinal Allen and Fr Persons. Over Christmas three priests and four laymen were put to death. Next year 'Cecilian Inquisitions' were conducted in every shire; and about the same time the Exchequer completed its reorganisation of the machinery for collecting recusant fines. Special attention was paid to Lancashire where the Stanleys, after escaping involvement in the Rising of the North, ran the county through a successful working compromise with Church Papists (or Catholics who occasionally attended Anglican services) such as Sir Richard Shireburn. Now Cecil took advantage of their involvement in Hesketh's Plot to undermine their power. Simultaneously, local Puritan groups were encouraged to demand stronger measures in this heartland of Catholicism, provoking several dangerous disturbances. Finally, when Parliament met in 1593, two bills were promoted: In the Lords an Act for Restraining Popish Recusants to Some Certain Place of Abode and, in the Commons, an Act for Reducing Disloyal Subjects to Their Due Obedience. The latter contained the following vital item:

> Clause VI: Children of recusants above seven years of age are to be committed to others to be educated; and they are to be kept and maintained at the third part left unto the recusant parent, the committing of them to be due either by Council Ordinary or Justices of Assizes.

That Cecil was behind the bill there can be no doubt. When it 'fell asleep' in committee at a conference with the Lords on 30 March he announced that the Upper House would introduce a similar measure, which his political ally Thomas Heneage and son Robert Cecil urged the Commons to support. We also know that such a scheme had long been in his mind. The Somers Tracts contain a position paper of 1583 entitled 'Lord Burghley's Advice to the Queen in Matters of Religion' advocating just such a separation of Catholic children from their parents adding 'by this means, you shall under colour of education, have them as hostages of their parents' fidelities, that have power in England, and by this their number will be quickly lessened'.

Fr Persons's reaction was immediate. At an audience with Philip II he obtained a grant worth 1,920 crowns a year to found a school for 16 boys at St Omer. But it is clear that he had been considering such a scheme for some time before. The bill was first read on 7 March and Philip's patent is dated 13 March; but, given the slowness of communications and the clumsy routines of the Spanish bureaucracy this seems far too quick. Fr Persons must have known about the Government's intentions beforehand. A letter from him to the Jesuit General Claudio Aquaviva hints that the idea may have been put forward in February; and if we go further back, Fr Cresswell's answer to the 1591 proclamation suggests that many suspected that just such a bill would be introduced. Nor is this surprising when set against the general background. From the beginning the Government had tried to regulate and control the education system. The Oath of Allegiance specified by the 1559 Act of Supremacy had to be taken by 'all and every other person which shall be promoted to a degree of learning in any university within this your realm or dominion'; the Act for the Assurance of the Queen's Majesty's Royal Power extended this to all schoolmasters; the 1581 Act to Retain the Queen's Majesty's Subjects to Their Due Obedience specified a year's imprisonment for teachers absent from Church on Sundays and imposed a fine of £10 a month on those who kept Catholic tutors; while clause V of the Act against Jesuits and

Fr Robert Persons SJ, founder of St Omers College, from a contemporary drawing.

Seminary Priests prohibited children from being sent overseas without special licence – penalty, a £100 fine.

This legislation was supported by a sporadic but intensifying campaign on the ground. The evidence for this supplied by J Simon and A Beales is detailed and impressive. The Government maintained the episcopal prerogative of issuing licences to teach first introduced by Cardinal Pole in 1557; in 1562 the Court of High Commission received the power to amend all school statutes; and a systematic programme of visitations and inspections purged and reorganised schools and universities. Nor was the programme entirely negative. Members of the Government were prominent in the foundation and reorganisation of grammar schools. The hope was that they would provide a new generation of Protestant gentry – hence their stress on religious education. Alexander Nowell's catechism became a standard text, and in many schools pupils had to attend and make notes on the Sunday sermons. The threat this posed to Catholicism

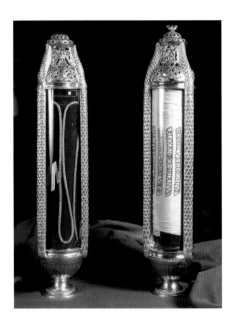

Two reliquaries, one containing the rope that bound St Edmund Campion to the hurdle at the time of his execution, the other a corporal used by five English martyrs in the Tower of London between 1581 and 1583.

is clear when we hear that two of Sir Richard Shireburn's children attended just such an establishment – Bishop Pilkington's foundation at Rivington – in 1575–6. Nor did the Government stop there. When parents proved uncooperative there had already been instances where the authorities had forcibly tried to separate children from their families and send them to Protestant schools.

It is no surprise, then, to find Fr Persons involved in educational schemes long before 1593. Born at Nether Stowey, Somerset in 1546, he had been educated at Stogursey and Taunton before going on to become Bursar and Fellow at Balliol. Forced out of Oxford in 1575 he travelled to Italy intending to study medicine. Instead, while stopping at Louvain, under the influence of Fr William Good he decided to join the Society. After a year in the Noviciate of Sant Andrea he read his theology at the Roman College and was ordained in 1578. While at the Roman College he became involved in the 'Broyles' between English students and their Welsh Rector Dr Owen Lewis – events that led to the 'take-over' of that institution by the Society in 1579. In 1581 he organised and led the first Jesuit Mission to England; but, after the arrest and execution of his companion Edmund Campion, he retired – temporarily as he thought – to Rouen. There, under Guise protection, he busied himself with a variety of projects: organising a printing press, writing his *Christian Directory* – a best seller that ran to 46 Protestant and eight Catholic editions before 1641 – and setting up clandestine routes in and out of England for books and priests. He even planned to convert James VI of Scotland, if necessary after forcible abduction, and then use his kingdom as a springboard for invading England. Among these schemes was the establishment in 1582 of a small preparatory school at Eu. Early in 1579 Fr Claude Matthieu had been negotiating with Henry, Duke of Guise to set up a Jesuit College there. Guise assigned the Hôpital Normand; but, when this proved to be unsuitable, on 9 July 1581 Fr Matthieu obtained leave to erect new facilities in the adjoining garden. The Duke was therefore able to offer Fr Persons the vacant building, supported by a yearly pension of £100. The plan was for the boys, numbering 30 by 1584, to lodge there under the supervision of Fr Chambers, an elderly secular priest, and attend classes in the French Jesuit college near by.

Now, in the past these events have been seen as the first steps towards the foundation of St Omers. However, Eu was intended to 'feed' the Douai Seminary that had recently been moved to Rheims, though some boys were also sent to Jesuit colleges at Verdun and Pont à Mousson. Unfortunately, the school ran into difficulties. In December 1588 the assassination of Henry of Guise deprived it of his protection and financial support, while the revenge killing of Henry III the following year led to an escalation in the French Religious Wars. Fr Persons responded by appealing to Philip II; and in 1589 he secured a grant of 3,000 crowns for the Rheims Seminary, 500 of which were earmarked for Eu. Unfortunately, in September Henry IV captured Dieppe and, with the arrival there of an English squadron, the area became highly unsafe. So, from November 1590, the boys were gradually withdrawn in stages, the last reaching Rheims on 1 February 1592.

It was this situation that led to the suggestion that a new preparatory school be opened at St Omer. Accordingly Dr Barrett, the President at Rheims, made no less than three petitions to its magistrates. The last, backed by a letter from the local bishop (both were dated 18 September 1592), envisaged a school for 12 to 15 boys housed opposite the Jesuit Walloon College and attending its classes. But, although successful, the petition was not followed up, for at this time the Rheims

Seminary was being transferred back to Douai. Since Douai already possessed a Jesuit college, there was no need for a separate establishment at St Omer and no boy from Eu went there. The English Jesuit College at St Omer then was not a continuation of the Eu foundation; in fact it was intended to meet quite a different situation. We have seen how the proposed legislation of 1593 had stung Fr Persons into action; and it is also pertinent to note how, in the interval between 1582 and 1593, he himself had changed. Compared with his other schemes, Eu had been a minor sideshow; and he still hoped to return to England. But Professor John Bossy has shown that by 1586 Aquaviva had convinced him that quiet missionary work was better than glorious martyrdom. In this context his tertianship, or period of study and meditation at Sant Andrea prior to the taking of his final vows in 1597, is especially significant. Persons was now settling down to the long haul of creating a viable English Jesuit Province. His first job was to restore order after a new bout of trouble at the English College. Next, in 1589 and 1592, he established two seminaries at Valladolid and Seville in Spain. His plan was that, while recruits from Douai went on to complete their studies in Rome, St Omers would supply the new seminaries in Spain. It is to the practical details concerning the foundation of this institution that we can now at last turn.

One of a collection of St Edmund Campion's letters still at Stonyhurst. The College also has original MSS by Robert Southwell SJ and others closely associated with the history of English Catholicism.

First Steps

As we have seen, Fr Persons's first step had been to obtain from Philip II an annual grant of 1,920 crowns (approximately £432 in Elizabethan money) for the education of 16 pupils. According to Fr Flack, the first Spiritual Father, he chose St Omer because 'no part thereof liked him better than the Low Countries in regard to their nearness to England and ayr most like unto the ayr of an English climate: especially France being in garboiles and the jarres between the two crowns being like frequently to hinder theire passing out of one King's dominion to another' (This is a reference to the French Religious Wars, in which Spain took an active part). All other suggestions, notably Douai and Courtrai, were met with the reply that this was the express wish of the King. To make the initial preparations Fr William Flack set out from San Lucar in southern Spain on 8 April 1593 with 500 crowns privately raised by Fr Persons. Other staff were supplied by the Gallo-Belgian Provincial, Fr Oliver Manare. To soothe local prejudices, at the suggestion of Fr Persons, a Fleming, Fr Jean Foucart, was made Rector. He was to be supported by Fr Nicholas Smith as Prefect of Studies, Fr Henry Bray as Minister and Fr William Holt agreed to act as the College agent in Brussels. However, while Fr Manare was away at a Jesuit Congregation in Rome, Fr Foucart had to act as Socius, or general counsellor, to Fr Oranus, the Vice-Provincial. Fr Flack, then, was at first left in complete charge.

On his arrival in May he established his headquarters in the Walloon College; and, before long, he had to find accommodation for the first contingent of boys – four Worthingtons and three Rookwoods. His first solution was to send them to local inns; but 'after a while he hired Mr George Persons' corner house from about autumn til Candlemas following for some 14 florins: whither he got Mr Persons himself [brother of Fr Persons] to come from Doway for a time to be their caterer.' By 1 October the number of boys had risen to 19 and, with the arrival of Fr Smith two days later, they may have started to attend classes in the Walloon College opposite. However, it was not until 23 November, the same day that Fr Foucart came, that Frs Smith and Flack took over the management of the 'Maison de Berghes' from its 'caterer'.

These steps were not taken without difficulty. In the first place Dr Barrett, the President of Douai College, did not welcome a competitor; and matters were not helped when Fr Flack had to turn away a dozen boys sent up from Douai because Dr Barrett was short of space. There also seems to have been some confusion in Dr Allen's mind between Dr Barrett's abortive plans for St Omers and the College that eventually emerged. Nor were relations with Fr Oranus without strain. 'He has shown himself colder about this business than anyone I have ever seen in my life,' Fr Persons complained. Then there were the feelings of the English Catholic exiles. Many were destitute because the Spanish pensions on which they depended were in arrears. Now they had the galling sight of money they might have received going to St Omers. English spies had also to be considered. In February 1594 one Simon Knowles, entrusted with letters by Fr Holt for Fr Bray, took them to the English Government instead! Ironically, at the same time the St Omer's magistrates, fearing the presence of an English fifth column, objected to the expansion of the school beyond the 16 boys originally stipulated. The Maison de Berghes, possibly the same building as that hired by Dr Barrett in 1592, proving inadequate, Fr Flack took out a three-year lease at £25 per annum for a house belonging to the Sieur de Croix in the Rue de Dunkerque on 12 December 1593. When it proved unsuitable, he then offered to purchase the Hôtel du Comte de Fressin. This was blocked by the magistrates. Finally, there had been a complete failure to get the Brussels administration to disgorge Philip's pension.

Fr Persons' reaction was characteristic. Philip customarily gave audience to Jesuits about to go on the English Mission; accordingly, when Fr Walpole came to take his leave on 2 November, Fr Persons encouraged him to raise the matter of St Omers. The result was spectacular. Within a month the first warrant for 700 florins (£70) arrived; then, on 20 March 1594, Fr Persons announced to Aquaviva the acquisition of a new grant worth 2,000 gold crowns (about £600) secured against 'the licences and passports at Gravelines or if these be hindered out of more sure licences in the country'. This was confirmed by royal letters patent dated 6 May. Its acknowledgement by the Archduke Ernest, Philip's governor of The Netherlands, on 29 May effectively made it the foundation deed of the College. To expedite matters further, Philip wrote three letters between 29 and 30 July to the Bishop of St Omer, the magistrates and Duke Ernest. On the strength of this the College was able to secure the Hôtel du Comte de Fressin from the Dean of the Chapter, Canon Louis Bersacques, for 7,500 florins (£750). Seisin was granted on 24 October, and by the following February the College had moved into its new quarters. 'This', wrote Fr Flack in 1635, 'is the house and ground which the Seminary now enjoys, containing then the house and Refectory, ye kitchen and Rooms over it, the bake-house Infirmary as it was antiently, and part of the bake-house with the garden: which bargain caus'd much muttering, when it came to be divulged.'

With this purchase the first phase of the foundation was now over. There then followed a period of rapid expansion. In 1594 the Annual Letters mention 33 boys, by 1595 this had risen to 50. A forced removal to Courtrai to avoid the plague left the figure unchanged in 1596–7: but by 1601, with numbers standing at 120, growth had resumed, reaching a peak of 135 in 1610. Thereafter, there was a slight fall, so that by 1621, when the Dutch-Hispanic conflict resumed, there were 121.

One reason for this expansion was the sheer pressure of persecution. This, when combined with the threat of forcible separation from their children, impelled many to take up the offer of an education abroad. As an English priest, writing to Fr Persons on 1 November 1593, said: 'what has gladdened their hearts above all things is the news of the Seminary at St Omers in Flanders for small boys from there: for this will afford a remedy for the greatest evils, and already many of the leading Catholics have determined to send their young sons there in order to set them free from the hands of the heretics.'

Secondly, Douai College, St Omers' main competitor, became infected with the same trouble as that at the English College in Rome following Allen's departure in 1585. This was compounded by subsequent quarrels among English Catholics in the Wisbech Stirs of 1594–5 and the Archpriest Controversy of 1598–1602. Indeed, a report compiled by its Vice-President Fr Worthington and Dr William Percy for Caetano, the Cardinal Protector of England, suggests that this was one of the reasons for the foundation of St Omers in the first place. Nor was the situation helped by the problems attendant on its transfer back to Douai, as letters by Dr Barrett to Fr Persons, Dr Lewis Bishop of Cassano, Cardinal Laetare and Monsignor Malvasia between 1594 and 1596 clearly show.

A third factor was the tremendous boost provided by Fr Giles Schondonch after he had replaced Fr Foucart as Rector on 2 July 1601. A native of Bruges, after joining the Society in 1576, he held several teaching posts before becoming Rector at Cambrai in 1593. As Rector at St Omers he delighted in classical scholarship, music and drama. A master of public relations, Fr Schondonch made the St Omers chapel one of the principal attractions of the town. 'More English than the English', he enjoyed the backing of a highly efficient and loyal staff. These included Fr Lee, Minister until 1614, Fr Cresswell, who between 1614 and 1618 sorted out the financial embarrassments created by his Rector's over-sanguine enterprises, and, last but not least, Fr Henry Thunder, an Old Boy who returned in 1615 to hold a variety of posts, including that of First Prefect, until his death in 1638.

Fr Schondonch was also a vigorous builder. In this he was helped by the extra grant of 2,000 crowns which Fr Baldwin, a future rector, secured from Philip III in 1599. 1607 saw the opening of a new chapel dedicated to St Thomas of Canterbury, the patron saint of the College. Next year Fr Schondonch bought the Hôtel de Régnauville and, despite local protests, replaced it with a new church, opened on 9 September 1610. At the same time he obtained the adjoining building to house the St Omers Press. Still not content, he bought further property in 1610 and 1613; and would have continued on the same lines had not the General, Mutius Vitelleschi, prohibited all further enterprises until the accumulated debt of at least 20,000 florins had been paid off.

This expansion exacerbated tensions with the Walloon College. At the start St Omers had essentially been a boarding house attached to this college. The Walloons had tried to resolve the contradiction by suggesting that St Omers be run by a Superior subject to their authority; but instead it had been put under its own independent Rector. To whom were the boys responsible – the Walloon Prefect of Studies or their own masters? As early as 1594 a dispute involving Ambrose Rookwood in the Syntax class had led to a boycott by the entire English contingent, and the matter had to be taken up to the Provincial. One result was that the boys were allowed to use their own chapel instead of being compelled to attend services at the Walloon College. But, despite every effort by both sides, incidents continued to recur as the English establishment grew. Prizes, for instance, were a bone of contention. The English boys were too successful! In the eighty exams taken between January 1612 and December 1613 only on five occasions did an English boy not come first or second. Rumour suggested that this was because they had been put in the wrong classes. Whatever the reason, from September 1610 the Cathedral Chapter insisted that the prizes they donated be given to local children only. A week later, when the Abbot of St Bertin celebrated the Exaltation of the Holy Cross in the English Church, Fr Schondonch retaliated with his own Academies and prize-giving ceremony. What really decided matters, though, was the growth of the English Jesuit community from 11 members in 1604 to 27 in 1615. In 1614, then, the logical step was taken and the two colleges separated, though at first the Provincial tried to ensure that all five Classmasters were Walloons. A further break came in 1617 with the death of Fr Schondonch. His successor Fr Philippe Dennetiers, of lower calibre, could not get on with his English staff; so, when in 1621 he asked to retire, he was replaced by Fr William Baldwin, the first English Rector.

These alterations were complemented by the creation of a separate English Province. Hitherto, English Jesuits on the Continent had been largely subordinate to the Provincials of the districts where they resided, and St Omers had been no exception to this rule. What co-ordination there was had been given by the Prefect of the Mission, a post created for Fr Persons in 1598 and held after his death by Fr Thomas Owen. But, between 1610 and 1620, the number of English Jesuits exploded, rising from 53 to 240. Simultaneously much of the structure of a full province was put in position. In 1608 Fr Persons helped to establish a noviciate at Louvain. Transferred in 1614 by Fr Gerard to Liège, it sprouted a house of Philosophy and Theology. In 1622, thanks to the good offices of Bishop Blaise and Fr Schondonch, the noviciate was moved again, this time to the derelict abbey of Watten, five miles from St Omer. Finally, in 1620, a House of Tertians, where Jesuits prepare for their final vows, was opened in Ghent. Clearly, it was time to recognise the English Jesuits as a distinct entity. Accordingly, in 1619 England became a Vice-Province instead of a mission, and Fr Richard Blount, its Superior since 1617, became Vice-Provincial. Four years later the Vice-Province became a full Province and he was appointed Provincial. In turn this allowed Fr Baldwin to replace his remaining Walloon Classmasters with an all-English staff. St Omers College and the English Jesuits attained their majority together.

The 'St Omers Charter' of 13 March 1593. This is one of two documents, sent to Paris and Rome in 1762 and 1763 respectively, at the time of the first migration. One of them was given to Fr Thomas Talbot SJ, the Secular Priest appointed to take charge of the building. Through him it came to the Westminster Diocesan Archives where it was rediscovered and returned to the College after Fr Browne SJ became Provincial in 1910.

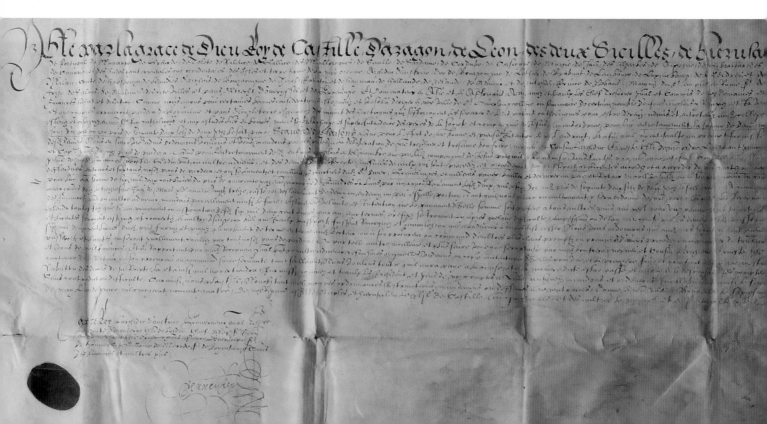

JESUIT EDUCATION

LIKE ALL JESUIT schools St Omers was stamped by the personality of St Ignatius Loyola; and his spirit still runs through the veins of its lineal descendant. The many distinguished soldiers and martyrs produced by the College are testimony to a strong sense of duty, a concept of service for others, and the idea of being used by God – all typically Ignatian virtues. This spirit is expressed by and articulated through the educational system he and his followers devised. The Society has acquired an enormous reputation for pedagogy – rightly so – because first, it was the principal means by which Rome consolidated the gains made by the Counter-Reformation in Europe. Second, it introduced many educational innovations which are now taken for granted. Third, at St Omers it gave English Catholics the necessary steel to withstand decades of persecution. Moreover, as one of the few Jesuit boarding schools in existence, St Omers had to tackle the problem of what to do with its pupils outside the classroom from first principles. The Playroom system that was devised is still a real alternative to the House system that haphazardly evolved in other schools during the nineteenth century.

But, although its importance has long been recognised, little effort has been made to understand how the system really worked. The same clichés, flattering or otherwise, continue to be repeated by interested parties; and there is not much sense of how the system evolved over the centuries. Partly this has been the fault of the Society. Success discourages change, and a strong reverence for the past tends to make former customs and regulations seem sacrosanct. So the history of Jesuit education is one of long periods of apparently rigid immobility punctuated by brief but sharp upheavals. And on each occasion change – or reaction – has been justified by referring back to the original intentions of the founder. This is right and proper, since without sensitive adaptation the animating spirit would disappear. But it can lead to controversy. Ignatius led a varied and active life, and he would have been the first to admit that his views – though not the overriding objective – changed during that time. Any assessment of his legacy, therefore, has to start with a brief analysis of his career.

He was born at Loyola in Guipúzcoa, a province of north-eastern Spain, sometime before 23 October 1491. Basque was his native tongue, one reason for an awkwardness when expressing himself in Spanish. The son of Bertrand Yanez, Lord of Ognoz and Loyola, by birth and temperament he seemed destined for

Title page from Ludolph of Saxony's Life of Christ. *This edition dates from 1581; but the College also possesses an earlier version of the 1478 from Nuremberg, printed in Gothic script with hand-drawn illuminations.*
St Ignatius used a Castilian translation by Fray Ambrosio de Montesino printed at Alcala in 1502–3.

25

Silver head of St Ignatius, originally made for the altarpiece of the Gesù, Rome, after the Restoration of the Society in 1814. It was purchased by the English Province in 1870.

the role of a soldier knight. Polanço, his secretary for nine years in Rome, recalled that 'though he was attached to the faith, he lived nowise in conformity with it and did not avoid sin. Rather he was much addicted to gambling and dissolute in his dealings with women, contentious about using his sword.'

All this was changed in 1521. At the siege of Pamplona his leg was broken by a cannon-ball and he was forced to convalesce for several months in the castle at Loyola. There he read two works: A *Life of Christ* by Ludolph of Saxony (d. 1377) and a four-volume *Lives of the Saints* compiled by Jacobo de Varazzo, Bishop of Genoa (d. 1298), otherwise known as 'the Golden Legend'. This had been translated into Castilian and supplied with prologues by Fr Gamberto Vagad, a Cistercian from Saragossa. Under their influence Ignatius resolved to make a pilgrimage to Jerusalem. But before doing so preparation had to be made. In February 1522 he set out for Montserrat.

We must not underestimate the importance of Ignatius's early life; for in some respects he simply transformed the medieval notion of courtly love into the ideal of service to God and the Blessed Virgin Mary. Vagad had described his saints as 'Caballeros de Dios' while Ludolph declared that 'Our Sovereign Lord and army commander [caudillo] Jesus desires that the eyes and the countenances of his devout Caballeria should ever be raised to his life-giving wounds, so that by looking in the mirror of his passion they may become the more valiant for the sufferings and hardships of battle.' Ignatius was quick to follow this example. Like a knight of old, on his first evening away from home he persuaded his brother 'to join him in a night of vigil at the shrine of Our Lady of Aranzazu'; when he reached Montserrat, after a three-day preparation for confession, he exchanged his clothing with a beggar and hung up his sword and dagger in the church before the altar of Our Lady.

Ignatius spent only a few days at Montserrat before moving on to nearby Manresa. Legend has it that for most of the next ten months he lived in the celebrated 'cave' of Manresa (really a rock overhang). Alas, this idea was originally derived from statements made by Widmanstadt in 1556. Instead, Fr Broderick has suggested that he mainly resided either at the public hospital or at a cell in the Dominican Convent, or in private houses. What is certain is that he practised some remarkable austerities – including flagellation five times a day – which permanently weakened his health. He also saw visions: Polanço describes how 'in this same time a serpent of great splendour with seven or eight eyes used to appear to him every day, without missing a single day, twice, thrice, five times, six times. He drew comfort from its presence and became disconsolate when it faded away.' More constructively perhaps he wrote the first draft of the *Spiritual Exercises* which, according to Ribadeneira, his first biographer, was 'so replenished with excellent documents and instructions in the highest points of a spiritual life, that it is most clear and evident that the Holy Ghost was his master therein'.

This work is so important, forming the inspiration behind the Retreat and the Sodality – two peculiarly Ignatian devotions long practised at St Omers and Stonyhurst – that some technical description is essential. The Exercises consist of a course of meditations divided into four 'weeks' that can be lengthened or shortened as circumstances require. Week 1 lays down the general principles and describes how to examine one's conscience and face the fact of sin; Weeks 2, 3 and 4 are meditations on the life of Christ, his crucifixion and the events between the Resurrection and the Ascension. Implicit in this is the call to follow him. There then follows an appendix of scriptural passages suitable for further meditations. Interspersed with all this are notes and advice on such topics as the 'Three Modes of Humility', 'Scruples', 'Rules for the Discernment of Spirits' and 'On How to Make a Wise and Good Choice'.

The work is suffused with the spirit of late medieval mysticism. Ignatius himself recommended study of The Imitation of Christ; while his choice of vocabulary, echoing passages in the Golden Legend, more than hints at a crusading knightly ideal:

> Second point: I will consider how this King [i.e. Christ] speaks to all his subjects saying 'It is my will to conquer all infidel lands. Therefore whoever wishes to come with me must be content to eat as I eat, drink as I drink, dress as I dress etc. Third point: I will consider what the answer of good subjects ought to be to such a generous and noble King, and consequently, if anyone would refuse the request of such a King, he would deserve to be despised by everyone and considered an unworthy knight.

But these elements are regulated by hard practicalities. The technique of meditation is clear and systematic, usually proceeding from a recollection of the history of the subject, through 'a mental image of the place', to asking 'God Our Lord for what I want and desire'. And for the examination of conscience Ignatius recommends the keeping of a numerical record of all sinful thoughts. These features have sometimes led to criticism: the approach is said to be too rigid and mechanical, a possible example of this being the massive three-day retreats held for the whole school at the beginning of the academic year in Stonyhurst until the 1960s. On the other hand, Paul Johnson, who himself experienced the full force of this as a boy in the late 1940s, claimed that it cleansed the mind of the holidays and gave a clear signal that the serious business of the term was about to begin. Perhaps also it is worth remembering that the Exercises were never intended to be given through a fixed set of rules. The earliest surviving version, 'The Autograph', dating from 1541, is full of

St Ignatius Loyola. Anonymous portrait, probably contemporary. It was presented to Mount St Mary's College in 1991 to mark the Ignation year. The College possesses two other originals as well as a large seventeenth-century picture similar to but not a copy of Ruben's famous work.

The Spiritual Exercises. The edition, printed in 1553, must be one of the earliest in existence.

marginalia added by the Saint. It is really a flexible set of guidelines for use by a spiritual director. A marvellous example of their adaptability can be heard in the Cave of Living Streams record produced by Fr Hewett and Wilfrid Usher at Stonyhurst in 1974; and the wide variety of Playroom retreats now given by the College shows a similar spirit.

To some the most jarring feature of the Exercises is the section entitled 'Rules for Thinking with the Church', almost certainly produced after Ignatius had encountered Protestant ideas in Paris. Its most celebrated passage comes in clause 13:

> If we wish to be sure that we are right in all things, we should always be ready to accept this principle: I will believe that the white I see is black, if the hierarchical Church so defines it. For, I believe that between the Bridegroom, Christ our Lord, and the Bride, his Church, there is but one spirit, which guides and directs us for the salvation of our souls, for the same spirit and head who gives us the commandments, guides and governs our Holy Mother Church.

Even more controversial for contemporaries would have been his attitude towards predestination and justification by faith. In Paris he had been a contemporary of Calvin; and, like Luther, he was obsessed with sin. How near he gets to their views and the dangers this posed can be gauged from clause 14: 'Although it be true that no one can be saved unless he have faith and grace, still we must be very careful of our manner of discussing or speaking of these matters', a point reiterated in clauses 15, 16 and 17. Perhaps this is a confession that he was not very interested in academic theology. Nonetheless, the proximity of his spiritual ideas to Protestant doctrine may explain why so many committed Calvinists, including possibly Fr Persons, joined the Society. However, such passages should not be taken outside their proper context and a fuller statement of Ignatius' position can be found in the prayer at the beginning of the Second 'Week':

> Eternal Lord of all things, I make this offering *with thy grace and help,* in the presence of thy glorious Mother and of all the saints of thy heavenly court, that it is *my wish and desire, and my deliberate choice,* provided only that it be for thy greater service and praise, to imitate thee in bearing all injuries, all evils, and all poverty both physical and spiritual, if thy most Sacred Mejesty should will to choose me for such a life and state.

It was this remarkable document then that Ignatius took with him on his pilgrimage to Jerusalem (1523–4) and started to expound when, at the age of 33, he decided to go to university. After a two-year Latin course in Barcelona he went first to Alcala and then to Salamanca. In both cases his activities aroused the suspicions of the Inquisition. For this reason in 1528 he resolved to leave Spain and study in Paris. Even there he did not escape scrutiny; but in spite of that, he completed his MA in Philosophy and took the Divinity course. There too he gathered around him the 'founding fathers' of the Society – Pierre Le Fèvre, Francis Xavier, James Laynez, Alfonso Salmeron, Simon Rodriguez and Nicholas Bobadilla. On the Feast of the Assumption, 1534, at a Mass celebrated by Le Fèvre (the only priest among them at that time) in the chapel of St Denis on Montmartre, they vowed to live lives of poverty and chastity, visit Jerusalem, convert the heathen and assist the Pope. Unfortunately, when they all met again in 1537, war between Venice and Turkey precluded sailing to the

Holy Land; so, at this point, the nascent Society took a new direction. While the tasks of converting the heathen and caring for the unfortunate were not forgotten, perhaps as a result of their experiences in Paris, the conversion of the Protestant became a paramount aim. It was on this basis that Pope Paul III formally approved the new Society on 27 September 1540. The following Lent Ignatius was elected Superior General, a post he held for the next 15 years, three months and nine days, according to the exact computation given by Ribadeneira.

Thereafter, the story is one of expansion. At his death (31 July 1556) the Society consisted of 12 Provinces or administrative areas; by 1600 this had grown to 23 Provinces and two Vice-Provinces containing over 300 Colleges. Ribadeneira aptly summarised its many activities:

> For who is not witness of the care and solicitude, with which St Ignatius' children employ themselves in teaching Christian doctrine; in instructing youth in liberal sciences and good manners; in visiting and comforting those that are detained in prison; in helping the poor and needy, and helping them to die well.

Scenes from the Vita Beati P. Ignatii Loiolae *of 1609, printed in Rome. The College also holds the second edition dating from 1622 as well as the original copper plates from which the engravings were printed.*

Left: Ignatius recovers from his wounds after the Siege of Pamplona.
Right: Ignatius sails to Italy on the first leg of his pilgrimage to Jerusalem.

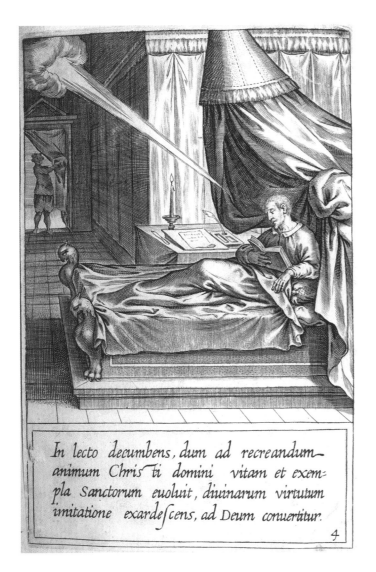

In lecto decumbens, dum ad recreandum animum Christi domini vitam et exempla Sanctorum euoluit, diuinarum virtutum imitatione exardescens, ad Deum conuertitur.

4

Nauigaturus in Italiam sola DEI fiducia pro uiatico munitus emendicatam pecuniam in littus abijcit.

22

Hence the need for organisation. But this created the dangers of stultification and distortion; a problem that vexes Jesuits to this day. Were the aims of the Society that emerged in the 1550s the same as those that had inspired Ignatius thirty years before? And if there had been a change did this really matter? As the Society grew, Ignatius and his successors developed an elaborate organisational network of structures and officials (see Appendix C: Table I); and as the number of Colleges multiplied, so a standardised system of education and training became a more urgent priority. Between 1547 and 1551 Ignatius laid down detailed regulations in Part IV of the Constitutions, forming a touchstone against which all other proposals would be tested. However, it was not until 1584 that Aquaviva began the immensely long and complicated gestation – itself a sign of how bureaucratic the Society had become – that produced a definitive *Ratio Studiorum* in 1599.

At once there is a paradox. From his earliest student days Ignatius was antipathetic to some aspects of the Renaissance. The *Spiritual Exercises* insist on praise being given to positive and scholastic theology; and this support for St Thomas Aquinas, Peter Lombard and a suitably pruned Aristotle was reiterated in the Constitutions and the Ratio. This was not unusual. Many Catholics blamed Erasmus and his followers for the spread of Protestantism, an attitude well summed up by Bobadilla's tag 'Qui Graecizabant, Lutheranizabant'. Had not the English Government seen Renaissance learning as a means towards Protestant indoctrination? Yet, while Thomist theology and Aristotelian philosophy were taught in their Colleges of Higher Studies, lower down, where the grammatical foundations were laid, the Society used Renaissance techniques. The emphasis on Latin grammar, on learning Greek and even Hebrew, an insistence that Latin be spoken on virtually every occasion, these surely are symptomatic of the New Learning. The result was a very curious compound. Ignatius himself wrote: 'The order to be observed in the subjects is that a solid foundation should be laid in the Latin language before the Liberal Arts, in the Liberal Arts before Scholastic Theology, and in Scholastic Theology before Positive Theology, the Sacred Scriptures can be studied at the same time or later.'

But even this is too simple, since Jesuit education in its Lower Studies contained many medieval features – the love of disputation for example, or the monastic habit of having readings at meal times. In one sense of course this is not surprising, since all Renaissance education contained a fair dash of medievalism; and the Ratio itself was an unashamed synthesis of current educational methods. Thus, although the Society made many educational innovations, St Omers bore a striking resemblance to other contemporary schools. The system of contests between rival teams in class – later known as 'Romans and Carthaginians' – was used at Westminster, which also put a similar emphasis on drama as a way to develop rhetoric. Even the class curriculum, which seems so unusual today, was commonplace. Under the influence of Cranmer, King's School, Canterbury for instance, was organised as follows:

I.   Rudiments
II. Cato and Aesop
III. Terence and Mantuan
IV. 'Letters of Learned Men and Studies from the Poets'
V.   'Choicest Poets and the best Historians'
VI. Erasmus' *De Copia,* Horace, Cicero.

So what made Jesuit education so distinctive? One answer lies in its Catholic emphasis. Renaissance educators were concerned with 'the whole man', but there could be no Terence, because of his corrosive effect on moral standards; textbooks and texts should have a Catholic slant, in much the same way as Cecil and his friends had prescribed works with a Protestant tendency; and the catechism, biblical study and other ecclesiastical writings were integrated into the classical curriculum. To take an extreme case, in its 'Rules for the Professor of Hebrew Language', which was periodically taught at St Omers, the Ratio requires the teacher to defend the Vulgate, teach Grammar in the first year in conjunction with an easy book of scripture, and 'consider nothing more important than to explain, with very great accuracy, the first words of sacred scripture'. More generally, the 'Professors of the Lower Classes' were enjoined to 'so instruct the boys who are entrusted to the discipline of our Society, that they will thoroughly learn, along with their letters, the habits of Christians. Let this particular purpose be kept in mind, as much during lessons, when opportunity is offered, as outside, in order that the plastic minds of the pupils may be directed to a reverence and love of God and the virtues which should please him.'

So, at least in the Lower Studies, Jesuit education was Renaissance education with its Protestant detonators removed: provided proper safeguards were maintained the Society felt it could beat such opponents at their own game. First, this would be achieved by a more systematic method of study designed – and here is another difference with other schools – to bring the average and not just the best pupil forward; second, Jesuit schools had far higher teacher-pupil ratios (*see* Appendix C: Table 2). Instead of a master and his usher struggling, with the aid of monitors, to control six or more classes simultaneously, as was the common practice in most other schools, St Omers had a master assigned to each class in separate classrooms. So although 'Decurions' – or boy prefects – were used, they were not as important, their job being merely to observe and report disorders or irregularities to the master. Moreover, the whole system was backed by a proper system of in-service training. Indeed, the Ratio even considered the erection of separate teacher-training colleges, an idea not adopted in England until the nineteenth century. As many staff had been educated in Jesuit schools this came naturally; and, although it may have exposed them to the dangers of inbreeding, at least it ensured consistency. Also Scholastics, after leaving the noviciate, were expected to take lower classes before moving on to their Higher Studies; so they were in effect pursuing a sandwich course. Seen in this light the peculiarly Jesuit practice of the master staying with his class as it moved up the school makes sound sense, and of course it allowed him to build up close relationships with the pupils.

But if Class masters were undergoing 'on the job training' then they had to be properly supervised. The Ratio required the Prefect of Studies to visit each class once every 15 days (in seminaries this was once a month) and in addition scrutinise the records kept by its master. There was a most elaborate system of exams, on the basis of which the Prefect of Studies assigned places in every class. These were of three kinds: a written exam taken at the end of the academic year, compositions, and an aural 'examen' of three boys from each class. The Ratio explains exactly how such an examination should be conducted. The pupil was expected to read out part of his composition, correct his own mistakes, and then, if he was studying grammar, translate something off-hand from the vernacular into Latin, answer questions on the rules of

Detail of books in the Arundell Library.

The Bay Library, incorporating the College Archives. Nearby are the Square and Arundell Libraries. The contents of the latter were presented by the widow of Everard, Tenth Lord Arundell in 1837. The whole complex was built up primarily for the use of the Jesuit community, though it was made available to the Gentlemen Philosophers.

grammar and give a short explanation of any book he had studied in class. Records from Liège and Stonyhurst in the late eighteenth and early nineteenth centuries show that examens and compositions took place towards the end of each of the four terms in the academic year. Thus, in 1788–9 compositions were taken in November, March, May and July, examinations in December, March, May and August, and reports read by the Prefect of Studies to the boys on 23 December, 3 April, 27 May and 13 August. Those who failed were expected to revise in the Study Place during the holidays and take a second examen at the start of the new term!

Examinations were complemented by Academies, or public displays of academic skill and entertainment. In 1788–9 there were five: Rhetoric gave theirs in December, Poetry in February, Syntax in March, Grammar in May, and members drawn from the whole school gave a 'Great Academies' on 6 August. This last included prize-giving for which the Ratio made clear specifications:

Rhetoric: 8 Prizes – 2 each for Latin Prose, Latin Verse, Greek Prose and Greek Verse.

Poetry: 6 Prizes – 2 each for Latin Verse, Latin Prose and Greek Prose.

Lower Classes: 4 Prizes – 2 each for Latin Prose and Greek Prose.

In addition, one prize was awarded for Christian Doctrine; and we also know that at Liège and Stonyhurst, medals were presented to the 'First Six' in every class.

Close supervision and intensive testing, while good in themselves, are not sufficient to ensure consistently high standards from a possibly inexperienced staff. This was one reason why the Ratio specified such things as the times of school terms and holidays, daily routine (Appendix C: Tables 3 and 4), the curriculum (Appendix C: Tables 5 and 6) and even teaching methods. In a 'Prelection' (clearly some form of construe) the Professor of Higher Grammar was told:

> First he will go through the subject book in Latin and in the vernacular; secondly he will so interpret each sentence that the vernacular explanation will be given immediately after the Latin; in the third place going through it again from the beginning . . . he will explain the force and derivation, and confirm his explanation by one or another example taken especially from the same writer.

Similar instructions were given for Concertatios and what were later known as 'Romans and Carthaginians'. Concertatios, or disputations, were frequently held at meal times and often used as a form of academic display. When they were given in class by senior boys the Ratio expected junior boys to attend. In his *English Spanish Pilgrim* the renegade James Wadsworth, himself a former St Omers boy, gives a racy description:

> After the boys have ranged themselves a while, the Rector and Fathers enter, the elder says grace himself, or ordains another, which being done, he placeth himself at the upper end of the table, the others in their order. All this while the students' mouths are shut, not from eating but speaking, bestowing their ears upon six of their companions disputing three against three in two pews overthwart the other, of such things which may help digestion to the Fathers than benefit their own understanding . . . and this begins and ends with their dinner.

'Romans and Carthaginians' is best described in the testimony given by Fr Kingdon, then Prefect of Studies, to the Taunton Commission on 15 December 1865. Ten years before this practice had been revived by Fr Gallwey, an earlier Prefect. The parallel with Westminster should be remarked:

> 12,228. You have a system, which seems a peculiar one, of exciting the boys' emulation amongst themselves by public competition among them, in which one of the boys is set to examine the others, partly as is done in Westminster. Would you give us a short account of the system?
>
> In the ordinary lessons in school there is a certain amount of this. The class is divided into two sides, which go by the name of Romans and Carthaginians, and each boy on one side has a rival opposed to him on the other. When any boy is put on in his lesson, his rival stands up to him and detects any mistakes he may have made. If these mistakes are detected rightly on each occasion, there is a mark made for the conqueror. Then the rival is put on, so as to

give his adversary the opportunity of doing the same for him. At the end the marks are counted up and whoever has the most is declared victor in that particular engagement.

These passages raise the question of how strictly the Ratio was applied at St Omers. Superficially, the answer seems quite simple. The records show that it was used at the Walloon College, and when in 1614 St Omers became separate, Aquaviva made this conditional on the use of the Ratio. Until the late nineteenth century it remained a touchstone of good practice. Fr Gallwey's reforms of 1857–9, with their emphasis on classical learning, on the revival of Concertatios, 'Romans and Carthaginians', and even the changing of class names to Higher, Middle and Lower Grammar were a deliberate throwback to the Ratio. But, even in the earliest days, the translation from theory into practice must have involved some adjustment. We can see this in the class names (Appendix C: Table 7) and in the way prizes were supplemented by 'Good Days', a tradition that still survives in attenuated form with the Choir Good Day at Stonyhurst. Thus 27 January, the Feast of St Chrysostom, was set aside for 'the more skilled and diligent in the Greek language', and 7 November, the Feast of St Cecilia, was for musicians and altar staff. On these occasions the selected boys were free for the whole day and had a special table at dinner. Then there was the practice of taking the 'First Six' from the end-of-year exams out for a special holiday and meal at the Blandêques Villa outside St Omer. When the College migrated, first to Bruges and then to Liège, similar houses were obtained at Momelbeke and

The Do Room, so called because of the 'Dos' or celebrations held there.

Chèvremont; and during vacations these villas were used by the teaching staff as a holiday home. Confusingly, at Stonyhurst a Blandyke (the title derives from the original Blandêques) came to be the name given for the monthly whole holiday otherwise known as a 'Month Day'. By the 1990s, it was simply a special meal the Jesuit community occasionally had, with or without lay staff and other guests.

But the clearest sign of practical adjustment can be seen from a glance at the timetable drawn up in the St Omers Custom Book by Fr Schondonch (Appendix C: Table 8). When taken with the other differences this emphasised St Omers' unusual character as a boarding establishment. Most Jesuit schools at this time were for day-boys. Yet, from the beginning, St Omers was intended for boys living away from home, and not just during the term but even in the holidays. Indeed, it was by no means unusual for them not to see their parents for years at a time. This posed unique problems, since a full routine for every day was essential; and special arrangements had to be made for feeding, hygiene and discipline. Breakfast, according to Wadsworth, consisted of 'a peece of bread and beer, and beere as pleaseth him'; dinner was 'served in by seven of their own rancke weekely and by course [i.e. in rotation], and according to seniority each man hath first brought him a messe of broth which is the antipast: afterwards halfe a pound of beefe which they call their portion, and after an aple, a peece of cheese for their postpast, bread and beere as they call for it.' Cleanliness, strongly emphasised in the Custom Book, included the regulation that no one was allowed up into his dormitory during the daytime except 'on certain days the boys may be allowed during the summer to cleanse their beds from fleas and vermin'.

Charles Waterton captures an adult cayman in Guiana, *by Captain Edward Jones OS. This painting now hangs in the Do Room bay area – between 1851 and 1888 used as a washing place.*

All this required a staff distinct from the teaching establishment (Appendix C: Table 2). Feeding was the responsibility of the Minister; and he was supported by lay brothers in the kitchen and on other menial tasks. A St Omers' catalogue for 1609 even mentions a 'Braxator' (Brewer) and a 'Pistor' (either a miller or a baker). And although such officials were present in other Jesuit colleges and the Ratio has some rules for a beadle – his task was to keep the classrooms clean – the job they had to do at St Omers was much greater.

Nowhere can this be seen more clearly than with discipline. In the Constitutions Ignatius took one vital decision; he insisted that Class masters should not administer punishments: 'We wish, however, to recommend in this place that the externs should be given the corporal punishment which they need; which, however, will not be exercised through any one of the Society itself.'

But at St Omers this had a rather curious sequel. Punishments were administered not by a non-Jesuit 'corrector', as the Ratio had specified, but by a new official, later known as the First Prefect of Discipline. The procedure at Stonyhurst in 1865 is described by Mr Bryce in his report to the Taunton Commission:

> The teaching staff of the establishment is entirely distinct from that to which discipline, and the care of the boys during the hours of play, of meals, and of sleep is entrusted. This is carried so far that the teacher does not even inflict a punishment for an offence committed in the classroom. If he desires to punish a boy, he says to him, 'Go to Mr So and So (a prefect) and ask him for four (i.e. four blows on the hand)' . . . The boy rises from his seat, leaves the room, and proceeds to that of the prefect named . . . He knocks on the door and enters. 'Well, what is it?' 'If you please sir, I was told to ask for four.' 'By whom?' Then the boy gives the name of his teacher. The Prefect records it in the punishment book, and duly administers the strokes

This is similar to the rather cryptic account given in the *Memoir* of Edmund Matthew alias Poins who died at St Omers in 1667. When late for Studies he voluntarily 'went to the Prefect's chamber and desired him to strike him five times on the head with a stick'.

But the Prefect of Discipline's role went far beyond this. The job description given by Wadsworth reads: 'Father Thunder, who appoints chambers and studies, makes them render account of their studies, keepes hours of study and recreation, and exercises many of his claps upon their breeches.' In fact 'Praefecti Cubiculorum' had existed as early as 1597. However, Fr Thunder did more than anyone else to establish the role still carried on by his lineal descendants, that is the Deputy Headmaster, the Assistant Headmaster and the Playroom Masters, House or Playroom Mistresses. In addition to the dormitories he ran the Study Place, 'a large hall under the First Gallery, where according to order each takes his seate, where they study one houre, and in the midst walks Father Thunder, and sees they all keep silence and be diligent at their bookes' (Wadsworth). And on half-holidays after 'dinner ended we march forth of the College by 2 and 2, Father Thunder carrying up the reare untill we are distant about a mile from the towne, where we walk, or play at ball or bowles or other such games, till the clocke and our stomackes strike supper time, wherein, repairing to the College roast mutton is our provision most ordinary.'

The principle, then, was constant watchfulness. This may have stultified individual initiative, but it greatly reduced the possibilities of bullying and fagging so endemic in other public schools. Another advantage was that in a boarding school it enhanced the opportunities for shaping religious habit and belief. The day opened and closed with prayers, including short points for the morrow's meditation: 'They shall be read twice, in a clear voice' (St Omers Custom Book); all classes, following the dictum of the Ratio, opened with a short prayer; readings at meals, always religious in character, were usually taken from a martyrologium, and intended to stiffen youthful resolve against persecution; true to the *Spiritual Exercises* (Rules for Thinking with the Church, clauses 6 and 8) religious pictures, crucifixes and relics were everywhere. Amongst other items Stonyhurst still possesses the bones of St Gordianus, the relic of the Holy Thorn, and the rope that bound St Edmund Campion at his execution. The *Memoir* of Edmund Poins describes how 'as he passed along the galleries he would kiss the pictures hanging on the walls which he could reach unto and those that are fastened to the doors'.

On a more public plane, again in accordance with the *Spiritual Exercises,* there were the religious services. Fr John Wilson, in the Annual Letters for 1614 describes how:

> During the Litanies and Sundays, throughout the whole of Lent, representations were exhibited in the church of the prayer of Our Lord in the garden on the first Sunday, the blindfolding and mocking of the second Sunday, the scourging on the third, the crowning with thorns, or Ecce Homo, on the fourth, the carrying of the Cross on Passion Sunday, and on Palm Sunday the crucifixion. These representations so excited the people to devotion that each time they were observed to shed tears in great abundance. After the Litanies Fr Schondonchus, on a certain day, delivered a short discourse to the people present, speaking briefly of the vanity of the world, the method of examining conscience etc. [another echo from the *Spiritual Exercises*].

As the passage implies, such ceremonies bordered on the theatrical. The Ratio had said that dramatic performances 'must not be given except in Latin and on very rare occasions, ought to be sacred and pious, and nothing should be introduced between the acts which is not in Latin, and is not becoming; nor is a feminine role nor feminine attire to be introduced.' But despite this, perhaps because St Omers was a boarding school, a dramatic tradition quickly developed under Fr Schondonch. Usually plays were produced by the master of Poetry and, true to the spirit of the Ratio, religious subjects were often chosen; but on occasion, such as when Philip II's daughter, the Archduchess Isabella, and Cardinal Cueva visited the College in 1625, classical topics were introduced, in this case the masque *Saturn and Astrea* allegorising her reign. Entertainment, the development of rhetoric, religion and good public relations were thus fused together. Fr Joseph Simons' *Zeno,* first performed in 1631, not only enjoyed performances in Rome, Naples, Bologna and Spain but was pirated to form the basis of the *Imperial Tragedy* as late as 1669.

Zeno was performed 'clangentibus tubis, tympanis sonantibus'; and music was a valuable ancillary for theatrical or religious display. As one would expect Fr Schondonch did much to encourage it, the Custom Book referring to four music halls: one for singing and strings, another for psalmody, a third for Gregorian chant, and the fourth for instrumental music. There is a detailed list of instruments – viols, viola de gamba, flutes, recorders, hautbois, theorbos, zithers, lutes, harps, a bassoon, an organ, and a harpsichord. Careful instructions are given about how

A St Omers Playbill. Leonidas *was produced by the College in 1755.*

they are to be organised into 'Whole' and Broken Consorts and the occasions when they are to be used. 'The music of wind instruments', for instance, 'is full of Majesty, especially for Church services, for the reception of persons of high rank and for the theatre.'

Religion, then, pervaded every aspect of life; but it was at its most profound in the Sodality established at St Omers in 1609. In its chapel were stored the most precious relics, including the bones of St Martina, the inspiration for the annual Mass for Health still held on 30 January (her feast day) at Stonyhurst. The idea was started in 1563 when Fr Jean Leunis, a professor at the Roman College, encouraged his students to honour the Virgin Mary with pious exercises at the end of his classes. The idea caught on and, at the prompting of Aquaviva, was given canonical status by Pope Gregory XIII in 1584. The Ratio urged every Rector to establish one, and the regulations in the St Omers Custom Book are most extensive. To these were added a further supplement of no less than 75 pages in 1629 at the instance of Fr Baldwin. Associated with it was the 'Bona Mors' confraternity set up by the Jesuit General Vincent Caraffa in 1648 and brought to St Omers in 1681 by Fr Thomas Stapleton. As the title suggests its purpose was to encourage postulants to 'die well', a theme clearly relevant for those about to return to England. In character the Sodality was essentially a prayer group, many of its practices being inspired by the *Spiritual Exercises*. Members were supposed to set a good moral example; and as such it fitted in with the disciplinary system. The *Memoir* of Edmund Matthews describes how 'a companion once let fall some words which signified that rather than he would lose all his means, and become a beggar, he would temporise and go to church with heretics. This was a two-edged sword in Edmund's heart and he did so bestir himself to bring his companion to understand the indignity of his saying and the danger he exposed himself to, that being quite ashamed of his words said he spoke only in jest and not only then endeavoured to persuade Edmund as much but also at other times came and excused his rash and inconsiderate words.'

But the Sodality also met deep psychological needs. Physically separated from home for years at a time and caught up in a rigid formal routine, individuals needed a quiet refuge. The *Memoir* of Edmund Matthews describes how 'you would never find him long absent from this place, when the order and discipline of the house obliged him not to be otherwise employed'. It is also pertinent to remark that his mother was dead, for there are clear references to his treatment of the Virgin Mary and a St Encratides (whose bones rested in the Sodality Chapel) as maternal figures: 'From that time [of hearing of her life] he considered St Encratides as his mother, every day asked her blessing, [and] committed all his affairs to her.'

Here then, refracted through the pious phrases of his hagiographer, lies a pathos. But there is something more; for Edmund Matthews, by focusing his filial affections on God, was taking the first steps on the road pioneered by St Ignatius some 140 years before. He was becoming a Jesuit.

Facing page: The Sodality Chapel. Note the relics of St Gordianus below the altar. They were taken from the catacombs in 1670 and presented to St Omers by Fr Christopher Anderton SJ, who had hoped they would come to his native Lancashire. In 1773, following the Suppression they were placed in the care of Augustinian nuns, and taken by them to Hengrave Hall, Suffolk, during the French Revolution. In 1834 they at last found their way to Lancashire, and in 1862 they were ceremonially translated to the Sodality Chapel.

TRIALS AND TRIBULATIONS

WHEN FR SCHONDONCH died he left St Omers in a thriving state. The splendour of the services, the quality of its classical training, the excellence of the music and drama had given the College a reputation second to none. The only blemish, a debt computed at 80,000 scudi (£8,000) in 1621, was mainly due to the non-payment of the Spanish pension.

Progress continued under Fr Baldwin (1621–32). His early career had been adventurous. Of Cornish stock, he studied at Oxford and Rome; ordained in 1588, he entered the Jesuit Noviciate at Tournai in 1590; five years later, while escorting six St Omers boys to Spain under the pseudonym of Ottavio Fuscinelli, he was arrested on suspicion by the English authorities. But, despite all their efforts, they could not get him to betray himself and, after some weeks in the Bridewell prison, he had to be released for sheer lack of evidence.

Sometime between 1600 and 1601 he was involved in the drafting and implementation of the St Omers Constitutions. Later, in 1610, while travelling between Brussels and Rome as Vice-Prefect of the Jesuit Mission, he was kidnapped by the Elector Palatine and sent to James I. He spent eight years in the Tower for alleged complicity in the Gunpowder Plot before, at the instance of the Spanish ambassador, being released and banished. After two years work in Brussels he became rector at Louvain, whence he was transferred to St Omers to replace Fr Dennetiers (1617–21). Although his health had been sapped by these experiences, and this showed particularly towards the end of his rectorate, numbers rose to an all-time high and the financial position improved (see Appendix C: Tables 9 and 10). Moreover, he enjoyed the favour of the Archduchess Isabella. One sign of this was her state visit to the College in 1625. It was her influence that helped to secure his appointment and that of his successor, Fr Thomas Worsley (1632–6), against the opposition of an anglophobic St Omer magistracy. Her death in 1633 was an important loss for the College.

One reason for this success was the relaxation of persecution in England. In James' early years, due to the fears associated with the Gunpowder Plot, this had been severe, one victim being the St Omers protomartyr St Thomas Garnet (put to death in 1608). Three new statutes consolidated Elizabethan anti-Catholic legislation. Particularly relevant for St Omers was the 1606 'Act to Prevent and Avoid Dangers Which May Grow by Popish Recusants'. Clause XI stated that anyone educated abroad in Catholic seminaries would be disinherited unless he

Facing page: The Mill and its associated cottages.

41

took an oath of allegiance at the age of 18; while clause XIV disabled recusants from holding wardships or having custody of children by any other means. But, with the subsidence of the panic and the death of Robert Cecil in 1612, James was inclined to pursue a more pacific policy. Advised by the Howards, and fearful of the prospect of a new European religious war, he promoted a marriage alliance between his son Charles and the Spanish infanta. To be sure there were some brief flurries. In March 1615 St Omers was mentioned in a proclamation to prevent Catholic parents sending their children abroad for their education under pain of losing all their property; but even this was not followed up and Catholics continued to enjoy the benefits of a more relaxed regime.

Unfortunately, this could not last; for the years when St Omers grew to maturity just happened to coincide with a lull in the conflict between the Habsburgs and their enemies. In its first phase, reaching a peak in the 1590s, Spain found herself waging a three-front war against England, France and her rebellious Dutch subjects. However, due to its exorbitant costs, from 1598 onwards Spain seemed to be withdrawing from these excessive commitments; but this did not mean that the sources of tension had been removed. So, when the Dutch-Hispanic truce expired in 1621, a second phase of fighting began; and since by this time Spain was much weaker, she stood mainly on the defensive, particularly after 1635. St Omer therefore became part of a war zone. Moreover, these troubles coincided with renewed bouts of persecution in England. In the course of the seventeenth century these factors combined, on at least three occasions, to bring the College to the verge of disaster.

But at first the war did not seem to have much effect, for the Dutch-Hispanic conflict was mainly fought overseas. As far as St Omers was concerned the only consequence was that the Spanish pension, never very reliable, was hardly ever paid. Secured against the Gravelines customs dues, it was hit by the stringent embargo and counter-embargo imposed by Madrid and the United Provinces. However, as long as numbers continued to rise, the losses could be made good from parents' fees.

In 1624 the war escalated. Irritated by the failure of the Spanish match and alarmed by Habsburg successes in Germany, Parliament – encouraged by Buckingham and Charles, Prince of Wales – pushed James into a declaration of war. James still hoped to avoid fighting, but by 1625 he was dead and his place taken by Charles. At once new security measures were taken against Catholics. The Proclamation of 14 August 1625 recalled all Catholics from seminaries and reactivated anti-recusant legislation. In 1628 Parliament passed an 'Act to Restrain the Passing or Sending of Any to be Popish Bred across the Ocean', clause II stating that offending parents would forfeit for life all their goods and chattels. Clearly St Omers was a primary target! But in 1629, with the restoration of peace and under the influence of his catholic queen, Henrietta Maria, Charles reduced the pressure.

Thus, the real challenge was postponed till 1635. In that year Richelieu, having failed to undermine the Habsburgs by covert means, formally declared war on Spain. This immediately put St Omer in the firing line. A French army invaded the Spanish Netherlands and the boys were set to work repairing the town defences. At the same time numbers fell sharply from 200 to about 145. 1636 saw no fighting, since the French had to concentrate on defeating a great Habsburg invasion; instead bubonic plague killed 8,000. Although the College escaped, perhaps because of the hygienic regime laid down by Fr Schondonch, parents became alarmed and numbers slumped again to 115. The following year the French returned to Douai and Arras. St Omer's turn came in 1638; 25,000 men under Gaspard de Coligny camped at Blandêques and besieged the town for six weeks. A few shots from the bombardment hit the College and 40 boys were evacuated to the Jesuit house in Ghent. Immediately afterwards the sweating sickness struck, one of its victims being Fr Thunder. Later, when Hesdin fell the following year, hundreds of refugees poured into the town and the College found itself feeding up to 20 people a day. As in 1635, boys were requisitioned to repair the defences. Then, in May 1640, the French besieged the neighbouring town of Aire, capturing it on 27 July. At once the Watten community took refuge in their town house; and, until Aire was retaken six months later, marauding bands of cavalry roamed the countryside. On one occasion two bands of novices and boys were surprised while rashly taking a walk outside the walls: the novices escaped but three boys and their escort, a scholastic by the name of Henry Poulton, were drowned. During the next few years the French, helped by revolts in Catalonia and Portugal, gradually overran the whole of Artois; but, except for a plot to betray the town in 1647, St Omer was not directly threatened.

Meanwhile in England the summoning of the Long Parliament and the outbreak of the Civil War released the pent-up frustrations caused by Charles's High Church policies. Between 1641 and 1644 16 Catholics, laity as well as priests, were formally executed for their faith and several others died in gaol. They included two Old Boys: Fr Thomas Holland (SO 1615–21) and Fr Ralph Corbie (SO 1613–19), both betrayed by their fellow schoolmates James Wadsworth (SO 1618–22) and Thomas Gage (SO c.1615). Two years later, in 1646, three more met their deaths: Fr Thomas Whitaker (SO 1630–6), Fr Edward Bamber (SO 1618–21) and Fr John Woodcock (SO 1628–9). The previous year Fr Brian Cansfield (SO 1598–1601) died in gaol.

The combined effects of war and persecution were catastrophic. Income fell to 6,040 scudi as numbers declined and parents failed to pay their fees, an issue that had been raised as early as 1623 by the Provincial Fr Blount (see Appendix C: Tables 9 and 10). In 1644 the Poetry and Rhetoric classes departed leaving only 24 boys and 12 Jesuits in the community the following year. In the Province matters were little better. No Scholastic was admitted for two years and appeals had to be made to other Provinces for assistance.

Looking at this decline one has to face the possibility that the Catholic community was not as vigorous as it had been earlier. In the 1590s St Omers, along with the rest of the English mission, had seemed to thrive under persecution; but in the 1640s the opposite happened. The chance of picking up thousands of waverers, still open in the 1590s, had evaporated; James had not turned out to be a Catholic monarch after all, and the Civil War struck directly at the wealth and power of the Catholic gentry on whom the mission depended.

Nevertheless, there was still sufficient resilience to make a recovery when opportunity offered. Between 1648 and 1653 France was paralysed by the Fronde disturbances; while in England the execution of Charles I marked the end of the Civil War. Numbers began to grow, finances improved and efforts could be made to restore academic standards (see Appendix C: Tables 9 and 10). In 1641 the Prefect of Studies, Fr John Turner, had complained that interest in Greek had declined since commentaries on the Church Fathers, to the exclusion of 'profane works', had begun to be explained in the Refectory; but visitations by Fr Alexander Gottifredo from Naples and Fr Joseph Simons in 1648 and 1668

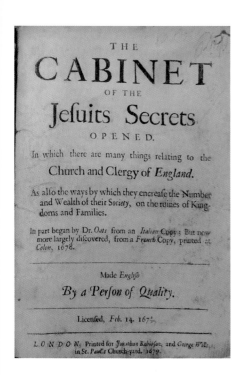

The Cabinet of the Jesuit Secrets Opened, *London 1679, one of a mass of anti-Catholic propaganda associated with the Popish Plot.*

produced good reports, and under the Rectorate of Fr Thomas Cary (1669–72) Greek was revived.

It has to be said, though, that this recovery was very halting. One difficulty was a regulation made in 1646 by Pope Innocent X. Until reversed in 1658 rectors had to be changed every three years, with obvious effects on continuity. Then there was the smallpox epidemic of 1650 killing three boys and affecting 47 others. After 1653 the revival of France and her alliance with England brought more fighting to the vicinity. A document of 1659 describes how 'Last year this house [Watten] suffered very serious damage when an army of French and English for fully eleven days camped in the house and surrounding grounds. During that period grain of almost every kind was laid waste, various flocks and herds driven away, timber cut down, everything ruined. The cost of repairs will not be less than 8,000 crowns.' Since the College depended on Watten farm for provisions these losses were a serious matter.

The war finally came to an end in 1659. Under the Treaty of the Pyrenees France secured the whole of Artois except the towns of Aire and St Omer, henceforth known as Artois Reserve, which remained under Spanish control. The restoration of Charles II was also a hopeful sign. But France had not abandoned her ambitions in Flanders. In 1667 Louis XIV provoked the War of Devolution; five years later he invaded Holland. Aire was taken in 1676 and the following year, while Louis besieged Valenciennes, the Duke of Orleans attacked St Omer. His troops camped at Blandêcques causing 600 crowns' worth of damage. William of Orange's relief attempt was defeated at Mont Cassel and on 1 May, after a siege of 25 days, Louis entered the town in triumph. At the treaty of Nijmegen (1678) St Omer was permanently ceded to France. Naturally, the Spanish authorities refused to continue paying Philip II's pension; but for years this had proved virtually valueless. Between 1660 and 1684, out of the 250,000 florins due, only 1,577 had been received. Accordingly representations were made to Louis, and in 1680 an annual grant of 8,000 livres was secured, the exact equivalent to the amount offered before.

Unfortunately, by this time the College had become entangled in the tentacles of the Popish Plot. Its central figure was Titus Oates. The son of an Anabaptist preacher, his early career had been a litany of expulsions from school and college, academic failure, a fine of £1,000 for perjury and the loss of several posts through intemperate behaviour. Chance threw him in the way of the Provincial, Fr Richard Strange. He applied to join the Society and, under the pseudonym of Titus Ambrose, was packed off to the seminary at Valladolid. He did not last long, for he lacked the Latin requisite for the course. Five months later 'ob pessimos mores', as the register puts it, he was removed. Even then Fr Strange did not desert him, and he was sent, at the age of 28, to St Omers where he arrived on 10 December 1677. The College, loath to accept him, did what it could. 'Sampson Lucy' (Oates' new alias) was put in Rhetoric 'by reason of his age and on no other account' according to Henry Thornton, then a Syntaxian; and he was given a separate table between the Community and the boys at meals. But it could not work. In the first place his appearance was totally against him; and then there were his strange habits. The tales told of him by his contemporaries in the courts are legendary. Anthony Turbeville 'saw a little boy beat him up and down with a fox's tail', William Parry (veré Conway) 'broke a pan about his head for recreation' during 'a peculiar recreation which they call "sawing the witch" ' held in mid-Lent. Thomas Billing deposed how, while walking in the garden with him,

This Blunt (Richard Blunt veré Barnaby) and one Henry Howard (veré Haggerton) were playing with one another, throwing stones at one another's shins. At which he was displeased and said, if they would not be quiet, he would tell the Rector. Howard was hasty, and spoke angrily to him, and said, if he would not be quiet, he would beat him. But Mr Oates persisting, and daring of him says he, 'what, do you dare me?' and comes up to him, and throws up Mr Oates his heels. Upon which Mr Oates lookt fretfully upon him, and withdrew himself into the infirmary.

Not surprisingly, he became the laughing-stock of the school; and, as a further delectation, the nightly rule of silence was occasionally shattered by the loud intonation of some imprecatory psalm. When the new Provincial, Fr Thomas Whitbread, came on visitation his days were numbered. On 23 June 1679 with a suit of clothes, a periwig, and £4 in his pocket he was expelled. According to Fr Stapleton, Rector between 1679 and 1683, 'on the night of his departure, late at night, he was found in the Sodality, leaning on his elbows over the altar like a priest at Mass. Asked what he was doing there, he replied "I am saying farewell to Jesus Christ".'

Oates went straight to London still hoping, by ingratiation or blackmail, to re-enter the Society. When this failed, in collaboration with Israel Tonge and Captain Blood, notorious for his attempt to steal the Crown jewels, he concocted his *True Narrative of the Horrid Plot*. In its 43 articles he alleged that the Society, at a 'consult' held in the White Horse Tavern, Wild St, off Drury Lane on 4 May (NS) planned to assassinate Charles II, massacre the Protestants, and bring in a French army of 50,000. Through Israel Tonge's friend Christopher Kirkby the conspiracy was brought to the attention of Charles and the Council in September 1678. Oates also deposed his information before Sir Edmond Berry Godfrey, a local Justice of the Peace. So, when Godfrey was found dead at the foot of Primrose Hill on the evening of 17 October (NS), panic set in. The offer of a reward brought forward a 'Captain' Bedloe to substantiate Oates's claims, and when Parliament met shortly afterwards, at the prompting of Shaftesbury, committees were set up to investigate. They uncovered what the Council had already been sifting, the possibility of a real plot in the correspondence between Edward Coleman and the French Government. This was dynamite, for Coleman had acted as secretary for both James, Duke of York, and his wife Mary of Modena. In November Oates and Bedloe gave their evidence before the Commons and extended it to implicate the Queen. As a final touch, on 19 December Ralph Montagu, formerly ambassador in Paris, revealed the secret clauses of the Treaty of Dover. With his first minister Danby facing charges of impeachment, Charles had no choice but to prorogue and dissolve Parliament.

To the modern mind it seems preposterous that a group of unbalanced perjurers could set a nation by the ears. But this does not do justice to the effect of decades of statutes, proclamations and other forms of anti-Catholic propaganda. For the public the Bull of Excommunication, the attempts against Elizabeth's life, and the Gunpowder Plot formed the groundwork for a continuing saga of Catholic iniquity. Israel Tonge was by no means unusual in believing that the Great Fire of London had been caused by Popish agents; and in 1641–2 Pym and his followers, in exactly the same way as Shaftesbury, had used such fears, backed by the news of massacres of Irish Protestants, to whip up an atmosphere of hysteria just before the Civil War. In such conditions it was virtually impossible for Catholics to get a

Titus Oates shown confounding the 'Romish stratagems' of the Pope and Jesuits in a contemporary print.

Two of the playing-cards printed by 'Robert Walton at the Globe' in 1678 illustrating various scenes from the Popish Plot:

Above: *Fr William Ireland SJ being drawn to his execution*

Facing page: *Fr John Fenwick SJ, St Omers London agent, sending students to St Omers.*

fair hearing before the law, something that under penal legislation was never very easy in any case. Unlike most informers Oates had the tremendous advantage of having actually visited Jesuit seminaries; so it was very easy for him to give a touch of verisimilitude. He was also lucky with the discovery of Coleman's correspondence; lucky too because there really had been a 'consult' on the day he mentioned. This, the triennial congregation of the English Province, had been held in James, Duke of York's apartments in St James's Palace; but being illegal, could not be used in the defence.

Charles' actions also had not helped. To be sure, he owed his life to Catholics after the battle of Worcester; and, even before his deathbed conversion, he was sympathetic to their cause. Many were part of his Court circle, some of them sharing his scientific interests. For instance, Edward Sherburne (this was how he signed himself), a distant relative of the Shireburns at Stonyhurst, was Master of the Ordnance and dedicated his astronomical work, *The Sphere of Marcus Manilius,* to the king; Fr Francis Line, Professor of Hebrew and Mathematics at Liège, engaged in controversy with Newton and even came over in 1669 to erect an elaborate sundial at Whitehall Palace.

But Charles did more. In the Declaration of Breda, issued just before the Restoration, he had promised 'liberty to tender consciences'. Unfortunately, the 'Cavalier' Parliament would have none of this and instead enacted the Clarendon Code. As early as 1662 Charles had tried to reverse it with a Declaration of Indulgence and introduced a toleration bill the following year. All that did was to set off a sharp anti-Catholic reaction, forcing Charles to issue a Proclamation ordering the expulsion of Jesuits and Seminary Priests by 14 May.

Undeterred, at the next opportunity Charles tried again. In 1667 the fall of Clarendon allowed him to create a new ministry appealing to Catholics and Dissenters. This was known as the Cabal, a term popularly derived from the names of its principal leaders – Clifford, Arlington, Buckingham, Ashley Cooper (later Lord Shaftesbury) and Lauderdale. By this Catholic-Dissenter alliance Charles hoped to free himself from his dependence on the Anglican Church and gentry. Instead, he heightened anti-Catholic alarms. By the secret Treaty of Dover Charles, in return for French subsidies, undertook to fight the Dutch, announce his conversion at the appropriate moment and in the meantime do all he could to promote the Catholic cause in England. An intermediary in these negotiations was none other than Humphrey Weld, an ancestor of Thomas Weld the donor of Stonyhurst. His career illustrates the continuity between Catholicism at the court of Charles I with that of his son. In 1638–9 he had been cup-bearer to Henrietta Maria; in 1647 he acted as Charles I's agent in Rome; while, under Charles II, as Governor of Portland Castle he received £1,000 in Secret Service money for forwarding letters to and from D'Estrées, Louis XIV's foreign minister.

In accordance with the treaty Charles issued his Second Declaration of Indulgence. It aroused a storm of protest; and because the Third Dutch War was going badly, Charles was in no position, financially or otherwise, to withstand demands for a Test Act debarring Catholics from holding any form of office. A chastened Charles, guided by his minister, Thomas Danby, at last reverted to an Anglican alliance. But he had left too many hostages to fortune. First there was Shaftesbury, implacably hostile after his dismissal; then there was Louis, who could blackmail him with the secret clauses from the Treaty of Dover; and third, there was his brother. As the events of his own reign all too clearly prove, James had by no means given up the idea of a Catholic-Dissenter alliance. Through

Coleman he conducted a correspondence encouraging Louis to hope that, in return for more subsidies, he could keep England at war with the Dutch and promote Catholicism; and if this was not generally known, the announcement of his conversion in 1676 can scarcely have been reassuring for Protestants.

Oates's revelations, therefore, ignited a highly explosive situation. Already, a Second Test Act had been passed in 1678; now both Louis and Shaftesbury saw their opportunity. Charles had recently sent an army of 20,000 to support the Dutch at Ostend; Louis, anxious to secure the Treaty of Nijmegen, struck back by getting Montagu to reveal the secret clauses in the Treaty of Dover. Meanwhile Shaftesbury pressed for James's exclusion from the succession hoping to substitute Monmouth, Charles's illegitimate son in his stead. To do this he had to maintain an atmosphere of hysteria, hence the constant ramification in the scope of the plot, the show trials and the executions of Jesuits and other suspects.

Into this trap fell some very distinguished Old Boys. On 27 December 1678 the Procurator of the Province, Fr William Ireland (SO 1647–55) and the St Omers' London agent, Fr John Fenwick, were brought to trial; and it is significant that Oates arrested them first so that their papers could not be used to disprove his fabrications. Next came the Provincial – Fr Thomas Whitbread (SO 1630–5), Fr William Harcourt (veré Barrow) (SO 1628–32) and Fr John Gavan (SO ?–1660) – known as 'the angel' at St Omers. To these can be added Fr Edward Mico (SO 1643–7), Socius or assistant to Fr Whitbread, who died from the complications of fever and maltreatment in gaol, Fr Edward Turner (SO 1647–8) who also died in gaol, Fr Thomas Thwing (SO c.1650), Fr Philip Evans (SO ?–1665), Fr John Plessington (SO c.1665) and James's former chaplain at the battle of Sole Bay, Fr Thomas Downes (SO 1630–6).

Naturally, every effort was made to save them. Since evidence on oath taken by Catholics overseas was inadmissible in court the Rector sent over 14 boys and two lay brothers to give testimony. They were joined by a gardener, a mason and a bargeman from Watten and two lay brothers from Liège. Nine of the boys testified in the trials of Frs Whitbread, Gavan, Turner and their legal agent, Mr Richard Langhorne, on 23 June 1679. Some also gave evidence during the impeachment proceedings of five Catholic Lords in April and May. On both occasions their object was to prove that Oates could not possibly have attended the 'consult' on 4 May 1678 as he claimed because he was still at the College; but, in a rigged court dominated by a vituperative Chief Justice Scroggs, they had little chance. Their own position was not without danger: on one occasion Oates arrested two of them at a chance meeting in the street, and on one was found a letter written by James's chaplain, Fr Edward Petre, who was promptly imprisoned.

Coinciding as it did with the loss of the Spanish pension the Plot had severe effects on the College itself. Channel communications were cut for five months and the arrest of Frs Ireland and Fenwick disorganised the finances. Fr Warner, the new Vice-Provincial, actually considered closure and was in part dissuaded by the attitude of the boys themselves. 'Not a single one out of their number', he records, 'thought of returning to his native land: all preferred to beg alms from door to door, or to enter the service of some nobleman in any capacity whatever rather than trust themselves into such a manifest danger of losing the faith while uncertain of their constancy.' With rumours circulating that closure was imminent the senior boys went to the Procurator, Fr Busby; on hearing that existing resources could last for only three more months they offered to extend it to six by eating bread and water only at meals. Certainly, there was an upsurge

Fenwick at Dover sending Student to St Omers

Right: *Fr William Ireland SJ, Scholastic and Prefect of Studies at St Omers, 1672–7. At the time of his arrest he was Procurator of the English Province.*

Far right: *Fr Thomas Whitbread SJ, Provincial of the English Province 1678–9.*

in religious fervour; the Community had a special fast on Fridays which many of their pupils voluntarily shared, relays of four boys each took turns 'watching' the Blessed Sacrament exposed every Sunday, and the number of vocations doubled from an average of ten to twenty-two.

These measures bought just sufficient time until the French Pension was granted and fees, supplemented by gifts, began to arrive from England. During the rectorates of Fr Thomas Stapleton (1679–83) and Fr John Warner (1683–7) there was some recovery. In England it proved impossible to sustain the initial hysteria. By a masterly policy of delays and dissolutions Charles fended off demands for an Exclusion Act until the time was ripe for a counterattack. It came in 1683; Whig excesses and fear of a new civil war fuelling a Tory backlash. Despite acquittal on a charge of treason by a Middlesex jury, Shaftesbury had to flee abroad. At the same time the revelations of the Rye House Plot completed the rout. At last action could be taken against Oates. On 10 May 1684 he was put in the Counter and then transferred to the King's Bench prison pending libel charges brought by James. The jury duly awarded £100,000 damages plus 20s. costs, and since there was no possibility of payment he returned to gaol. Then, on 8 and 9 May 1685, he faced charges of perjury in Westminster Hall. Twenty-two St Omers boys, only three of whom had testified in 1679, were sent up by Fr Warner. Oates was sentenced to be flogged, put in the pillory five times a year (one of the days being 24 April (OS) the date of the 'consult') and life imprisonment.

On 22 December 1684, scarcely after the College had got over the effects of the Plot, there was a dangerous fire. Writing to the Brussels Internuncio, the Procurator Fr Warren stated that 'It destroyed kitchens, dispensary, refectory, a large hall where the lesser plays are produced, the Community recreation room, the procurator's room, and an entire dormitory not to mention furniture of various kinds.'

The rebuilding, which cost 17,000 scudi, took three years to complete. Although Père La Chaise encouraged Louis XIV to send 4,000 scudi, a number of unpleasant expedients had to be adopted, including the plundering of the College bursaries. Nonetheless the prospects seemed to look good. With James II's accession the

Province planned to open no less than 12 schools in England, two of them being the celebrated interdenominational foundations at the Savoy Palace and Fenchurch Street. These would have to be staffed in part from St Omers and for a time it seemed as if a Continental school was no longer necessary. But these hopes proved premature. In 1688 William of Orange landed at Torbay; and within a few weeks the 'Glorious Revolution' was triumphantly completed. Forty-six Jesuits fled the country. Among them were Fr Warner, appointed only the year before as James' confessor, and Fr Petre (SO 1644–52), the only Jesuit Privy Councillor in English history. Oates, the 'Saviour of the Nation', was released from Newgate, awarded a pension and, by marrying a Miss Rebecca Weld, secured a dowry of £2,000.

Steps were at once taken against Catholics: Acts 'For Amoving Papists and Reported Papists from the Cities of London and Westminster, and ten mile distance from the same', and 'For the better securing the Government by disarming Papists and Reported Papists', targeted Catholic Jacobite sympathisers like Sir Nicholas Shireburn of Stonyhurst who were busily stockpiling arms. Twelve years later another 'Act for the further preventing the growth of Popery' was passed. It imposed a £100 fine on anyone sending a child overseas to receive a Catholic education, life imprisonment on anyone caught saying Mass or running

Below: *St Omers after the fire in 1684. Print by Monthard in 1689. The key at the sides gives a useful guide to particular parts of the building.*

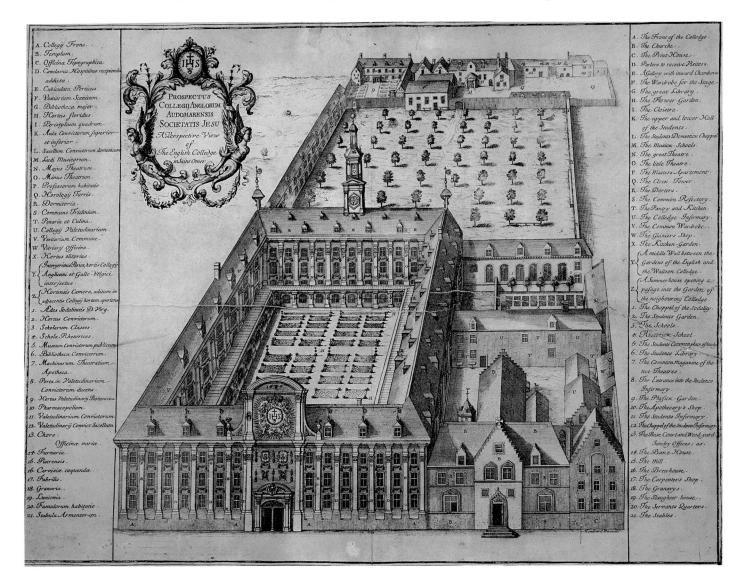

'The Scientific three-horned Doctor, Fr Peters SJ, a great labourer, in the works of darkness.' Engraving of 1679, now held in the Farm St Archives. Fr Petre SJ, Rector of St Omers from 1693 to 1697, has the distinction of being the only Jesuit Privy Councillor in English history.

a Catholic school and, unlike in previous legislation, gave the whole £100 reward to the informer. Catholics were also prohibited from buying property and, if aged 18 or above, disabled from inheriting their estate unless they took the Oath of Allegiance prescribed by the Test Act. According to the Provincial Fr Henry Humbertson 'certainly no laws more effective for rooting out the Catholic religion have ever been passed; and unless God hinders the execution of them, it will be impossible for religion to survive long in that kingdom.' Proof of this can be seen with the Calvert family. In November 1713 when Benedict Calvert, Lord Baltimore, apostatised to save his American property, he removed his four sons from St Omers and had them brought up as Protestants. The letters of Fr Louis Sabran, Rector between 1713 and 1715, show the difficulties encountered during this period. Boys crossing over to the Continent are referred to as 'packs'; and on one occasion his London agent Fr Coxon reported that Mr Deale the College apothecary had informed on him, arrested Fr Hanmer while he was saying Mass and deposed on oath 'that Mr Sabran who goes about by the name of Wittmore sent him [Deale] over to poyson a great person, and several other things relating to the Pretender'.

At the same time the War of the League of Augsburg (1688–97) and the War of the Spanish Succession (1702–15) broke out on the Continent. Luckily, the only direct consequence for St Omers came in 1696–7 when the Community worked with an Irish brigade wintering in the town: but Fr Sabran's letters and Appendix C: Table 10 show how the finances were affected. In 1714 appeals by Père La Chaise, Père Le Tellier and Lady Jersey were needed before Desmaretz would pay the French Pension, and efforts to restore the bursaries were sabotaged in 1713 by the French Government's cut in interest rates from 4% to 2½%. In a letter of 9 January 1715 Fr Darell, Sabran's Paris agent, mentions that capital worth 39,300 livres had been reduced to 23,580 livres by this expedient and that a further 3,930 livres interest was owing. Not surprisingly numbers were also erratic (see Appendix C: Table 9); but the most serious problems were caused by the non-payment of fees. In 1693 the Rector, none other than Fr Petre, did not mince his words:

Very Rev Father in Christ (The General),

Ever since Your Paternity has been pleased to lay upon me the over-whelming burden of this College, I have spared no pains in communicating to you the state of affairs, such as it is. To my intense sorrow, I have found things in so deplorable a condition, that I am borne out by other competent judges in the opinion that we may scarcely hope to avert the downfall of this house. This untoward state of things can be traced to two sources (1) a large number of scholars have been admitted without due selection, from familes in such straitened circumstances, that it was, even at first sight, idle to expect them to pay their sons' pension. . . . (2) English Catholics have been so ground down by fines and extraordinary impositions, that they enjoy scarcely a third of their income, so that even the wealthier ones find it hard to pay for their children the moderate pension we demand. I say moderate as the cost of living and clothing has increased threefold beyond what it formerly was.

Ten years later Fr Sabran's letters show that matters had improved little. Writing to Fr Coxon on 6 June 1714 he reckoned that fees worth £800 per annum were unpaid; and the following month Fr Coxon estimated losses of £8,375 or £400 per annum in the past two decades. Its magnitude becomes fully apparent when one realises that the fee was still only £25, the same as in the 1590s!

Ruthless measures were called for. As a matter of course, bonds were taken from parents, and sometimes resort was even made to the law. On 29 November 1714 Fr Coxon proudly announced he had secured £28 less £4 legal costs outstanding 28 years before from the late Lord Abergavenny. The coming of peace also allowed Fr Sabran to play the currency markets of London, Antwerp and Paris. Some idea of his industry can be gauged from the fact that in 1714 he sent 443 letters and received 504. When he retired on 20 October 1715 he could announce that he held 3,000 florins more cash in hand than he had found, that numbers had risen to 146, and that seven of the eight free places had been refounded. Like many of his predecessors he proved effective at public relations. When the Duke and Duchess of Norfolk (née Mary Shireburn of Stonyhurst) visited the College on 12 and 13 May 'ye badges of [the] Earl Marshall' were in position and a stage entertainment was provided by the boys before the guests repaired for dinner at the Abbey of St Bertin. The total cost for the College was £35.

St Omers, then, bounced back from the effects of war after the Treaty of Utrecht. Nowhere was vigour more clearly apparent than in the response to the fire of 4 October 1725; which may have been caused by arson. This was much more serious than that of 1684. According to Fr Edward Gage, procurator of the Province

The fire broke out at the further end of ye study place towards the Scholars' Infirmary: by that time people were got out of their beds, it had gained the space of two windows, and went on with that violence that in 8 minutes that whole range of building was in a flame: and what is more surprising, in half an hour's time the fire had seized the 4 corners of the New Square, scholes and [the] whole New Square was burnt down. The main walls of ye Square are standing; but to be sure, must be pulled down, at least to very near ye ground.

The fire, therefore, destroyed the classrooms, the Study Place, private rooms of the fathers, the boys' dormitories on the top floor of the New Square, the Great and Little Theatres and most of the College Library. It could not have come at a worse time. Fr Hyde, the College Procurator, wrote 'we had not 180 livres in ye house; all our winter clothing for Fathers and schollars' bedding with most of the Fathers' all burnt; all their gowns, books, musick instruments, in fine all lost: so that I count ye loss of moveables greater than that of the house.'

Emergency arrangements were immediately put in hand. Sixty boys were placed in another Jesuit building in the town, 23 others put in a Canon's home, beds were borrowed from a local barracks and the remaining 27 put in the Infirmary. Normal routine restarted on 11 November and rebuilding began the next day, though the roof was not slated until April 1727. The operation was expensive, but the College was helped by some benefactions: Pope Benedict XIII gave 1,000 crowns, the king of Portugal provided 5,000 guilders, in February 1726 £2,200 was raised from friends in England and another £100 contributed by Fr Turbeville. Louis XV eventually produced 30,000 livres, and even the Roman College found 80 scudi from its attenuated finances in 1727. One result was better facilities. The Study Place, completed in April 1727, had brick walls 38 in. thick, was 34 ft. high and 24 ft. long with 15 windows on each side; the classrooms which, like the Study Place, only had flagstone paving, were 14 ft. high and each had two windows 8 ft. by 4 ft. and a half-size window over the door; the Refectory, completed in May 1727, had marble paving and a new wainscot. There are references to a Buyer's, Singing and Violin Rooms and the Court was crenellated. For the Infirmary we have a particularly detailed description from the pen of Brother Henry Bartlet written some time before 1742:

> I judged worth our notice an apothecary's shop exquisitely beautiful, and furnished with most costly drugs and medicines from Holland. Some of the drawers are made to represent pillars in several orders of architecture, and have fine splendid carved work, gilt on the top, seeming as so many stately supporters to the place. Adjoining this is a room set apart for surgical operations, which apartment makes a very neat appearance. In this we observed two very compacted skeletons, and near them a handsome set of surgeon's instruments in 'fine order'.

Rebuilding may have delayed plans, first mooted in 1726, to start a Preparatory School at Boulogne. Hitherto, the College had relied on elementary schools in England. But although the 1599 Constitution had prescribed the age of entry to be 14 and deemed an elementary knowledge of Latin essential, during the previous century numerous exceptions had been made and it was not until 1742 that decisive action was taken. The Château de la Cocheuse, a few miles outside Boulogne, was acquired and placed under the control of a Superior, Fr William Blackiston. From St Omers Fr John Heatley and two lay brothers were sent to help. The new establishment aimed to teach up to 40 boys the three Rs, English, French and the rudiments of Latin. Finding these quarters inconvenient, in 1747 the school moved to an old brewery within the town. Four years later a building-plot 2,900 sq. yds. in area was acquired by a Mrs Panting, whose son was a Jesuit novice, with the intention of presenting it to the Society. However, since by this time the College was taking French pupils, the local curé and the Oratorian school, fearing competition, protested vigorously. So, despite support from the local bishop, the school had to be refounded at Watten the following year. Nonetheless, until the suppression of the Society in France, Jesuits continued to use Mrs Panting's house as a staging post for their journeys across the Channel.

But if these were signs of strength there were also some symptoms of weakness. Tables 9 and 10 (in Appendix C) show that, during this period, numbers and finances remained sluggish; and this at a time when, despite anti-Jacobite alarms, the English Catholic community was beginning to grow. Nor was everything well academically. It is true that Fr Edward Slaughter introduced the study of Hebrew during his rectorate (1705–9), but this was a short-lived experiment. From the days of Fr Warner and Fr Petre onwards there were complaints about the over frequent rotation of staff. Fr Charles Shireburn, the Provincial between 1740 and 1744 and a distant relative of the Shireburns at Stonyhurst, recommended that Prefects, if capable, should be retained at their posts for a minimum of three years.

Further signs of change, not necessarily for the worse, can be found in the first appearance of small but significant numbers of foreign, mainly French-speaking pupils – about 15 in all before 1762. The Sabran Letters for instance contain a note dated 3 January 1714 from a Monsieur Geraldin of St Malo sending his son a louis d'or as a new year gift to 'pay for washing that he may not want clean linen'. Other items show that by this time communications with Paris were well established, particularly as a source of 'acting suits'. It has been suggested that these might have been a code for altar vestments. However, on 23 April 1714 we find Fr Eyre sending 33 sets of rubies, feathers, shirts and embroidery worth £46.3s. Clearly such items were intended for the theatre. Some saw this sort of thing as a sign of decadence. The General, Fr Retz, had no doubts. During the rectorate of Fr Joseph Constable (1737–9), and acting on information supplied by Fr Thomas Lawson, he complained of boys taking riding lessons, being allowed to spend the night away from the College on shooting expeditions, and thought that the masters at Liège, whence St Omers got most of its teachers, ought not to wear wigs or possess watches. The Bedingfeld accounts from the same period show that the charges were not unfounded. On 2 December 1740 Richard and Edward 'Clay' received silver cups, spoons, knives and forks to the value of £7.17s.; on 8 January 1743 4s. was spent on some snuff boxes; and for 27 January 1744 we read that £9.14s.7d. was spent on an excursion with one 'Blount'– presumably a school friend. In other words St Omers was becoming a more gentlemanly school. Its effects on scholarship can be gauged from a letter Fr Sabran received on 5 February 1715 from Monsieur Brugneel 'to free his son from Greek that he may learn to dance, and if [he] hath a genius and liking musick'. Whether these changes were really a sign of decay must remain a matter for conjecture. After all it could be said that the Society was simply moving with the times: but the trials and tribulations of the previous century do make the placid atmosphere of the eighteenth look very like lassitude. It remained to be seen whether the College, and the Province it supported, still had the energy to face a new challenge, namely the total suppression of the Society. Before that some attention must be paid to its relations with the Catholic community in England.

ST OMERS, THE SHIREBURNS
AND THE ENGLISH MISSION

SCHOOLS DO NOT exist in isolation; and nowhere is this more true than at St Omers. This explains why, despite its small size, the College had so much impact on English society. This chapter then looks at the Catholic community, the mission that served it and the contribution made by St Omers to the whole.

The bedrock of that community was the gentry. Money, protection and future priests all came from this source; through their households they set the tone for their extended families of relatives, servants and tenants. Fr Persons' *Directory* was only one, albeit very successful, example of a mass of literature designed to develop a 'godly discipline' – Catholic or Puritan – in such homes. Moreover, since priests could not legally hold property, gentlemen as private individuals did it for them, usually in some kind of trust. St Omers' scholarships were sometimes held in this way. But there was a price. Gentlemen could and did regulate the behaviour of 'their' chaplains. They may also have distorted the balance of the mission. Too many clergy were left isolated amid seas of Protestants in the aristocratic households of the South and East; too many opportunities in the North, West and Wales went a-begging for lack of manpower. But these were facts of life. Given the shortage of priests it seemed right to deploy them where they would do most good, and in a hierarchical society that meant with the rich and powerful. Had not Protestants succeeded by going to the top? And if the 'commanding heights' could not be scaled, were not lesser nobility of some account in a society believing that its country was its county? A gentry-based strategy had much to commend it.

These points are admirably illustrated by the Shireburns at Stonyhurst, especially by Sir Richard 'the builder'. Not that there had been no building before; but in this, as in other respects, his achievements mask those of his ancestors. Succeeding as a minor in 1537 he did not begin to make his mark until the reign of Edward VI. Knighted for services in the Scottish wars his subsequent efforts to accumulate wealth and power rested on two pillars – the development of estates originally put together by Robert Shireburn in the days of Edward II, and the exploitation of family connections going back to the marriage of another Richard Shireburn (d. 1441) to Agnes daughter of Sir William Stanley of Hooton. These proved especially valuable under Mary Tudor and continued to yield dividends in the reign of her sister. Sir Richard was treasurer and later chamberlain of the Stanley household; he acted as their deputy governor on the Isle of Man; he

The Shireburn Tombs at Mitton. Above are Richard Shireburn (d. 1629) with his wife Catherine, daughter of Lord Stourton. Richard was largely responsible for the Jacobean building commenced by his father at Stonyhurst in 1592. In the tomb below lies his son, also called Richard, who died in 1667–8. This photograph was taken by Fr Lawrence SJ, in 1941.

Facing page: *Rear view of the 'Eagle Towers'. A contract of 1712 shows that they were put up by 'Richard Rydeing' of Waddington for £40. Directly below the photographer lies 'Quality Street; 'Siberia' is on the opposite side of the quadrangle.*

55

was keeper of Greenhalgh Castle and Park; he was steward of their estates at Bolton in Lonsdale and Ewecross; and he was Forester of Ingleborough Chase. Sir Richard also built up connections with other gentry in Stanley service. The best example of this was his first marriage to Maud, daughter of Richard Bold, Sheriff of Lancashire between 1577 and 1590. He even had his son, also called Richard, betrothed to Catherine, daughter of Charles Lord Stourton and niece of Henry Stanley, fourth Earl of Derby. It is hardly surprising then to find him a member of the third Earl's funeral cortège in 1572.

In addition, the Stanleys helped to further his official career by securing his election to Parliament for Lancashire in 1553, Liverpool in 1555 and Preston in 1554 and 1557–8. Sir Richard also obtained several local offices – Butler and Searcher for the Port of Liverpool, Master Forester of Bowland, Deputy Lord-Lieutenant in 1569 and 1585, Commissioner for the Muster in 1579 and Subsidy Commissioner in 1585. Last, but not least, he obtained the wardships of the Langley and Talbot families.

Nevertheless, there was a change of emphasis between the reigns of Mary and Elizabeth. Under the former he could hope to rise into the ranks of the nobility, an ambition betrayed by the sheer scale and quadrangular arrangement of his building at Stonyhurst – quite unlike most of the other smaller gentlemen's houses in the area. But from the 1570s it is clear that the Stanleys would not or could not do so much for him. True, they still needed families like the Shireburns to help them run what was still a very Catholic county; but, unlike his father, the fourth Earl was a strong Protestant and, under increasingly close scrutiny from the government, he cannot have felt happy about their religious loyalties.

So Sir Richard turned to estate management and, like many Catholic gentlemen, became very good at it. His estates, scattered in a great arc from Dent, through Bolton, Chorley and the Fylde down to Liverpool, were enhanced by a succession of purchases – Bailey Hall, West Esholt (where he kept an iron-foundry), Leagram (bought from the Earl of Leicester) and a cluster of properties around Stonyhurst itself. As Deputy Lord-Lieutenant he is even alleged, according to a spy's report of 1592, to have threatened a Simon Haddock with violence if he refused to sell him property near Chorley.

Revenue from land could be very high. In 1571, for instance, Sir Richard's lands around Stonyhurst generated about £305; and his will was valued at £4,240. Financially this put him in the same league as a great nobleman; and the same point applies to his descendant Sir Nicholas Shireburn in the eighteenth century. Through his marriage to Catherine, daughter of Sir Edward Charlton of Hesleyside, Nicholas received valuable properties and, through their links with the Widdringtons, built up his power in Northumberland. But, like Sir Richard before him, his career was blighted by a change of ruler. During the Revolution of 1688 his father was arrested and died in gaol the following year. A staunch Jacobite, in 1698 he showed his true loyalties by sending his daughter to St Germain – not Whitehall – to be 'touched for the king's evil'. Later, the house became a veritable arsenal. In 1715 the accounts show that one John Mason supplied a pan for casting bullets from 20 lbs of lead for the several pistols subsequently discovered in secret places during later building work.

His estate management was extremely ruthless. A list of several hundred leases from the Long Preston area shows him to have tripled the yield between 1689 and 1716. This enabled him to engage in substantial building work and marry off his daughter to the eighth Duke of Norfolk at fabulous expense. Wealth and powerful connections could also help Catholic and philanthropic causes. In 1686,

Sir Nicholas's father had founded a school and even begun an almshouse at Hurst Green. Sir Nicholas completed the work, but moved the almshouse to Kemple End. In addition, between 1693 and 1700, £140 was spent relieving poor Catholics, a dispensary was opened by his wife in the coach-houses and people of the neighbourhood were encouraged to spin jersey wool in the house itself. Further afield, in 1700 £100 was sent to help the Franciscans at Douai and another £100 given to Fr Dicconson, Superior of the Society's Lancashire District. Two distant relatives – Charles and 'Dick' Shireburn – had their St Omers school fees paid for them. Later Charles went on to become Provincial. Sir Nicholas himself, like his father, but only very possibly his brother, was an Old Boy.

A similar pattern can be seen with Sir Richard. Accounts for 1571 and 1572 show regular payments to Fr Richard Gradell, a former chantry priest brought in to confess his second wife, Isabell, when she fell ill. Using his position as chantry commissioner, he bought up half the endowments of the Mitton chantry to build a family mausoleum on the opposite side of the chancel. William, later Cardinal Allen, probably visited Stonyhurst during his Lancashire tour of the 1560s and his brother was a Shireburn tenant. Like his father-in-law and many other Catholics Sir Richard even sat on the Ecclesiastical Commission that was supposed to identify and prosecute recusants. When all else failed he resorted to a mixture of violence, concealment and bluff of the most brazen kind. The spy's report of 1592 states that he and his family stuffed wool in their ears during church services, threatened informers with death and removed Richard Startevant, a suspected Jesuit, from the Subsidy Book. At Stonyhurst the chapel, part of which is now the Bayley Room, was openly 'concealed' in the 'Blind' Tower, which then had no windows opening on to the Avenue to prevent prying strangers from looking in. And if there was a search – one was actually made during the Popish Plot – then the House contained several hiding places. From the sacristy adjoining the chapel (now the Headmaster's study) two escape routes ran in opposite directions; one into the garden, the other to a secret 'hide' behind the shield above the main

'Stepped into a barn of ours, a great shadowy barn . . . and looking at the rudely arched timber branches . . . I thought how sadly beauty of inscape was unknown and buried away from simple peoples and yet how near at hand it was.' Journal of Gerard Manley Hopkins, 1872, probably referring to the fourteenth-century Shireburn Barn, here photographed by Fr King in 1927.

Above: *Sir Nicholas Shireburn (d. 1717), by Sir Godfrey Kneller.*

Above right: *Elizabeth Weld (d. 1688), sister of Sir Nicholas Shireburn. It was through her that the Welds inherited the Stonyhurst property. Portrait by Sir Geoffrey Kneller.*

entrance. Another priest hole, 11 ft. long, 3ft. 6 in. wide and 2 ft. 6 in. high, was found above the bay window in the Main Quadrangle between the Long Room and the top floor. In the Duchess's Rooms a space behind a bookcase worked by a spring contained a bed, mattress, a bottle of rum and 90 King James II guineas. Likewise Sparrow's Hall, standing on the site of the Arundell Library, produced two more caches, one containing a further 30 King James II guineas.

But, as suggested at the beginning of the chapter, this protection could be used to dictate the terms and conditions under which their chaplains worked. In a deed that was later witnessed in 1724 Richard, father of Sir Nicholas Shireburn, specified that 'Hee [the priest] is to celebrate three times a weeke, offering upp one Masse for Richard Shireburn of Stonyhurst esq, and Isabel his wife. Another for their children and grandmother, and all whom they in dutie are bound to pray for the living. A third for friends departed.' Sixteen members of the family were specified and the priest was further required, if necessary, to serve parishioners in Leagram, Mitton, Long Preston and Giggleswick. Even more autocratic was Mary (née Shireburn), Duchess of Norfolk. After the death of her former chaplain, Fr Thomas Hunter, she insisted that Fr Thomas Lawson, then rector at Watten, take his place; when he objected to her questionable relationship with Peregrine Widdrington (it was probably ratified by some kind of morganatic marriage) he was sacked and the Society excluded from Stonyhurst till after her death.

Nonetheless, there were some limitations on Shireburn power. Sir Richard 'got away with it' because he was a church papist, or a Catholic who attended

Anglican services; but his more stiff-necked descendants ran into trouble. In 1648, during their march to and from the battle of Preston, Cromwell and his Ironsides quartered themselves in and around the house, the future Lord Protector himself allegedly sleeping on the great table that still stands in the Top Refectory. Three years later this Richard Shireburn temporarily lost nearly two-thirds of his estates for sending his sons to St Omers. Even Sir Richard found that friends and allies could turn against him. In the early 1590s the delicate balancing act maintained by the Stanleys between the Government and Catholic gentry like the Shireburns broke down in the face of vociferous agitation from Puritan communities in Manchester, Bolton and other South Lancashire towns. Simultaneously the extravagance of the fourth Earl's wife landed him in serious debt – a situation that was compounded by the succession struggle that followed his death. Partly this was due to Hesketh's Plot, a half-baked Catholic scheme to further the royal claims of Ferdinando, Lord Strange, son of the fourth Earl. Ferdinando saved himself by betraying his backers; but then died shortly afterwards in highly mysterious circumstances. It is hardly surprising then to find that the most damaging accusations against Sir Richard date from this time; and, although under James I, the situation was partially restored by the sixth Earl, during the Civil War Stanley power collapsed completely. For once they could not sit on the fence. They had to choose between Puritans in the towns and a partially Catholic gentry supporting the Crown. In the event the defeat of Charles I ruined the seventh Earl and destroyed the umbrella under which the

Above left: Mary, Eighth Duchess of Norfolk (d. 1754), daughter of Sir Nicholas Shireburn.

Above: Thomas Weld (1750–1810) the 'donor' of Stonyhurst, aged 15.

Sir Nicholas Shireburn's buildings of 1699.

Shireburns had sheltered. This goes far to explain the eclipse of their fortunes in the mid-seventeenth century.

Turning now to the Catholic clergy, we find that they can be divided into three groups: the secular priests, the Society of Jesus and the other Regular orders. On paper the seculars seem to have been the most important. Trained at Douai, Valladolid and the English College at Rome they stepped into the shoes vacated by the Marian clergy. Not only were they the first to enter England, they were also the most numerous. Unfortunately, they were poorly organised and riven by dissension. The celebrated 'Broyles', which erupted when the Society was invited to run the English College, are an early example of this. Later, between 1595 and 1598, a group led by Dr Bagshawe waged a virulent campaign against the Jesuits and other priests within the confines of Wisbech Castle. These 'Wisbech Stirs' developed into arguments over the appointment and powers of bishops. Thus, the Archpriest Controversy of 1601–2 began when the Pope appointed an Archpriest, instead of a bishop, to co-ordinate English Catholic affairs. Such quarrels, as we shall see, left lasting wounds that affected the development of the College and the Society for centuries to come.

In essence the issue was about resources. People complained that the Society took the most money, secured the best livings, used unfair methods of recruitment and planned to take over all the training-centres as a prelude to governing the

English Mission by itself. The foundation of St Omers was part of this argument. In his *History of the English College at Doway*, published in 1705, Charles Dodd, whose real name was Hugh Tootel, asserted that 'Persons had all his eye-teeth . . . for he so managed his business as to become banker to the Doway College, so that the collections were continually to pass through his hands. This management afterwards proved very fatal to the clergy; for Persons having a long time been hatching a design to erect a College for his own body . . . he applied part of the collection designed for Doway College, towards founding a College at St Omers.'

But Dodd's argument rests on the mistaken assumption that St Omers was founded in 1592. Thus, in reply, the same Fr Hunter who acted as chaplain for the Shireburns wrote a *Modest Defence of the Clergy and Religious*; and in it he assembled many documents proving that the correct date was a year later.

This kind of distortion is also apparent when wider issues are considered. If the Society was planning to take over the English Mission then naturally it would oppose the appointment of bishops. In turn this would jeopardise the prospects of toleration; for some priests hoped for a deal whereby the Crown would get some control over episcopal elections run by a chapter in return for the expulsion of the Society. Thus, Persons was blamed for the appointment of an Archpriest, instead of a bishop. Indeed, according to Dodd, 'by this means Persons had cunningly invented a way to govern all the clergy by proxy'. The trouble with this view, though, was that, whatever might be the practice in Catholic countries, no Pope could countenance any Protestant government exercising control over the choice of bishops. Moreover, an episcopacy that dictated the selection, deployment and discipline of individual clergy ran clean against the interests of the gentry. One reason why the Society got the better posts and more money was because it recognised this fundamental fact. Gentry were well aware that the presence of Jesuits and other Regulars, by widening the range of choice, strengthened their control. Rome knew the facts of life too. An Archpriest evaded the whole question of episcopal relations with the gentry and regulars. Unfortunately, such tactics aggravated the tensions that already existed.

The result was that, even when a bishop and chapter were finally appointed in the 1620s, there was too much distrust. Some seculars, notably Dr Bagshawe, were so eaten up with hatred that they betrayed Jesuits to the authorities; and a few decades later Dr Sergeant played a major role behind the scenes during the Popish Plot. He was therefore indirectly responsible for the deaths of some of the St Omers Martyrs. More immediately, between the resignation of Bishop Smith in 1631 and the appointment of Vicars-Apostolic in 1688, secular clergy lacked an effective organisation on the ground.

So the field was left clear for the Regulars. The Benedictines, after establishing their first house in the Low Countries in 1602, set up two colleges or houses of probation at St Malo (1611) and St Gregory's Douai (1605) – the ancestor of Downside. Three other monasteries were founded at Chelles (1611), St Lawrence's at Dieulouard in Lorraine (1606), which later moved to Ampleforth, and St Edmund's in Paris (1615), which eventually became Douai Abbey at Woolhampton. Later, in 1643, the house at Lambspring, near Hildesheim, was incorporated into the English Benedictine Congregation. The Franciscans had two houses, one at Gravelines (1614) and the other at St Bonaventure's Douai (1618); while the Dominicans possessed a house of studies at Louvain and a college (*c.*1660) and noviciate (1657) at Bornholm near Antwerp. However, as Table 11 makes clear, the most successful Regulars were the Society. One reason for the failure of the secular priests to organise themselves was their reluctance to switch from a 'Church in Exile', awaiting the next swing of the political pendulum, to a fully fledged denominational Church. In contrast the Society was quick to appreciate this and set about creating the first national organisation. On the Continent the groundwork was laid by Fr Persons. It was he who set up the seminaries and colleges, pioneered safe routes in and out of England and provided some central direction as Prefect of the Mission. Meanwhile, in England Fr Henry Garnet and Fr Holtby busily created a network of safe houses, secret communications and supporting finances.

Even so, there were some unsatisfactory features. It was difficult to reconcile the need for permanent endowments with a vow of poverty or St Ignatius's clear preference that the Society should live on alms. There were also arguments over jurisdiction. Should English Jesuits living on the Continent be controlled by the Prefect of the Mission or by the Provincials of the districts where they resided? So long as Persons was alive his dynamism, the personal role he played in setting up the seminaries and his close friendship with General Claudio Aquaviva, glossed over the problem. But this *ad hoc* approach aggravated rifts between the Society and secular priests, particularly on questions about how to pool resources and establish a regular chain of command; when he died, no one was there to take his place.

The solution then, was to create a separate English Province in 1623. This envisaged a district network of 'Colleges' and 'Residences' served by a central London office to which was attached an agent to collect St Omers' school fees. To prevent any dislocation caused by the possible capture of the Provincial, a Vice-Provincial held responsibility for establishments on the Continent. Colleges in England would be run by Rectors and sufficiently endowed to look after themselves. Residences, subject to Superiors, had fewer endowments and less independence; but it was hoped that they might eventually grow into Colleges. Both were expected to run preparatory schools, some of which, like that established by Fr Metham at Osmotherly in Yorkshire, were intended to supply St Omers. Co-ordination and a common sense of purpose would be achieved by regular conferences of clergy in their districts and at a triennial assembly of representatives for the whole Province.

These dispositions removed the jurisdictional anomaly of having English Jesuits subject to a Gallo-Belgian Provincial; but they did not resolve a similar difficulty in Spain. Here, English Jesuits remained under the control of their Spanish colleagues; and some historians have argued that this was one reason why these English seminaries declined later in the century

Whatever its defects the Jesuit system did work, and by so doing, helped English Catholicism survive the difficult years of the seventeenth century. What then was St Omers' part in this? The answer is fourfold: first, it educated many of the gentry; second, it was the main feeder of the seminaries; third, it had close links with many English nunneries and schools on the Continent; lastly, through its printing press, it supplied much of the literature consumed by English Catholics.

As far as the gentry were concerned, it is clear that the College was solidly orientated towards their needs. Annual fees of £25, although remaining unchanged throughout its history, when taken with the cost of travel, eliminated the poor unless they received sponsorship or a free place. Furthermore, a classical education was the perquisite of those with leisure, a point reinforced by the

Shirk from the Boys' Chapel sacristy.

provision of optional tuition in riding, dancing, fencing and other gentlemanly activities during the eighteenth century.

This emphasis could clash with the second purpose of the College, namely the supply of vocations for the priesthood. Indeed, for most of the seventeenth century Jesuits always referred to it as a seminary. 'College' only starts to appear in Fr Warner's correspondence of the 1680s; and even then the General and his officials continued to use the old terminology right up to the end. In particular, St Omers was supposed to supply Valladolid; accordingly its constitutions were directly modelled on those of that institution. However after 1604, Valladolid, along with the other Spanish houses, fell into decline; so most of St Omers' output went to Douai, Watten or the English College.

Recruitment to the English College was affected by the divisions within the English Mission referred to earlier. For instance, complaints by secular clergy led to the imposition of an oath forbidding any candidate from joining the Regulars without permission from the Holy See. This policy, embodied not just in the College oath but also in the more detailed questionnaire introduced by Cardinal Barberini in 1658, discouraged St Omers pupils, who might have wanted at a later date to join the Society, from coming forward. Immediately numbers slumped. An analysis of the *Responsa* to the English College shows that, between 1651 and 1660, St Omers supplied 44 of its 73 students; but in the following decade these figures fell to 17 out of 38. Despite repeated complaints to Fr Warner and his successors the situation only worsened. Thus, in the 1670s, St Omers supplied only six of the 46 scholars.

Elsewhere, St Omers' contribution remained considerable, and nowhere more so than within the Society. For instance, during recusant times nine of the 18 chaplains resident at Stonyhurst were educated at the College, and the proportion would probably have been higher but for the quarrel with the Duchess of Norfolk. To get a fuller picture we can add up the names supplied in Fr Holt's admirable *Biographical Dictionary of English Jesuits*. Between 1650 and 1829 the College educated 866 Jesuits. Of these 698 went to St Omers, 33 to both St Omers and Bruges, a further 18 to Bruges alone, two more went to both Bruges and Liège, another three attended Liège and then Stonyhurst, while the remaining 111 were at Stonyhurst after 1794.

Given the size of this contribution it was inevitable that many priests would be gentlemen. Nine Plowdens from Shropshire went to St Omers before joining the Society; and to this figure can be added six more from their relatives the Dormers and other recruits from the Drummonds and Cottons. Or, if we just look at Stonyhurst, we find Edward, son of Sir Charles and Mary Carteret (née Fairfax), who taught at St Omers between 1725 and 1727, serving as the Duchess's chaplain till 1730. The *Responsa* for the English College give an even fuller picture; though it is pertinent to remark the declining proportion of gentlemen in the latter half of the century. Maybe this was not unconnected with the fall in the number of pupils coming from St Omers. According to John Bossy, 52% of the students attending the English College between 1592 and 1600 can be classified as gentlemen; and by 1611–20 the figure had risen to 70%. In the three subsequent decades the proportions were 58%, 65% and 73%; but in the 1660s this fell to 38%, recovered somewhat to 40% in the 1670s and finally slumped to 17% in the 1680s.

It was inevitable, then, that snide remarks would be made about the methods of recruitment used at St Omers. James Wadsworth, for instance, remarked that:

> For those scholars who are nobly descended and of rich parentage, they strive to allure by their honied words and flattering imbracings, inducing them with pictures, beads, meddals, Agnus Dei, which they have from Rome: Also that their baites may take effect, they licence them to participate of all their wine and juncates provided for their own pallates, and if white boyes of a comely feature they bestowe on them (though ill deserving) the preheminence of their schools.

But the advantages were obvious, for chaplains from well-connected backgrounds were far more likely to get on with their hosts; and even when they were of lower social status, they were often sponsored by gentlemen, as the case of Charles and 'Dick' Shireburn shows. Moreover, donors and their descendants frequently retained control over their rights of nomination to free places at St Omers. Thus a bequest worth £800 left by Frances Holden in 1647 continued to be administered by the Welds until 1710, the two Godolphin scholarships were limited to Cornishmen, and in 1706 the Gerards of Bryn agreed with the Provincial that their nominee could only be rejected if he were found to be palpably inadequate in his studies.

In another direction, namely through its relations with English Continental nunneries, St Omers also played a significant role. Many of the boys' sisters, cousins and aunts were educated or worked in them. John Gerard's *Autobiography* mentions how in 1592 he sent Dorothy, sister of the Rockwood brothers, who were among the first pupils at St Omers, to the Augustinian Convent at Louvain; and the registers of the abbey of Our Lady of Consolation and the Benedictine Nuns at Brussels contain Gages, Rookwoods, Plowdens, Darrells, Bedingfelds, Blundells and, after their transfer to Winchester, Mary Joanna Weld. Even closer were the links with the Poor Clares of Gravelines, originally founded at St Omer by Mary Ward. Through the good offices of Fr Schondonch, Fr Lee and Fr Baldwin, then chaplain to the Archduchess Isabella, they bought land at Gravelines. Under the guidance of Fr Lee, who acted as their chaplain, they even went through the *Spiritual Exercises*. After 1609, when Mary Ward left to found her Institute, the chaplaincy was transferred to the Franciscans; but three St Omers names appear in their list of chaplains: Fr William Rookwood (1620–48), Fr William Warner (after 1658) and Fr Gervase Birkbeck (1771–3).

St Omers' closest connections though were with the Institute of the Blessed Virgin Mary founded by Mary Ward. When she left the Poor Clares, Mary founded a girls school at St Omer. Fr Lee, after some initial hesitation, actively worked as their chaplain and spiritual director. He even helped draft the petition that led to their commendation by Paul V to Bishop Blaise of St Omer in 1615. Unfortunately, this was not approved, and in 1631 the Institute was temporarily suppressed. Nonetheless, despite such obstacles, progress was rapid. Schools were founded in London (Hammersmith), Cologne, Trier, Rome, Naples, Perugia, Vienna, Munich, Pressburg and at the Bar Convent at York in 1686 .

St Omers' fourth contribution to the Catholic cause was through the printing press, set up in 1608 to counter James I's college of preachers and divines. Thanks to Fr John Wilson, a secular priest and former secretary to Fr Persons, it dominated the Catholic book trade until the 1630s. Many of his activities directly benefited the College: his *English Martyrologie* of 1608 was used in the Refectory; he regularly gave prizes, the last occasion being in 1645; and profits from the press paid for the Community's private garden, the villa at Blandêcques, the enlargement of the sacristy to form a Sodality Chapel and the construction of a side chapel within the church dedicated to St Thomas of Canterbury. Thereafter, there was a considerable decline, with nothing at all being produced between 1642 and 1672. However, it was then revived and, under the direction of Brs Thomas Hales (c.1691–1726) and Nicholas Joseph Le Fèvre (1726–61), continued to operate on a reduced scale up to the Migration.

Naturally the output of controversial works has attracted most attention for, as the Annual Letters for 1615 state:

> Their production in pamphlet form, written in the vernacular tongue, are circulated throughout England with the most happy results. They effect what could scarcely be done by priests, for to persuade a Protestant to forsake his sect and be reconciled to the Church is a capital offence, and the fear of the law makes Protestants shrink from the mention of a priest; so that it is a difficult and dangerous matter to treat with them about religion. But nothing is easier than to call their attention to a new book, which they eagerly accept and devour, especially if, as is sometimes the case, it contains an attack on some Calvinist minister or divine.

But the bulk of the work was spiritual; for even Fr Persons recognised that 'battles of books' were not very effective. The main object was to confirm the faith of

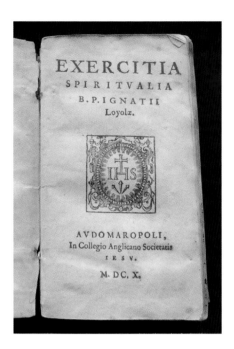

Another edition of the Spiritual Exercises, *this time from 1610, the only work before 1700 bearing the imprint of the St Omers Press.*

Catholic sympathisers through the medium of the household. Here the wife, as manager of the domestic economy, played a significant role; so much of the work was directed towards feminine tastes. Fr Clancy has calculated that half the Jesuit output was spiritual and a further one-fifth devoted to saints' lives. Often translations of Flemish and Spanish authors were published. Examples of native work include *The Mirror of Christian Perfection* (1632) and a life of St Catherine of Sweden (1634) – both by Fr Falconer, socius or assistant to the Master of Novices at Watten in 1633.

Books required distribution, and in times of persecution all sorts of expedients were adopted. The same point applied to letters – hence the use of codes – and of course special arrangements had to be made for the movement of people. St Omer's location near the Flemish coast made it a natural terminus, and the Annual Letters contain several accounts of Protestant visitors being converted by Jesuits at the College. The most important communication of course was with England. One of the jobs of the St Omers agent in London was to arrange the safe passage of new boys to the Continent. Early accounts show that this could be hazardous. Fr Gerard described how 'once I sent over two boys. They were to go to St Omers and I gave them letters of commendation. I had written them in lemon juice, so that no writing should appear on paper, and then I wrapped the paper round one or two collars to make it look as if it was being used to keep the collars clean.'

When Gerard was in the Clink prison the boys travelled via Ostend; however under the guidance of Nicholas Fulwood the normal route was from Gravesend via Dunkirk. In April 1606 a spy reported to Cecil that:

> The priests of the country commend such youths as they make choice of unto him, who placeth them in some blind alley near the water, until the wind serves for a passage, which fitting, the vessel (which is some old hoy or such like to avoid suspicion) goeth down empty towards Gravesend, and provideth a pair of oars and boats, the passengers and carriage, and so ships them into the bark, commonly beyond Greenwich, and conveys the money which belongs unto them afterwards himself They ship them to Gravelines or Calais and take forty shillings for the passage (Cal SPD James I, Vol. XX, no. 47, p. 235, quoted by Foley).

Travel to Spain could prove even more dangerous, especially after the resumption of Dutch-Hispanic hostilities in 1621. Wadsworth made three such journeys. On the first, sometime in 1610, ten of the 12 ships in the convoy were wrecked and his vessel dismasted. Eight years later, on the return voyage to St Omers, his ship, a French vessel sailing from San Sebastian, was captured by pirates from La Rochelle, looted and left to drift for three days before returning to port. On the second attempt his ship, bound for Amsterdam, was forced to put into Milford Haven; but his Franciscan escorts, by concealing their identity, secured passports for Bristol and London, whence they sailed for Zeeland and St Omer. His third voyage in 1622 was the most dramatic of all. With 12 other seminarians he set out from Calais in a Dunkirk ship bound for San Lucar. Off Cape Finistère, after a seven-day battle, they were captured by a Dutch man-of-war and placed on an English vessel bound for Hamburg. They were then captured by a Moorish galley off Cape St Vincent and all sold into slavery at Sallee. However, they were ransomed by a French merchant and sent to Cadiz via Ramona. *En route* they were chased by three Algerian pirates so, not surprisingly, they disembarked and eventually reached Seville by land.

During the eighteenth century, especially after the Treaty of Utrecht, travel became significantly easier; but in some respects change was not always for the better. Paradoxically, and yet as so often happens in the history of the Church, the relaxation of persecution was accompanied by a decrease in the number of ordinations (see Appendix C: Table 11) and a rise in the number of apostasies from 45, or 1.5% of the whole, in the seventeenth century to 73, or 6.8% of the whole, in the eighteenth, according to Fr Clancy. These figures contrast oddly with the increase in the number of Catholics during the same period. What they reveal is a growth within the towns and a relative decline among the gentry. This suited the secular priests, especially since the establishment of Vicars-Apostolic in 1688 had at last given them a viable national organisation. Thus the way was being prepared for a radical shift of power in favour of a dominant episcopacy during the nineteenth century.

But this image must not be exaggerated. First, the number of apostasies was lowest among members of the Society, rising from 1.1% in the seventeenth century to only 2.6% in the eighteenth. Second, the number of vocations does not take into account the catastrophic effects of the suppression of the Society in 1773.

Throughout this period the American Mission, in which St Omers played a special part, went from strength to strength. In 1632 the Maryland settlement was organised by George Calvert, many of whose children and grandchildren were educated at St Omers. One year later four priests, led by another old St Omers boy, Fr Andrew White, set out for the colony. In 1685 the Mission still numbered only eight, but thereafter, despite the apostasy of the Calverts, progress was rapid. In 1649 Ralph Crouche, a Jesuit laybrother, established an elementary school at 'St Inigoes Manor' to feed St Omers. In 1653 this was transferred to Newton. Later, in 1745, this was moved to Bohemia Manor, which had been established as a Jesuit Residence in 1704 by Fr Thomas Mansell SJ, who had been a pupil at St Omers. Finally, in 1789, it became Georgetown University. Its first two university presidents were Robert Plunkett and Robert Molyneux. Both had been educated at St Omers and Bruges.

As a result of such activity, by 1771 the Mission had grown to 21 Jesuits. Prominent among them were members of the Neale and Carroll families. John Carroll (St Omers 1748–53) became Prefect of the Mission in 1774. Later, in 1789, he was consecrated Bishop of Baltimore at Lulworth. As such he became the first bishop in the United States; and eventually, in 1808, he became Archbishop of the same city. His successor was Leonard Neale (St Omers and Bruges 1761–7), whose brother was chaplain at Stonyhurst in 1773. The Carrolls were also active politically. John helped to draw up the American Constitution while his cousin Charles, a senator in the Maryland Assembly, was a signatory both of the United States Declaration of Independence and of his own state's Declaration of Independence.

Meanwhile, in 1753 Benedict XIV at last made a ruling that promised to end the endless bickering between Seculars and Regulars. *Apostolicum Ministerium* required all Regulars to show testimonials from their superiors to the Vicar-Apostolic or his deputy in whose area they proposed to work. Vicars-Apostolic also received rights of visitation; so no priest could hear confessions without their approval. These measures took much of the steam out of the old complaints formerly made against the Society. The result was that, when the Society was suppressed, secular priests were far more willing to extend the hand of friendship to their distressed colleagues.

A book of Latin Odes from the Arundell Library used by Charles Carroll and his cousin John while at St Omers. Top: Rubens frontispiece enhanced by grafitti attributed to Carroll; below: signatures of John and Charles on the title page.

THE MIGRATIONS

T HE LATE EIGHTEENTH century is a watershed in the College's history. Set in an urban environment, St Omers represented an isolated introverted community; by contrast, Stonyhurst is English, rural and shaped by the gradual integration of Catholics into the mainstream of British society. Moreover, for many decades it was the *de facto* centre of the English Province.

The catalyst for change was the sudden eclipse of the Society in France. It had been too successful, arousing not just the hatred of Protestants but the envy of Catholics. By mid-century a powerful coalition of Gallicans, Jansenists and enlightened Philosophes had been formed. Worse, the Jesuits lost some of their influence at Court. Threatened by Père de Sacy SJ, the king's confessor, Madame de Pompadour promoted the Duc de Choiseul, specifically to pull down the Society. The opportunity came in 1761. Père La Valette SJ, a brilliant but compulsive businessman, had exploited the currency differences between France and Martinique to set himself up as a middleman between the sugar-planters and their creditors. He also, on his own account, shipped sugar and Portuguese gold. The scheme might have succeeded but for the incompetence of his successor, the effects of the Seven Years War and his decision, in defiance of orders from his Provincial, to continue operations after 1758. When his agents, the bankers Lioncy and Goupe of Marseilles, failed, the French Jesuits were faced by a successful prosecution for damages from irate creditors. An appeal could have been made to the King in Council; instead the case was put before the Paris Parlement, notorious for its Gallican bias. Under the influence of Choiseul's ally, the Jansenist Abbé Chauvelin, an *arrêt* was issued in May 1761 ordering the Society to pay its debts within a year. When it looked as if the obligation would actually be met Parlement prematurely ordered the confiscation of its assets, declared the Society's Institute to be sacrilegious and impious, and demanded the closure of all Jesuit Colleges by 1 April 1762.

The Parlement of Artois was by no means happy to see its jurisdiction overridden by that of Paris; but on 19 April it sold the pass by closing the Jesuit schools in its area and replacing their staff with secular clergy. Following up its advantage, Paris, on behalf of the Lioncy creditors, began to seize moveables. On 9 July inspectors came to St Omers to draw up inventories. As an indignant Jesuit commented 'This was the first example I believe that a man, a House, a Royal College had been seized for debt without having been summoned to pay,

Facing page: *This statue of St Ignatius, now in the Pièta Gallery, once stood in the chapel attached to Chèvremont, the holiday villa owned by the English Jesuits just outside Liège. It was presented by the Carmelite Prior of Chèvremont in 1902.*

and without having been informed what the debt was, how it was contracted, to whom it was owing, and how much of it to be paid fell to our share.'

Nevertheless, there was still hope that the College might survive. An empty building could be refurnished, the local authorities, wanting to keep English business, had agreed at Fr Darell's request to keep the College open, St Omers was not part of the French Province, and the English Jesuits themselves had lent 200,000 livres to La Valette's enterprises. What sank St Omers was the actions of some of the English secular clergy. Many, horrified by the unfolding events, were most reluctant to take on the management of St Omers and other English Jesuit Seminaries; but their hands were forced by the consideration that the buildings might be put to some other purpose unconnected with the English Mission; and some, notably Dr Holden, ex-President of St Gregory's Seminary in Paris, and his successor Dr Charles Howard, openly intrigued with the Abbé Chauvelin to bring this about. It is significant that Dodd's *Secret Policy* and *History of the College of Doway* were reprinted in a French translation and circulated about the town at this time. On 6 August 1762 a final *arrêt,* denounced by Clement XIII as a 'most blasphemous attack of worldly powers on the sanctity of the Church and of learning', ordered the closure of all Jesuit houses in France, including St Omers. When rumours circulated that the boys would be confined to the house pending the arrival of a team of secular priests from Douai (the order was not issued till October) plans were made to evacuate the building.

At this point the Rector, Fr Scarisbrick, chose to go on retreat in a local convent. Matters therefore devolved into the capable hands of the Vice-Rector and Procurator Frs Darell and Lawson. Already, before the inspectors arrived to take their inventories, much property had been transferred over the border by Brother Blythe. Further advantage was taken of another *arrêt,* dated 13 August, allowing Jesuits to remove their personal belongings. On 9 August the carefully laid plans were set in motion. At 1 p.m. a contingent of 24 small boys, their personal possessions stuffed in their pockets, set out on a class 'walk'. Arriving at the Dunkirk Canal, they travelled by water to the noviciate at Watten where they spent the night; 5 a.m. the next day saw them set off in two market wagons for the frontier using unfrequented side-roads. There, after some difficulty with the local customs, they crossed the border and spent the night at the Benedictine house of Poperinghe according to arrangements made the previous day by Fr Darell. Owing to false turnings Bruges was not reached till 9 the following evening, by which time the gates had been closed. The ensuing delay meant that they did not reach their lodgings till 10 p.m. The scene, as described by Fr Reeve, was dismal indeed:

> By the glimmering light of a farthing candle they were conducted into a naked room, where not so much as a chair was provided to sit upon. In the middle stood a table made of rough boards, on each side a temporary bench which fell to the ground the moment they were sat upon. Three roasted legs of mutton were immediately set upon the table, but neither knife nor fork nor plate had been thought of The Fleming who produced the meat had luckily brought his great knife along with him, else the mutton might have remained untouched. Slices of bread and meat were cut and given to the scholars, who with their fingers and teeth managed as well as they could. This ceremony was soon over: from whence they were shown into an adjoining room, where they found mattresses with straw placed in a double

row upon the floor: here without a sheet or blanket they were to take their repose pell-mell together.

Similar contingents of 28 and 33 boys left on 10 and 11 August, leaving only Rhetoric and Poetry in the College. To conceal their departure the same quantities of food were ordered as before. Six Rhetoricians began their noviciate at Watten on 7 September; the remaining four, together with eight Poets, left St Omers on 15 September reaching their destination two days later. These Rhetoricians eventually became novices elsewhere. Finally, a party of 12 boys, led by Fr Reeve, after travelling by water through Watten, Berghe, Furness and Newport, reached Bruges on 18 September.

As for the Jesuit Community, most had been paid off on 17 October, seven fathers receiving 425 livres, five 300 livres and three lay brothers 225 livres each. Two days later they themselves set out for Bruges leaving behind a dignified *Protest* and three members who were too infirm to move, the last of whom, Fr Brown, died on 7 November 1764.

The result was that, when Fr Talbot and five other seculars arrived from Douai to take formal possession on 29 October, the cupboard was virtually bare. So, after travelling to England to consult with his superiors, Fr Talbot returned to Douai with three of his staff. Nonetheless, some attempt was made to continue the school. On a visit to St Omer in 1765 the Rev'd William Cole reported the presence of 30 pupils under the Presidency of Mr Butler. Indeed, his prognosis that 'there can be no doubt but it will increase after a time, as the present Governor of it has shown himself to be so able as well as so religious and pious a scholar' proved vindicated . The celebrated Irish politician and nationalist, Daniel O'Connell, was one of its pupils; and, at the time of its closure by French Revolutionaries in 1793, it had 52 pupils. These were transferred to Douai College. In 1795, after a period of imprisonment in Doulens, 94 students from the combined establishment came over to England and settled at Old Hall Green, where a school had been set up by Bishop Douglas.

Meanwhile, the migrants energetically set about restoring the College. Bruges had been chosen because, being under Austrian Habsburg control, it was beyond the jurisdiction of the French authorities. Moreover, as early as 18 August, the Brussels government, hoping to revive a decayed trading centre, had given permission to settle. Vienna confirmed this on 1 December; but on condition that the Jesuits did not teach that the Pope had any rights over the temporal concerns of Maria Theresa, that the government had the final say over any plans of education and that the staff were limited to 23 teachers and 18 lay brothers or servants. Following the evacuation of the Watten noviciate and preparatory school on 1 April 1763, three teachers and three lay brothers were deployed in a 'Little College' nearby. Steps were also taken to improve accommodation. Originally, the boys had been housed in the Maison D'Argille and the Hôtel de Commerce; the former was soon abandoned for another inn – the Fleur de Blé – and, later still, the guildhouse of the Arquebusiers de St Sébastien. Eventually, the College rented the 'House of the Seven Towers' on the Hoogstraet or High Street. Building plans were also made. In 1765 some property was bought bordering the Friday Market with a loan of 48,000 florins. In January 1768 the Little College was allowed to purchase a building on the Quay du Miroir which was then mortgaged for 70,000 florins (approx. £5,800) to finance the construction of a new wing. At the same time a farm at Momelbecke

The Protest of the English Jesuits, *deposited on their departure from St Omers in 1762.*

71

was bought to take the place of Blandyke. Of all these buildings only the Little College can now be positively identified.

Furnishing proved to be a substantial but temporary problem. In the first six months Fr Darell reckoned that 30,000 livres had been required for this purpose. One source of help was the Convent of the Austin Friars who not only lent furniture of their own but also 3,000 florins with which to make other purchases.

The result was that the College was soon established on an even keel. The first Ascensio Scholarum was held on 20 September 1762, a new rector, Fr Nathaniel Elliot, was appointed, and the saintly but ineffectual Fr Scarisbrick relegated to the Sodality. By 1766 numbers had risen to 176; and in 1773 they stood at 230. However, the situation remained uncertain. Building operations were hampered by a *shortage* of cash and, above all, the campaign to suppress the Society was continuing with full vigour.

Not that the situation was entirely without hope. Surprisingly, Louis XV, as well as his Queen and the Dauphin, continued to employ Jesuits as their confessors; Choiseul was replaced in December 1770, and his successor Aiguillon even drafted a proclamation inviting the Society to return, provided it accepted employment under the supervision of the bishops. But when the General, Fr Laurence Ricci, refused Bourbon pressure on the Papacy was renewed. In 1767 Jesuit colleges were closed down in Spain; Naples and Sicily followed suit the next year and the English College in Rome was lost in 1772. Finally, on 16 August 1773, in the brief *Dominus Ac Redemptor*, Clement XIV suppressed the whole Society.

The brief was executed in the Austrian Netherlands on 20 September. This time the authorities were determined that the College would not escape, particularly

The House of the Seven Towers, Bruges, from Sanderus's Flandria Illustrata *of 1641.*

The Little College at Bruges, as it is today.

as they suspected that Maria Theresa might exempt the English Province. Accordingly the staff, consisting of seven priests, seven scholastics and seven lay brothers were interrogated and confined to the house under the authority of a Flemish priest appointed by the local bishop, Monsignor de Caimo. At the same time the commissioner, Mynheer Van Volden, and his deputy, Louis Maroulx, searched the building for alleged Jesuit treasure and drew up an inventory of all they found there. Fr Charles Plowden describes how:

> At an unexpected moment Maroulx appeared at the house, attended by a riot of smiths, joiners and carpenters: he confined all the prisoners [i.e. the Jesuits] under guard in a separate room, while the workmen, armed with poles and iron tools, proceeded to beat up the quarters in order to draw imaginary treasures into light from supposed lurking holes and dark recesses . . . They searched, they probed, during a whole morning, every wall, floor, ceiling, beam, desk and table: they even pulled up the board on which the taylors worked, and at length they retired in the vexation of disappointment, leaving the prisoners to contemplate the odious scene in silent amazement and despair.

Amid the disturbance normal classes and studies were still continued; for the eventual plan was to replace the Jesuits either with secular priests or with Dominicans from Bornholm. On the night of 14 October the scheme was put into operation. A fresh contingent of troops arrived, arrested the staff and transported them to the Jesuit Flemish College near by. At once, according to Fr Plowden, pandemonium broke out among the boys:

> They were all at that time retired to study. The alarm was soon given, and in an instant the house was filled with confusion. More than one hundred boys were abandoned to the mercy of strangers and armed soldiers; muskets and bayonets were presented to them; the civil officers called to order; their words were drowned amidst screams and cries; the students grew desperate by military opposition; some forced their way through the gardens, some escaped over the walls and through the windows, others in excess of grief and resentment broke everything they found, and tables, chairs, desks, and

Above: *The Liège Monstrance was made in 1709 by Jean Francois Knaeps, possibly to the order of James Anderton, an old St Omers boy who joined the Watten noviciate in 1703 and died at his old school in 1710. However Gerard, citing Fr Plowden SJ, thought that it had been given by Lady Goring. Certainly the crystal and diamond pendant belonged to her.*

Above right: *Silver crucifix and four of the six candlesticks formerly belonging to the seminary at Liège. According to the inscriptions four of these date from 1667, the remaining two were made in 1711. One, the work of Geraud de Beche, was given by Bartholemew Dottrem, possibly related to Brother Hubert d'Ottrem of Liège who joined the English Jesuits in 1642 and died at St Omers in 1689.*

windows were dashed to pieces on every side of the house. The greater number that escaped ran up and down the streets in quest of their masters, and nearly all of them were humanely taken in and accommodated by the different families of the town, whose indignation at the violence of the proceedings was inflamed to a high degree.

The soldiers proved quite unable to cope, and to restore order in the dormitories Maroulx was reduced to recalling the Rector and Prefect of Discipline; but as soon as they left trouble broke out again. So, when Fr Underhill, accompanied by four Dominican priests and two or three lay brothers, arrived the next morning he faced an impossible task. Not even Alexian Brothers brought in from the local madhouse could keep control. There was nothing for it but to close the College. By this time, what with pupils escaping or being withdrawn by their parents, only 43 boys were left. Twelve were sent to the Little College, seven to the Alexian Brothers and the remainder went to the Dominican houses at Bruges and Bornholm, whence their parents recalled them. Groups of ex-pupils began migrating to Liège under their former masters.

The authorities were more hopeful about the Little College and even suggested that the former Superior, Fr Aston, might continue to run it as a Dominican. When he refused Fr Austin Noel (OP) was appointed in his stead. Unfortunately, the riotous condition of the Great College proved highly contagious. In a letter of 10 May 1774 an Austin Canoness reported how:

> Some Dominicans were on ye spot to take Mr Aston's school, which accordingly they did, but the boys could by no means be content under their jurisdiction, and I do not wonder, for they were so eaten with vermin that the poor things were in open sores: such complaints from the children, such discontent amongst the parents that Reverend Mother [Mary, sister of Henry More, the last Provincial] and Mr Berrington [the chaplain] were solicited on all sides to take them away, which they did, to about the number of fivety, yet not without great difficulty and trouble.

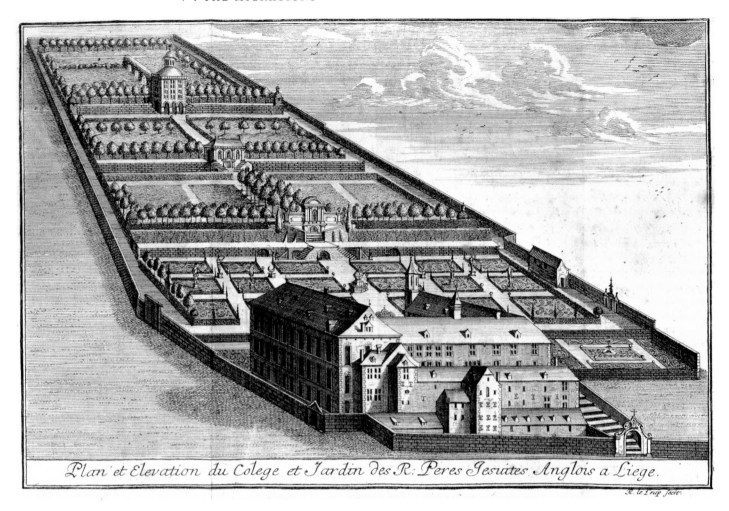

Plan et Elevation du Colege et Jardin des R: Peres Jesuites Anglois a Liege.

The English Seminary at Liège, taken from P-L de Saumery's Les Delices du Pais de Liège *1738.*

In January 1775 the Little College was therefore closed. By this time there were only 16 boys left. Some were sent to a small school at Wilhous and nine went on to Bornholm. There they staged yet another rebellion. Of the arrested Jesuits 8–10 were released within a few hours and the rest after a few days, all with orders to leave the Austrian Netherlands. However, in an attempt to recover school fees and money thought to have been secretly conveyed to England, the authorities kept Fr Angier [the Rector], Fr Aston and Fr Plowden under close guard for a fortnight at the Flemish House in Ghent. From thence they were transferred to the Convent of the Austin Friars, where they remained for a further nine months; but, when no money proved forthcoming, they were released on 25 May and set out for Liège. Their arrival caused a sensation. In a letter, dated 3 June 1774, Mary More described how the students 'rang ye bells, shot off cannons or whatever they could get hold of. The Gentlemen [i.e. the masters] used all endeavours to quiet them but to no purpose. To effect it they order'd ye bell ropes to be cut, but ye boys ran up ye towers and along ye ridges of ye houses, and made what noise they could upon ye bells.'

The English Seminary at Liège had begun with the transfer of the noviciate from Louvain in 1614. Fr Gerard, using donations given by, amongst others, Sir George Talbot and the ninth Earl of Shrewsbury, bought some land in the name of his cousin Sir William Stanley. Other grants were soon forthcoming, John Stonor, for instance, leaving 10,000 florins by will in 1626. The same year,

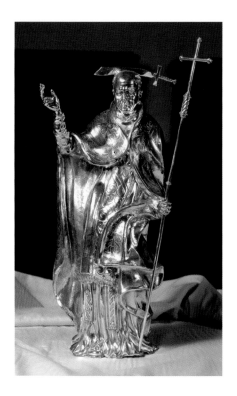

The silver statuette, the work of the celebrated Liège silversmith Henri Flemalle, of St Thomas a Becket of Canterbury, was presented to the seminary in 1666.

by a charter dated 8 September, Duke Maximilian of Bavaria awarded an annual pension, which in the eighteenth century was worth 5,000 scudi. By this time the noviciate had been moved to Watten; but in 1624 Liège became the main English Jesuit centre for the teaching of Philosophy and Theology. According to the Annual Letters, the first batch of five scholastics and 12 scholastic students from St Omers 'are for the most part sons of the principal friends of the Society in England, and some are eldest sons with splendid patrimonies'. It is interesting to note that sung vespers in the Sodality Chapel were accompanied by a string band formed from the students from St Omers.

As at Watten, scholastics were expected to help visiting soldiers, especially good work being done among English, Irish and Scottish contingents during the wars of Louis XIV. Just as effective was their collaboration with the local priests in evangelising the neighbourhood. Sometime between 1689 and 1691 Fr John Clarke reported that 'the common people of the country, and particularly the suburbs on every side of the town, come in through to the church on Sundays, and especially on great days, so that I think there come as many to us alone as to half of the town besides; that they sent their children to us as much as they could for their first confession, and that they and their children had a very great respect and reverence for us, wherever and whensoever they saw us.'

Thanks to the work of Fr Francis Line, Liège was also famous as a scientific centre. For instance, the Annual Letter from 1632 reported that 'A brass sphere, a novel kind of sundial, is suspended freely in the centre of a spherical vessel of water. On the side which bears the sun's image it follows invariably the course of the sun, and in twenty-four hours completes its course as the constant attendant on the primum mobile.'

Many of the instruments were placed in the gardens, arranged in three tiers above the Seminary. This was the work of another benefactor, Brother William Browne (1578–1637), grandson, brother and uncle of successive Lords Viscount Montague. His obituary notes that 'he studiously sought out and tenderly loved the lowest offices in our Colleges. For fourteen years he spent almost two hours daily in the kitchen, in washing the dishes etc. He cleaned out the out-offices, lit the fires, and performed other like offices.' Laying out the gardens he acted 'as a common hodman amongst the workmen. With a sack or a hodman's basket on his back, which he so fastened by a double cord over his breast as to leave his hands at liberty; in which he held his *Imitation of Christ* by Thomas à Kempis.'

Other gifts continued to be made during the seventeenth century. On 4 April 1678 Lord Castlemain, the cuckolded husband of one of Charles II's mistresses, bought the farm of Chèvremont for 4,400 florins as a rest-house. Here, in 1688, the Seminarians built a shrine which quickly became a local centre for pilgrimage. The Seminary also acquired several items of church plate, some of which the College still possesses.

Liège was fortunate during the Suppression to receive sympathetic treatment from the Prince-Bishop, the Comte de Velbruck. At first the procedure followed the usual pattern. On 9 September the Papal brief was read, priestly faculties were withdrawn, inventories compiled and M. Légipont, the local parish *curé*, appointed Superior. The shock was profound. The Philosophers and Theologians had gone to Chèvremont for their usual August vacation; the Day Book records how:

On our way back the Professors met us and broke the news that the Pope's decree had at last arrived whereby was suppressed and abolished for ever the Society of Jesus, our very dear Mother. Reactions varied: but on one point all were agreed that the matter must be left to God and his Providence as the basis of our trust. And if such a decree should actually take effect, then we could do nothing more pleasing to God than resign ourselves without reserve to his supreme will.

But there was no violence, no self-important posturing by officious civilians and soldiery. Although four ex-Jesuits returned to the American colonies, another six Rhetoricians and four novices went to Ghent to study Philosophy, while the remainder of the community, nominally under the authority of the local *curé*, carried on as before. The ex-Rector, Fr John Howard, had the key of the House returned to him and his faculties as confessor to the English Canonnesses of the Holy Sepulchre nearby were renewed. From there, where he seems to have resided for several years, he came up daily to transact whatever business was necessary.

It was on this unexpected refuge then that groups of masters and boys began to descend. Soon plans were being made to open an Academy. On Wednesday 15 December 1773 the log reported:

> Today his Highness the Prince gave public notice in the *Liège Gazette* that he had established in our English College an Academy in which youths of all ages would be taught a full course of subjects. On the same occasion to our great delight he named the Rev. John Howard as Director of the Academy. That this announcement might be more widely known he took steps to have it published in all the Gazettes of Holland and Germany.

News can travel fast. By October 1774 the Day Book listed a community of 47, of whom 21 were on the teaching staff, including Fr Aston as 'Principal' and Fr Richard Morgan as First Prefect. The school itself was organised into six classes, ranging from Rhetoric to Figures, with a Preparatory group below that. Meanwhile, the work of the Seminary continued, the Day Book referring to 12 Theologians, four Philosophers and three [later eight] students of logic. By 1776 there were 144 boys, including 11 Secular Philosophers or students who, without intending to become priests, attended the lectures and classes as a kind of university course or finishing school; a practice that seems to have begun in about 1672 among the local Liègeois. The list includes no less than 42 foreign names including two 'Nephews of his Highness' – presumably the archbishop – William and Adam de Loe.

It was now essential to devise a proper routine. As early as Christmas Eve 1774 the Day Book complained: 'House full of boys, no public discipline, no silence, no chapter.' The result was an interesting blend of Liège and Bruges customs. The annual eight-day retreat for the Community was retained, as was the Liège custom of saying a Mass against Fire on 20 October. Most of the other specifically Ignatian feasts were suppressed, but many crept back later in the 1780s. The Poets commenced their first three-day retreat on 3 October, celebrating its conclusion in true St Omers style with a Good Breakfast; while, at the end of the academic year, the 'First Six' were usually rewarded by a jaunt to Chèvremont. Details of the curriculum were outlined in the first prospectus:

> Boys are accepted from the age of six. They are taught to read, to write, and every part of literature and philosophy; English, French, German, Latin,

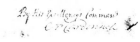

The Duke of Marlborough's Safeguard was issued in October 1702 when he visited the English seminary after capturing Liège.

Greek and Hebrew; sacred and profane history, geography, arithmetic, algebra, geometry, astronomy, experimental physics and mathematics.

It should be apparent, then, that to the traditional classical curriculum were added scientific subjects formerly taught as part of the Philosophy course. This was virtually unknown in English schools operating at this time. A further change was the shift from Latin to often lighter specimens of English drama. *The Faithful Friend*, for instance, was performed in 1789. The school uniform provides further evidence of a more relaxed gentlemanly attitude. At St Omers this had reflected the hope that many boys would go on to study for the priesthood. Wadsworth described it as 'a doublet of white canvas, breeches and stockings that had not troubled the weaver with much pains, cassocke and stockings of the same black and grave, the band precise and short, with a hat that might almost shadow all, and shoes correspondent'. This remained virtually unchanged, despite some alterations proposed by Fr Petre in 1693, ostensibly to reduce costs, but really to make it more attractive to the gentry. On this question Mgr Velbruck had no inhibitions whatsoever. The 1774 prospectus stated that 'the dress of his highness and the lords of his court in the country is that of the pensioner. It consists of a cassock, maroon in colour, with steel buttons.' By 1797 the dress had changed again, whether before or after the migration to Stonyhurst it is hard to say: 'The Sunday or holyday dress is uniform, and consists of a plain coat of superfine cloth with yellow buttons, red cloth or kerseymere waistcoats.'

Naturally, Velbruck was concerned to regularise the position of his new academy. Accordingly, in 1778 he secured from Pius VI the brief *Catholici Praesules* confirming the arrangements he had already made and recognising the establishment as a Pontifical Seminary with the right to present students to bishops for ordination and receipt of faculties. Further hope came with news of the survival of the Russian Province. At the time of the Suppression Catherine II had refused to permit the implementation of *Dominus ac Redemptor* and ordered the Society to continue as before. A noviciate was set up in 1780; and on 10 October 1782, with viva voce permission from the Pope, the first general congregation to be held in Russia elected Stanislaus Czerniewiez as General. Encouraged by this Fr Howard applied for affiliation; but the attempt was premature. Perforce, the Academy had to wait for another twenty years before success was achieved.

By this time, with numbers falling to 83 in 1786, much of the original impetus had been lost. Whatever his qualifications as a spiritual director of nuns Fr Howard, like Fr Scarisbrick before him, was no headmaster. Fr Charles Plowden thought 'it almost impossible to effect any improvements here unless Mr Director thinks proper to attend to the business of the house . . . Mr Howard answers to everything darkly and confusedly.' Financially the position was poor, and the English ex-Jesuits were in no position to help. An attempt to recover property bequeathed to St Omers and the English Province by Sir Tobie Matthew near Rome had failed in 1781, £80,000 had been lost in the La Valette affair, property of similar value had disappeared with the closure of the Continental colleges and the remaining funds had been squandered on ill-advised investments in French East India Company stock. Ironically, the Procurator responsible ended his days teaching book-keeping at the Academy. His successor, partly to keep the Vicars-Apostolic at bay, deliberately destroyed or concealed financial records, often confusing them with his personal finances, a situation that was not finally sorted out till the 1820s.

Real grip was restored after Fr Howard's death in 1783. His successor, Fr William Strickland, had been born at Sizergh Castle, Westmorland in 1731. He entered the Society in 1748, studied and taught philosophy at Liège and then held a variety of posts in England, including the chaplaincy at Stonyhurst, before becoming Superior of the Alnwick mission just before the Suppression. As Director or 'President' of the Academy he set out to restore flagging morale among staff, drafted a new code of rules in 1788 and, by the time of his retirement in 1790, brought numbers back to 104.

He was ably assisted by his Procurator, Fr Charles Wright, brother of Thomas Wright the London banker, 'a straightforward John Bull gentleman' as one Stonyhurst contemporary described him. For the first time since the foundation fees were ruthlessly raised to realistic levels, reaching £50 a year in 1783. One device was to use the system of extras defined by the prospectus. In 1774 the basic fee – 18 guineas – provided teaching, board and lodging, fire, light, table and bedlinen; washing, books, paper, pens, hairdressing and dancing lessons cost an extra 4 guineas; clothes, doctor's fees and medicines another 10 guineas; and further charges were levied for drawing, fencing and music lessons. Walter Tempest's expenses show how this could work out in practice. His outward journey to Liège cost £7.7s., the return £6.6s.; the uniform cost £4.6s., but with the addition of a greatcoat this rose to £5.9s.11d. Shirts cost £3.11s.8d., two wigs £3.15s., summer waistcoats £16.11s.4d., silk stockings £3.17s.4d., boots 17s., a trunk 16s.1d., 'Linen and clothing on going to Liège' £16.10s.

Fr Wright, helped by events in England, was also active in restoring endowments. At the time of the Suppression Bishop Challoner appointed the last Provincial, Fr Thomas More, Vicar-General of the ex-Jesuits. After much argument a congress held in 1776 ruled that each district and the Central Office should hold their money in a centrally managed fund which would be used to pay pensions to each of its members. At a second meeting in 1784 Fr Strickland was put in charge of the fund and persuaded the ex-Jesuits to subscribe money to enable the Academy to train new recruits to fill vacancies on the Mission as they appeared. Examples of such bequests were a gift by Mr Scarisbrick of £400 worth of 3% consols (consolidated annuities) earning £12 interest for the support of the library, £1,000 from Fr Lucas for the education of boys from the Suffolk District, and the donation of 40 guineas a year from 1786 onwards by Fr William Horne on behalf of the South Wales District. From 1787 Fr Wright systematically began to buy government stock. By 1795 his capital stood at £10,348.13s.9d. earning £354.4s.6d. worth of interest.

All this activity in London meant that Fr Strickland needed a deputy at Liège. At first he relied on Fr Wright and Fr Barrow his Prefect of Studies; but increasingly he groomed the former Second Prefect, Fr Marmaduke Stone, as his successor. An apparently unworldly man – Fr Wright once complained 'I think his reverence is too much absorbed in heavenly things to be fit for this mission' – he was an ideal foil for energetic but over-decisive subordinates like Fr Plowden. In the tricky situations he often encountered his very dilatoriness was perhaps an advantage. Confronted with a crisis his response was always, and usually rightly, to delay. On the other hand, his correspondence shows that he could be decisive enough when required. It is a curious fact that on each of the three migrations the man in command, whether Fr Stone, Fr Howard or Fr Scarisbrick, had to be prodded into action or bypassed by restless subordinates.

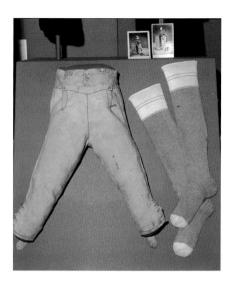

The early nineteenth-century Stonyhurst uniform. This is the sole surviving example.

Just such an occasion arose within three years of Fr Stone's appointment. In 1789, fired by the example of the French Revolution, 'patriots' seized the citadel and held the city of Liège for a year and a half. Fr Laurenson describes how the community, while holidaying at Chèvremont during Whitsuntide, were woken 'from their first sleep by a lawless drunken herd of cloutiers [nailsmiths]' who had to be bought off with some coins passed under the door. Next France declared war on Austria, won the battle of Jenappes and held Liège from 28 November 1792 till the following March. Troops were billeted in the Academy, but a holiday was granted on 6 March with the return of the Austrian soldiery. When Louis XVI was executed a Requiem Mass was said in the Academy. That year witnessed a further escalation of the conflict when France war on England. Faced by the new menace Fr Clifton, who had replaced Fr Howard as their chaplain, advised the Canonesses of the Holy Sepulchre, to rent a house in Maastricht. This proved most timely. In 1794, when Charleroi was besieged, some of the boys were sent home; but most stayed at the Maastricht house until it was judged safe to return. However, in June the French, under General Jourdan, won a decisive victory at Fleurus and prepared to occupy Liège. Clearly, the time to leave had come.

The question was 'where to?' Here changes in English law proved most timely. In 1778 and 1791 two relief acts had been passed. These gave individual Catholics the right to buy or inherit land, possess property and open schools, provided they swore an oath declaring that no Pope or foreign temporal prince had any civil or temporal authority in the land. For the first time, then, it was legally possible to transfer the College to England. So when Thomas Weld, himself a former pupil at Bruges, mentioned Stonyhurst to his former tutor and guide on the Continent Fr Charles Plowden – probably on a visit to collect his sons – the opportunity was quickly grasped. Stonyhurst had been inherited by the Welds in 1754; but since they lived mainly at Lulworth the building had been left empty for 40 years. Thomas, therefore, was more than willing to offer it to the 'Gentlemen of Liège'.

Right from the start, the journey, for which we have a detailed description by Fr Laurenson, was packed with incident (see map). The single cart used to convey the luggage down to the river was twice commandeered by the military. Next, the water level proved too low for the deep-laden barges, so Fr Wright held an impromptu auction on the quayside. At Maastricht the party delayed so long, presumably hoping to return, that they were nearly trapped when the retreating allies erected a pontoon bridge downstream. Later, Fr Wright was swindled into hiring an unsound vessel by a local Dutch Jew; its replacement, hired at thrice the normal rate, exuded 'a very distressing and unwholesome scent' of fermenting grain that had only recently been removed. On the crossing from Rotterdam to Harwich the Fathers scandalised Captain Scott of the *John O'Yarmouth* by 'not hindering some of the children from playing Beg O'My Neighbour with an old pack of cards which they accidently had with them. Shocked at this profanation of the Lord's day, one of the crew was heard to say that he should not be surprised if the ship were to go to the bottom, and the Captain took fervently to his Bible, to ward off the thunderbolts of heaven.'

From Harwich Fr Stone and Fr Wright journeyed to London before visiting Mr Weld at Lulworth to make final arrangements for the transfer. Several boys visited their parents before journeying northward. As for the others, a party consisting of three priests, four 'Juniors' or ecclesiastical students, two servants and 12 boys (later referred to as 'The Twelve Apostles') under Fr Kemper, the Prefect of Studies, sailed on to Hull.

It might be supposed that a leisurely summer cruise along waterways of northern England was the ideal way to travel. In fact nothing could have been farther from the truth.

> The slattern and neglected dress and haggard looks of our folks made them be, everywhere in their journey through Yorkshire, taken for Frenchmen. On their arrival at Selby, it being a Sunday, they were soon surrounded by an immense crowd of lounging idlers: some of them seemed to pity, but more to slight and insult them. Of the latter one was heard to exclaim with a curse, 'the rascals deserve all they have got for killing their King'.

At Skipton Fr Ellerker and Fr Semmens hired a chaise to take them to Stonyhurst. However, the rest of the party had no option but to walk. By the time they got to Clitheroe the 'children . . . were quite exhausted . . . resting themselves at every door where they could find a convenient seat, perfectly indifferent to the stare and surprise of the inhabitants.' One of them, Samuel Cox, is said to have been half-blinded when a sudden puff of wind blew some quicklime in his face. Turning aside to visit his father's house at Eaton Bishop he arrived in such a state that the servant who opened the door did not recognise him: 'You are not my Master's son, he was a fair, handsome youth, not a tramp like you.' The difficulty with this story though is that Eaton Bishop is in Herefordshire! A similar problem concerns the arrival of the first boy. According to Fr Laurenson, who incidentally was not a member of the party, George Clifford arrived by fly at the top of the Avenue with Charles Brooke, raced down to the house and, while the latter rang the bell, scrambled in through a window. Unfortunately this pleasing tale, though confirmed by Mr Tomlinson, who was working in a nearby field at the time, is probably untrue. His son, Fr William Clifford, said that he walked to Stonyhurst, forced open a door with an iron bar and explored the house; then, espying the deer park from the roof of the Tower, he rambled about there until the rest of the party arrived.

There they were met by Fr Stone and Fr Wright, who had been preceded the day before by the former Master of Poetry, the Marylander Fr Notley Young. On their first night, according to his son William, the irrepressible George Clifford 'observing his comrades, who knelt along the wallside, sideling to and fro, heavy with sleep, under pretence of arousing the one before him . . . gave him such a push that falling on his companions in front they were prostrated like a pack of cards, to the disturbance of the Master or Prefect who was saying the prayers.'

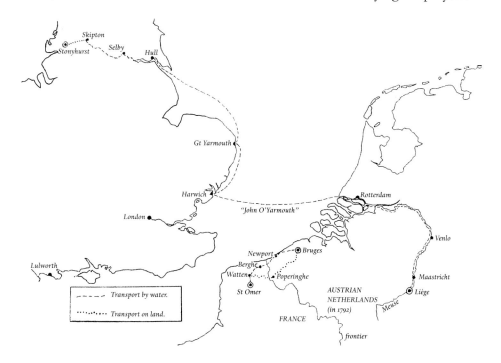

The migration from St Omers to Bruges and from Liège to Stonyhurst.

THE GENTLEMEN OF STONYHURST

THE BUILDING FOUND by George Clifford and his friends on the evening of 29 August was dilapidated but nonetheless impressive – a fitting symbol of the frustrated ambitions of the Shireburn family. Sir Richard probably and Sir Nicholas certainly had intended to construct a double court around the medieval hall they inherited. Instead, by the time work stopped in 1606, all that stood was the gatehouse, a range of buildings containing the 'Duke's Room' (now the Teachers' Common Room), the Bayley Chapel, the Long Gallery and a Great Drawing Room, now no longer standing, opening onto the refurbished Great Hall. To the south, linked by a staircase, stood a timber-framed edifice known as the Duchess' Rooms, erected by Hugh Shireburn in 1528. Later, Sir Nicholas had added the cupolas that give the Eagle Towers their name, the Avenue, Ponds, an ornamental Dutch garden and part of the west range of buildings that still make up the Shireburn Quadrangle, or Back Court, behind the Hall. In addition, a number of structures of indeterminate age and little architectural merit had sprung up haphazardly to serve the various needs of the household. The most important of these, denoted as Sparrow's Hall after Thomas Weld's steward, stood opposite the Long Gallery. The space between this building and the Gatehouse was enclosed by a high wall.

'The finest half house in England' (Oliver Cromwell). Watercolour of the Fronts in 1809 by J Buckler. The pillars are correctly arranged in Doric, Ionic, Corinthian and Composite orders. The marble shield was placed over the portal by Sir Nicholas Shireburn in 1705.

Facing page: '. . . acres of flat roof which . . . command a noble view of this Lancashire landscape.' (G M Hopkins to Robert Bridges, 1882). A view down the Avenue from the Eagle Towers.

Above: *The old entrance to the Top Refectory. Sparrow's Hall, shown on the left, was demolished in 1856.*

Above right: *The Great Quadrangle in 1809. Note the Palladian doorway added by Sir Nicholas Shireburn. He also laid down the paving-stones and in 1694 put up ornamental drainpipes with the armorial bearings of each branch of the family. Watercolour by J Buckler.*

Below: *'Sir Richard Shireburn's Parlour' a somewhat fanciful design by C S Beauclerk in 1885 for the restoration of the Bayley Room.*

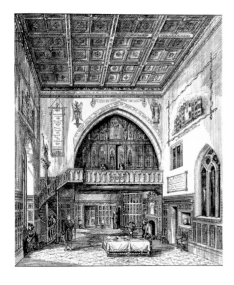

Sir Nicholas died in 1717; and because of the death of his only son Richard Francis – according to legend from eating poisoned berries in the garden – the house passed first to his widow and then, after 1728, to his daughter Mary, the eighth Duchess of Norfolk. Mary left no children; so, after her death in 1754, the entire property passed to the descendants of Elizabeth, sister of Sir Nicholas, who in 1658 had married William Weld of Lulworth. It was their great-grandson Thomas who offered Stonyhurst to his former masters.

With their property mainly in Dorset and Wiltshire the Welds were not particularly interested in Stonyhurst. Moreover, Fr Holt's researches suggest that the house was visited infrequently by the Duchess and her husband. Saving the presence of the steward and a few servants it seems to have remained virtually empty for at least 40 years.

The first task facing the migrants, then, was to make the buildings weatherproof and habitable. As this proved increasingly expensive drastic economies became necessary. Many of the garden statues had already been removed to Worksop manor by the Duke of Norfolk; now, with the exceptions of the statues of Regulus, St Mary Magdalene and St Jerome, all the others were melted down and the lead used to repair the roof. To all protests Fr Wright responded 'Stuff and Nonsense – I need the money'. For the masters' accommodation the Long Gallery and Duke's Room were partitioned into several compartments 12 ft. by 9 ft. reached by a passage 5 ft. in width; the Juniors, or ecclesiastical students, occupied 16 smaller cubicles ranged either side of a passage just 3 ft. wide on an additional floor inserted above. The senior staff, meanwhile, enjoyed equally cramped quarters. Fr Stone had a closet in the Duchess's House, the Master of Rhetoric Mr Spencer (alias Charnock) occupied the garret above, while Fr Kemper, the Prefect of Studies, was allotted a space partitioned from the Bread Room – an area between Sparrow's Hall and the bottom end of the Refectory. Sparrow's Hall itself was mainly given over to the boys, the first floor being used as a chapel, playroom and refectory as need arose. In the Duchess's House was another playroom with the Study Place near by. The Great Hall was not reopened till 1796. According to Fr Haly, who come to Stonyhurst as an eleven-year-old in 1807, the dormitories 'were damp . . . very badly ventilated and so economically supplied with even the most necessary articles of furniture that there was only one for every three or four beds'.

Clearly, the provision of a decent chapel was most important. At first this seems to have been on the top floor of the Gatehouse and confusingly referred to as the Museum, perhaps because of the curios stored there. Here the Sodality was reformed and transferred to the Bayley Chapel when it was reopened on 12 November 1796. With its 30 ft.-high pointed arch and tribune opening from the Long Gallery this was an even more impressive room than now. The altar, standing on the south side now occupied by Shirk, was flanked by the two massive paintings of St Thomas and St Augustine now hanging on the Lower Grammar Staircase. Alongside was a sacristy housed, according to Henderson, 'in a kind of loose box'. As for the benches, these were designed so that one row of boys could kneel while others in front used the flat tops as a seat. The following year the old stables were converted into a church standing at right angles to the present St Peters. As planned by Fr Darrell it was used by villagers as well as by the school. Inside were to be found the statues of St Mary Magdalene and St Jerome rescued from the gardens, where they have now been returned. The choir and organ occupied the hayloft; while on the High Altar stood some fine candlesticks made by Br Steerman, a Pole who had come over to Stonyhurst with Fr Korsak. Otherwise, according to a manuscript of 1820, 'the vestments were of the commonest material, some of which were called "ordinary" being made out of old dresses'.

Linking the church with the main building was a 'temporary' structure, known as Shirk, built in 1799. This masked the windows on the south side of the Bayley Chapel, leaving the light to filter through a much older medieval window brought from the Bayley chantry (at Bayley Hall nearby) by Mary, Duchess of Norfolk. At the same time the gateposts standing on the site that opened into the garden were removed to the front of the house, replacing the two couchant 'Lions' that still give that place its name. Opposite Shirk the old coach-houses

J M W Turner's view of Stonyhurst.

The South Front: above, as the Jesuits found it in 1794, and opposite, as it was in 1810, replacing the original front built by the Shireburns.

In 1877, after the present playground had been laid out, the handballs abutting the garden were removed and a new handball erected to the same design as the Great Handball of 1796.

The Old Study Place of 1810, just before its demolition in 1881.

were converted into a village school, while between and at right angles to this and the Gatehouse was built the first North Front in 1800. Like Shirk this was severely classical and much lower than the rest of the front. Indeed it was so out of keeping with the rest of the house that a startled Thomas Weld himself exclaimed 'Mr Wright must be a bold man, to set the criticism of all the world at defiance'. Here were lodged guests or 'strangers'.

Between 1808 and 1810 the new President, Fr Sewall, rounded off this spate of activity by constructing the Old South Front. According to Fr Wright it cost £13,000. With the Great Drawing Room and Duchess's House swept away the main gallery stretched 300ft in a straight line from the present Audio-Visual Room. As the Community still hankered for a return to Liège it was only intended to last for about 40 years and was therefore very plain: 'The work of a hodman and his dull industry alone' complained a youthful Thomas Meagher in 1855–6. The central block contained four storeys, the wings three. In a manuscript of 1824 the editor of the *Yorkshire Gazette and Blackburn Mail* says that the ground floor had three playrooms, six schoolrooms, music, drawing and dancing rooms. At the west end was a Study Place for 220 boys commanded by 'a lofty and spacious pulpit'. On the second and third floors the Superiors and Professors, now transferred from the Long Gallery, occupied 16 rooms in the central portion, while in the east wing stood a Philosophical or Science room. Sliding doors separated this from a lecture theatre with row upon row of seats rising to the ceiling. Along the top floor, according to the *Monthly Magazine* for July 1823, was 'the extensive dormitory, with its distinctly partitioned bed for each boy'. At the end of each dormitory, for there was more than one, was a room for the Prefect – 'Silence is here strictly enforced, no wilful consideration or communication whatever is at any time permitted.' Sadly, on 31 July, the feast of St Ignatius, and the day before its official opening, the ceremony had to be cancelled. Thomas Weld, urged on by the boys to sing, collapsed and died after a spirited rendition of the song. 'I am Mad Tom, behold me!' A Requiem Mass continues to be said in the College on his anniversary. Likewise the custom, originally laid down by him, of saying the Litany of Loreto on Saturday evenings is perpetuated as part of the Benediction service held in the Boys' Chapel at 6.00pm that same day.

Separated from it by two flower gardens and the Penance Walk the South Front looked on to a playground dominated by the Great 'Handball' erected in 1796. When they arrived the boys were at first permitted to range through the gardens. However, as the trail of devastation mounted, the authorities took determined action – 'great was the labour with spade and pickaxe to root out the ornamental shrubs and demolish the parterres on which Sir Nicholas had bestowed so much pains' lamented Fr Postlewhite. Thereafter, the garden beyond was declared out of bounds. Charles Waterton, who came that year, stated that 'at Stonyhurst there are boundaries marked out to the students, which they are not allowed to pass: and there are prefects always pacing to and fro within the lines'. To make their job easier a high stone wall was constructed. Two smaller 'Handballs' were let into this in 1820.

As Waterton states, the whole area was divided into two 'Lines' by the Prefects' Walk. Higher Line, the preserve of the senior boys, occupied the eastern end. Along its edge, starting from a line taken from (room) 'No. 10' in the present building, stretched a row of gardens behind 'Bond St', a favourite lounge. Each garden was owned by two or three boys with rights to pass on the property to selected 'heirs'. Some were cultivated carefully, others not at all. One, denoted the 'Haggory', was the haunt for members of the vociferous 'Young Ireland Party' and decorated with emblems proclaiming the demands of that pertinacious isle. Lower Line meanwhile had to make do with just three gardens, which rapidly fell out of use. The trees in the area also succumbed to the assaults of the little urchins and had to be removed.

Despite all these improvements conditions remained extremely tough. Heating, for instance, was a major problem. In a boy's letter home dated 25 October 1795 'the dimensions of the firegrate in the schoolroom' were described thus:

> Length 1 ft. ½ in., depth 8 in., breadth at the top 6⅜ in., breadth at the bottom 3⅝ in.: This, consider, to warm thirty persons in a large room, with two doors full of chinks, and the same number of windows; the floor paved with flagstones, and many other particularities peculiarly adapted to prevent the circulation of warmth.

Below: *Plan of the Old Playground.*

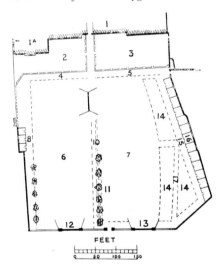

PLAN OF OLD PLAYGROUND, WITH GARDENS.

1. Front of old School-room Wing	9. Lower Line Trees.
1a. "Shirk."	10. Prefects' Walk
2. Lower-Line "Green."	11. Trees.
3. Higher-Line "Green"	12–13. Pavilion Hand-balls
4–5. Penance-Walks.	14. Grass.
6. Lower-Line Play-ground.	15. "Bond Street"
7. Higher-Line Play-ground.	16. Higher-Line Gardens
8. Lower-Line Gardens	17. "Ave Maria Lane."

87

Above: *The gasworks after their closure in 1922,* and above right, *the fully automatic 'Silverlite' plant installed at the same time to supply the kitchens and laboratories. It was the largest private installation of its kind in the world.*

Not surprisingly, in wintertime boys wore overcoats indoors. Colds, flu and chilblains were rife. As early as 1797 a boy died of pleurisy caught from sitting on a damp cricket-stone. Finding a decent supply of coal was therefore of the first importance. Under the Shireburns the house had obtained coal mined on the estate, but as the building expanded this quickly proved quite inadequate. Mr Hayhurst, for instance, the most productive of the local miners, brought in only 850 baskets during 1796. The obvious move then was to look further afield, and with Squire Lomax of Clayton, a local parent, the College found the answer. In February 1798 he produced 1,237 baskets for £20.12s.4d, in June 1799 1,793 for £29.2s.0d. and, six months later, 3,021 for £50.7s.0d. A peculiarity of these figures though is that, despite the expansion of the house and the installation of gas-lighting, they are higher than those recorded in a separate coal account for 1814–17. Either the price fell, or the coal account is incomplete or, in the interests of economy, people just froze. Moreover, turnpike charges took up one-third of the cost; hence Fr Wright's interest in road building. Between 1799 and 1803 £281.7s.6d.was raised by local subscription to repair Mitton Bridge; and in 1826 one of his last acts was to commission a new turnpike road between Lower Hodder Bridge and Hurst Green. Fr Gerard's claim though that this was designed and built by none other than John McAdam seems rather dubious.

Just as important as heating was the supply of light. In the earliest days, like everywhere else, the College relied on candles. The accounts show that these were usually made of tallow rendered down from the skins of the dozens of animals consumed every year. Not only was it inefficient and of course highly dangerous but, after the construction of the South Front, it was uneconomic. So Fr Sewall, encouraged by his friend Fr Dunn, formerly a teacher at Liège and now a most effective missioner in Preston, commissioned Samuel Clegg to install a gasworks in 'Tank Square' at the end of the South Front. Completed in 1811 at a cost of £480 it was a revolutionary step for, after Duxholme Mill, Stonyhurst became one of the first large buildings to be lit in this way. Its secret was Samuel Clegg's Lime Purifier. This removed the hydrogen sulphide which hitherto in confined spaces had caused headaches and in some cases affected the lungs. Following this up Fr Dunn helped to establish the Preston Gas Light Company in which the College took out shares. Preston thus became the first major provincial town to be lit by gas. Its implications for industrial practices – most notably the introduction of night-shift work – were profound. At a stroke, as Clegg's own estimates show, lighting costs were reduced to a fraction of their former level:

400 candles at 1*d*. each	£2.	10*s*.	0*d*.
20 lbs of tar at 2*d*. per lb		3*s*.	4*d*.
pint of oil		1*s*.	0*d*.
Sal Ammonia		5*s*.	0*d*.
Coke		2*s*.	6*d*.
	£3.	1*s*.	10*d*.

200 lbs Canal* coal		3*s*.	0*d*.
190 lbs common coal		1*s*.	8*d*.
Operator's time		2*s*.	0*d*.
Interest on £500 loan at 10%		3*s*.	6*d*.
		10*s*.	2*d*.

*i.e. 'Cannel coal' – so called because it ignites when a candle is held against it.

But if the lighting problems were largely solved those of feeding proved far more intractable. Robert Haly described his victuals as 'coarse but scanty'. Egg-cups and spoons were not supplied, a knife being used to transfer the contents to the mouth instead; 'Sunday dinner invariably was beef not roast but baked – and baked to a degree that deprived it of all juice . . . Mondays and Wednesdays were little better, as on these days the dinner consisted of a slice of fat bacon and veal that was truly and really what is called "Staggering Bob".' Other dishes received equally picturesque names. A species of round baked pastry was known as 'Race Course', 'Gas Pie' was a mince tart that when opened gave off an aroma of coal gas, while 'Shouting Cake' had currants so widely spaced that they were 'out of earshot' as it were. Hordes of rats made substantial inroads into what supplies there were. In 1823 no less than 1,067 of the vermin were caught; and in his autobiography Charles Waterton himself recalled how 'by a mutual understanding I was made rat-catcher to the establishment, and also fox-taker, foumant-killer and crossbow-charger at the time when the young rooks were fledged'.

Not surprisingly, complaints about the food were vociferous. On 8 March 1817 the Minister's Journal records that:

> All the boys of both refectories were assembled in the Great Refectory and the following order from the Reverend President was read.
>
> 'Reverend Mr President is much concerned to have observed of late among several of the scholars a disposition to rude behaviour and insubordination to their superiors, testified by frivolous and groundless complaints and by other transgressions equally forbidden by virtue and by honour. Now, to put an immediate stop to these disorders, Reverend Mr President first informs the scholars that he and their other superiors are taking, and will take, the best precautions to secure the good quality of their regular diet and to prevent wilful neglect in the cookery. The meat which is served to them is undoubtedly of as good quality as is found in the houses of the gentry of the country and attention shall be had that the other articles of their diet be likewise of good quality and that there will be no wilful neglect in preparing it.

Old pewter mugs, on display in the Do Room.

After this declaration, Reverend Mr President announces to all the scholars that in future no condescension shall be paid to their particular fancies, nor any change of victuals be allowed to anyone unless it be specially recommended by the physician of the College on account of health.

It is further declared that if any are detected in violating the decent order of the refectory by quitting their places, by throwing bread or other victuals about the refectory, and still more, by carrying out knives, forks, spoons or cups, they will incur exemplary punishment.

In fact, a few months later Fr Plowden took active steps to standardise the diet. The weekly menu given below is abstracted from the detailed instructions written on the first page of the new Minister's Journal started in September 1817:

Date	Dinner	Supper
Tues Sept 23rd:	Hashed sheep's head and liver, roast lamb etc.	Cold beef and mutton 'stakes'
Wed Sept 24th:	Beans, bacon, boiled beef, vegetables etc.	Cold meat etc.
Thurs Sept 25th:	Roast mutton and stewed hare	No information
Fri Sept 26th:	*Scholars:* Rice soup and apple pie *Community:* Flabby salmon, apple pie, rice soup	Eggs etc.
Sat Sept 27th:	Salmon and bread pudding	Butter, bread pudding, small hot loaves
Sun Sept 28th:	Roast beef and Yorkshire pudding	Mutton 'stakes', cold beef
Mon Sept 29th:	Baked mutton, turnips etc.	Cold mutton, beef etc.

To meet these requirements Fr Wright had to improve the yield from the estate. One of his first acts was to restock the farm. The accounts show that in 1795 at least 12 calves, 18 scotts – presumably Scottish cattle – 6 cows, 33 sheep, 46 lambs and some pigs were bought for £299.0s.5d. and a further £15.5s.5d. spent on hens, geese and other poultry. As numbers rose so did Fr Wright's expenditure. Thus in 1803 7 stirks or young bullocks, 1 fat cow, 19 scotts, 3 cows, 5 calving cows, about 40 calves and 144 sheep were bought. Excluding £41.19s.6d. for venison, £1,095.11s.3d. was spent on livestock that year. The diet was further supplemented by exploiting the local fisheries, £63.8s.10d. being spent on this item by 1803. At the same time the mill was reslated, new flagstones laid down and castings, ironwork, cording and new shovels supplied for £62.16s. Fr Sewall was thus able to buy American grain at Liverpool and grind it on the site, a practice that persisted into the 1960s.

Furthermore, Fr Wright was not averse to modern farming techniques. In February 1802 £31.10s. was spent on a new threshing-machine; the presence of turnips on the menu suggests up-to-date methods of crop rotation; while expenditure on lime fertiliser rose from £3 in 1795 to £26.6s. by 1803.

The most basic way to increase production, though, was to buy up more land. Originally, the College had been granted a 99-year lease on the house, garden and 100 acres for an annual rent of £30 in the first seven years and £60 thereafter. Three years later Thomas Weld remitted the rent in return for the annual right to present two 'fit and proper' persons aged between 10 and 18 for education at the

College. Then in 1809, when his son John entered the Society, he converted the lease into an outright gift. Two years after his death his son Thomas, later Cardinal Weld, sold to the College the rest of the farm, Lower Bridge Farm, Bankhurst Cottages, Throstle Nest, Stockbridge Farm, the blacksmith's shop, Greenfield, Perchfield and various allotments on Longridge Fell. Later, in 1828, Thomas sold another 3,250 acres including Bradhurst and Overhacking Farms, Mill and Loach Field Woods, the fields behind Judd Falls and the burial-ground at the top of the Avenue. Finally, in 1837, after the Cardinal's death, the College bought Hodder Wood, Pinfold Cottages, the Manor Warren, Timothy and Dilworth farms together with the lordship and manor of Aighton. These purchases not only made the College largely self-sufficient but gave it considerable prominence in local affairs.

The expenditure required for all these purchases was obviously considerable; and to this must be added the sums spent on the buildings and just keeping the house running on a day-to-day basis. Window tax, for instance, cost £119.3s.6d. in 1803; while the Day Book shows that between 1795 and 1803 annual expenditure rose from £4,327.14s.10d. to £9,979.15s.5d. One device was to recycle or resell unused items. For instance, the boys' shoes were produced from the skins of the animals consumed at table. Another resource was to tap the considerable sums accumulated by Fr Wright in government stock. This was managed as part of a much larger portfolio – worth £28,622 in 1801 – containing the funds of the ex-Jesuit Province and a number of private individuals. Of this £14,000 belonged to the College, yielding a useful £476 a year; and it was Fr Sewall who, pessimistic about the chances of a successful war against France, urged his Procurator to sell up and put the money into land and building work – a policy that was partially put into practice.

The most basic source of revenue, though, was the boys' school fees fixed, according to the 1797 prospectus, at 40 guineas p.a. for ordinary students, 37 for the under-12s and 45 for Rhetoricians and Philosophers. As numbers rose the situation steadily became more healthy. Geographically Stonyhurst was well placed to recruit from Ireland in addition to the traditional heartlands of English Catholicism. By Christmas 1794 nearly 40 pupils had joined the original 12; on 2 January an extra day's Christmas holiday celebrated the first 'half century'; and thereafter numbers rose to figures unheard of during the College's stay overseas: 100 in 1798, 150 in 1801, 225 in 1812 and just short of 250 a little later.

The curriculum they encountered was much the same as that offered by the Liège Academy. 21 October 1794 opened with the usual Ascensio Scholarum. In this ceremony, known at Liège as 'Knocking Day', the Prefect of Studies conducted the new members of Rhetoric to their schoolroom; one of their number was then sent to knock on the Syntax door and declare 'Poetry is empty'. In this way each class moved up to occupy the classroom vacated by the set above. Compositions, Examens, Academies and other scholastic routines then followed as usual. So strong was the classical tradition that attempts were even made to call the College 'Saxosylva', 'Collegium Saxosylvanum' or 'Saxosylvense'; but, as many boys were of local origin or sprang from the expanding Catholic middle class, adjustments had to be made. Thus, in 1814, Charles Brooke, the new Prefect of Studies, reported that 'on looking over the list of scholars, it appears that far the greater part of them are to be employed when they leave the College, in some sort of mercantile business. To all of these, Arithmetic is the science, which will be most useful and most interesting.' In the same document he recommended a

The Great Academies programme of 1807 which includes the names of several important future OS.

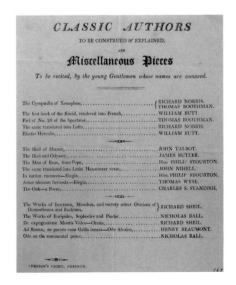

new textbook sent to him by Richard Clifford, demanded frequent repetition of the rules, addition tests every evening and urged staff to compare notes on their teaching methods – 'But each master is at full liberty to pursue any method, which by experience he shall find successful.'

The most revolutionary development, though, was in the teaching of Science. At Liège this had been actively encouraged, but during the migration most of the equipment had been lost; hence the inclusion within the South Front of a mathematical or philosophical room, the first of its kind in any English school. To equip it £2,239 was raised by subscription in 1808. In 1824 the editor of the *Yorkshire Gazette and Blackburn Mail* said this included a model of a steam engine, an 8-inch telescope, 'a beautiful and highly finished transit instrument 4 feet in length', an astronomical circle, a timepiece, electrical machines, an air pump and large handsome globes. At the same time a Chemistry laboratory was opened between the present South Front and Ambulacrum. This was surely unique, for not until 1857 did another English school – Rugby – have anything comparable. The building, which still stands, now forms part of the Art Department.

As before, the academic work was supported by a comprehensive routine. In 1817, when Fr Plowden took over as Rector – he was the first to use this title – the First Prefect's Log Book shows that this was thoroughly reorganised and carefully synchronised to take full advantage of the hours of daylight:

Monday

Morning

5.30 Rise, Wash, Vac till 5 [mins] before 6.00 Morning Prayers, then after these one of Bishop Challoner's meditations.

20 mins past 6.00 Litany of the BV then Mass.

6.45 Morning Studies.

20 mins before 8.00 Breakfast.

8.00 Return to the Study Place and from thence to schools.

10.30 Writing Lesson.

10 mins past 11.00 Washing.

11.30 Dinner.

Evening

12.00 Public Recreation.

1.30 Evening(!) Studies.

2.00 Schools.

4.00 Bread and Beer and Public Recreation.

42(!) mins past 4.00 Visit.

5.00 Night Studies.

6.30 Supper (presumably in Winter).

7.00 Supper (presumably in Summer).

8.00 Night Prayers.

8.30 Bed.

On a Month day or Blandyke the whole holiday routine was not dissimilar:

Morning		*Evening*	
6.00	Rising etc.	12.00	Recreation till
6.30	Morning Prayers etc.	1.30	Studies.
6.45	Mass etc.	2.30	Recreation till

7.15	Studies.	6.15	Visit.
8.15	Breakfast.	6.30	Supper.
8.30	Recreation till	7.00	Recreation.
11.00	Washing.	8.15	Night Studies (except
11.30	Dinner.		between April and August).
		8.30	To Bed.

The longer holidays were also carefully prescribed; the Christmas Vacation, according to the Minister's Journal, 'to begin on Christmas Day and continue to the 1st of January inclusive . . . the Easter Vacation . . . from the end of evening schools on Friday preceding Palm Sunday till Monday after Low Sunday' and 'the Pentecost Vacation consists of only 3–2 days, Saturday evening, Pentecost Sunday, Monday and Tuesday which are Villa days'. Due to the slowness of travel it was only during the Grand Vacation, which 'begins on the Wednesday coming nearest the 8th of August, and continues one calendar month', that the boys could go home. Several in fact remained behind, necessitating special arrangements for their supervision, including a certain amount of study, while the Prefects, along with the rest of the Community, enjoyed a well-earned rest at their 'Villa' in Blackpool. Otherwise for the boys the tedium was relieved by various privileges, rewards and entertainments. Thus, on 17 November 1818, the Prefect's Log reports that 'Master Anthony Clarke performed his feats in the magic arts for the amusement of the lower schools. Among other wonderful things he cuts a cock's head off and puts it on again; he did this so cleverly that the cock was as lively after it as before it.' More regular indulgences included 'Lemonades' – special meals subscribed to by the boys washed down with liberal potations of that home-brewed beverage. 'Good Breakfasts, Dinners and Suppers' were the perquisite of office-holders like torch-bearers or Green Room boys, 'finders' of keys and 'Walkers', who looked after people on their first day at Stonyhurst. A 'Good Day' – really a Blandyke – was offered to groups like the Choir, the Band, and the 'First Six'.

The whole system depended heavily on the energy and resource of the hard-worked Prefects of Discipline. As relatively junior members in the Community their relations with the Rector were not always easy. On the first surviving copy of their logbook, significantly entitled 'The Prefects' Checkbook Against Innovators', they inscribed their duties:

To see after the appurtenances of the game of football.
To attend the Dancers.
To superintend the Drawers.
To superintend the Musicians.
To distribute shoe-strings, garters, collars and caps.
To superintend everything connected with the Dormitories –
    – having them washed.
    – the sheet changed every month. To attend the lesson in writing.
To see after all the appertenances viz.:
    – bats
    – covering of balls etc to the game of cricket.
To see after the wine on Wine Days.

At the bottom they added in large letters: 'Ever to remember the BOTTLE when examining copy books.'

By 1817, though, this was the least of the problems facing Fr Plowden. Over 40 years had elapsed since the suppression of the Society. So, as the surviving ex-Jesuits got older and dwindled in number, young scholastics straight from the noviciate had to be deployed in the burgeoning playrooms, leading to major problems of discipline. Secular clergy and even laymen were also employed, weakening an already fragile sense of cohesion among the staff; Fr Plowden therefore had them removed. However, this did not solve the fundamental problem. If the College was to survive, the Society had to be restored and new recruits trained. This in turn depended on good outside relations; but from the start these proved difficult. It was not just that Stonyhurst was Catholic and suspected to be Jesuit; rumours also circulated that it contained a nest of Bonapartist agents. In 1803, for instance, Fr Hughes, writing to Fr Barrow at Liège, mentions that a Dr Collins, a local Anglican clergyman and JP, had discovered that no register of aliens had been forwarded to him. Consequently Frs Stone, Plowden and Laurenson, together with various foreign pupils and servants brought over from Liège, were summoned to attend him in Whalley. There Fr Plowden was mistaken for a Frenchman and Fr Laurenson for a German. When Plowden inadvertently mentioned that Fr Wright was the only person who had visited the coast in the last few months:

> The doctor insisted on a declaration to be made of this; first, who is this Mr Wright? Is he a foreigner? Secondly, what did he say respecting the coasts? and many similar questions were made. The doctor's scribes minuted the answers. Plowden wished to see what they had written. He found that they had greatly changed the sense of what he had said; upon which he wrote down what he had said, and took a copy of it, then tore the minutes made by the clerks.

Another complicating factor was the Paccanarist movement. In the late eighteenth century two French priests, Fr Charles de Broglie (son of the famous marshal) and Fr Nicholas Paccanari, despairing of the restoration of the Society, set up two new organisations, the Society of the Sacred Heart and the Society of the Faith of Jesus, to carry on the Jesuit tradition. In 1800, the year after their amalgamation, Paccanari sent Frs Broglie and Rozaven to England to secure recruits among the numerous French exiled clergy and set up a school in Kensington. The challenge to Stonyhurst was obvious, especially if they secured affiliation with the Russian Jesuit Province, since many English ex-Jesuits might be tempted to join them. In 1802 though, after a critical meeting at Stonyhurst with the two priests, their proposals for union were turned down. Further appeals, this time to rescue the Kensington school from debt, were wisely rejected and the rival establishment eventually collapsed in 1812.

Meanwhile, significant steps had been taken to improve the College's legal status. As early as 14 February 1796 Pius VII had renewed all the rights originally given to the Liège Academy in the brief *Catholici Praesules*. Then in May 1803, just after the Paccanarist appeals had been turned down, Stonyhurst successfully applied for affiliation with the Russian Jesuits. Fr Stone became Provincial and he, with a number of English ex-Jesuits, were readmitted to the Society.

On the strength of this a noviciate was opened on 27 September at Hodder Place under the direction of Fr Plowden. The site, occupied by a factory, was known as 'Hell's Gates', due to the extraordinary behaviour of its workforce. Thomas Weld therefore bought the lease from its bankrupt owner, Mr Emett, and presented it,

Two views of Hodder Place. The turrets were added in 1868–9.

together with 50 acres, to the College. In no time at all, the factory buildings were demolished and two new wings added to the private residence Mr Emett had left there. The conditions, aptly evoked by the vitriolic pen of Fr Plowden, were at first chaotic: 'I have been living two years and six months in dirt and cold, amidst slow-moving trowels and lazy carpenters, employed to erect a small and ill-contrived habitation for our ecclesiastical probationists and our nest of little boys.'

Nonetheless, despite these unpromising beginnings, Hodder offered the first real hope of relief for the hard-pressed Community at Stonyhurst. Here a contingent of novices, including several enthusiastic but ill-educated recruits from Ireland, began their studies. In 1807, partly to mask this activity, a Preparatory school for about 30 boys was established under Fr West. Hodder, through its lineal descendant St Mary's Hall, can therefore claim to be the oldest surviving preparatory school in the country.

The establishment of a noviciate could not fail to arouse suspicions, not only among Protestants, but also in the minds of the Vicars-Apostolic. Anxious to build up their own seminaries, they were naturally annoyed by the diversion of precious resources to a place whose alumni could be deployed wherever the 'President' of Stonyhurst chose to send them. Bishop Gibson, the Northern Vicar-Apostolic, reacted by trying to appropriate Stonyhurst for his own use as a diocesan seminary; but this cut across the interests of other Vicars-Apostolic, notably Bishop Milner of the West Midlands, who hoped to benefit from its recruits. A further consideration was the belief, widely voiced by members of the Cisalpine Club, that a revival of the Society might jeopardise the cause of Catholic emancipation. In this argument they were ably supported by the representations of Sir John Cox Hippesley, who advocated a restored Catholic Church in which the bishops would be supervised by the government in a manner not dissimilar to the system propounded by the Gallican party in France. These views were well calculated to appeal to a Catholic gentry anxious to keep control over their priests and suspicious of any of the Ultramontane ideas associated with Milner and the Society. Curiously enough Hippesley, hoping to get Stonyhurst on his side, had at first seemed well disposed and even subscribed to the building appeal for the South Front. Unfortunately, a sharp article by Fr Plowden, who well understood the parallel with the Archpriest Controversy two centuries before, had turned him into a bitter enemy.

This, then, was the very complicated and delicate situation that Fr Plowden inherited from Fr Stone. On 7 August 1814 Pius VII had restored the Society

Fr Charles Plowden SJ, Rector and Provincial between 1817 and 1819. Pencil drawing.

throughout the world but, in a letter to Bishop Poynter dated 2 December 1816, Cardinal Litta, the Prefect of Propaganda, made it clear that, as far as Stonyhurst was concerned, this was conditional on recognition by the British Government. Poynter also had an important ally at Rome in the person of Cardinal Consalvi. Consalvi felt that the restoration of the Papal States after the Napoleonic Wars was due to pressure from the British Government, acting on advice given by Poynter. Consalvi was therefore at one with Poynter in arguing that any restoration of the Society in England would do the cause of Catholic emancipation irreparable harm.

Plowden was not the right sort of man to deal with this. Unlike Stone, whose instinct was to wait, to blur over the differences and to compromise, Plowden was an inveterate controversialist whose thinking was dominated by the humiliating experiences he and his colleagues had suffered in 1773. Yet, surprisingly, at first it seemed that his efforts might be successful. Early in 1818 his agent, Fr Grassi, persuaded Litta to reverse the letter he had written to Poynter two years before and affirm that the Society was restored in England as well as in the rest of the world. But, within a few weeks, Poynter's agent, Dr Gradwell, drew Consalvi's attention to the unauthorised decision and persuaded the Pope to reverse it. Then Plowden, through the agency of Milner, and supported by a petition from many leading Catholic laymen, including some Old Boys, persuaded Cardinal Somaglia, the new Prefect of Propaganda, to issue a secret decree in December 1818 giving Stonyhurst the right, by virtue of its status as a Pontifical college, to present candidates for ordination to any bishop – in this case Milner – thus evading the hostility of any other Vicar-Apostolic. Once again this decision, after its discovery by an irate Bishop Gibson, was reversed by the Pope. Stonyhurst could only present candidates 'in titulo missionis' – that is the bishop would have sole control over their deployment in his area of jurisdiction, making them no different from any other secular priest. When he came to Rome for the election of a new General, Plowden made desperate but unavailing efforts to avert this. His failure – 'my heart and head are almost broken' – undoubtedly contributed to his death on the return journey at Joigné in Switzerland. Curiously enough the locals, thinking that he really was a military general, buried him with full military honours. He was aged 79.

The result was a swift collapse at Stonyhurst. The younger teachers, smarting under the tighter regime imposed by Plowden, did not know whether they were proper Jesuits or not; the Hodder noviciate became virtually extinct; while parents, sensing a fall in standards and discipline, declined to send their children. By 1822 numbers had plummeted to about 99. Chastened, the General accepted Plowden's dying recommendation that Fr Sewall become Provincial. Despite claims that he was burnt out and exhausted, Sewall's letters from this period show grip and incisive ability. Equally important was the work of the Prefect of Studies, Fr Charles Brooke, and his successors, Frs Glover and Brigham, in reversing the decline of academic standards. By 1840, despite the fashionable attractions of Oscott under Monsignor Weedall, numbers had staggered back to 183.

At Rome, meanwhile, the recovery of influence began. In 1825 Fr Glover was appointed as an agent representing the interests of the English ex-Jesuits. Next year the process was accelerated when Fr Brooke became Provincial. Milner's death was more than counteracted by the conversion of Bishop Collingridge, Vicar Apostolic of the Western District, to the Jesuit cause after a severe illness.

Poynter's death the year after led to the withdrawal of his able lieutenant, Gradwell, from Rome. Under the influence of Bishop Baines, Collingridge's coadjutor, the new Pope Leo XII proved more friendly, especially after the death of Consalvi. While on retreat at Subiaco, Baines, using materials supplied by Glover, drew up a memorial petitioning for the restoration of the Society in England. On 6 January 1829 it was presented to Leo as he left the Sistine Chapel and approved forthwith.

This brief, together with the passage of Catholic Emancipation Act later that year, seemed to remove every obstacle from Stonyhurst's path. But there was a flaw. Section 34 of the Act, while tolerating existing members of the Society, forbade it from recruiting new members. Panic ensued, and every potential postulant over the age of 16 was recruited before the Act came into force. But these precautions proved unnecessary. At an interview with Sir Robert Peel, the Home Secretary, Fr Scott the London agent was told: 'You a Jesuit, and not see through that. We must throw a tub to the whale, and this is it. But observe, no one can proceed against you except the Attorney-General – and I can undertake that he will have something better to do.'

Nevertheless, despite the reassurance, for a long time afterwards proceedings for the enrolment of novices at Stonyhurst took place in great secrecy. For instance, in 1870 Gerard Manley Hopkins described how 'In a tiny chapel upstairs, lit by a skylight . . . Fr Fitzsimon sat near a small table on which stood a crucifix, and we entered singly one after another, as though going to confession, and kneeling took our vows in secret . . . the Master of Novices merely answered Amen, took the written formula of the vows and the young religious withdrew.'

Meanwhile, anticipating the restoration of the Society by two years, work had begun on a new house of philosophical and theological studies. Hitherto, potential ordinands had either been taught within the College or sent to seminaries abroad. Situated on the site of the old Shireburn piggeries and fishponds, St Mary's Hall was opened in 1830. Nicknamed 'Thin Drink Hall', due the low quality of beer supplied to the workforce, it then consisted of only the central block in the present building. Of the three persons who had done most to make it possible none actually saw it. Fr Plowden had long been dead; without his contacts with Thomas Weld it is probable that the Society would never have come to Stonyhurst. Fr Wright, active to the last, succumbed in 1827, aged 76. At his funeral all the servants of the house and farm lined the Avenue from the front door in order of seniority. That same year Fr Stone gave up his post as Minister and retired to the mission at St Helens where he died, almost totally blind, at the age of 86 in 1834; but for the rest of the Community the time of waiting was over.

Hodder Chapel.

BASKERVILLE HALL

The Avenue opened into a broad expanse of turf, and the house lay before us. In the centre was a heavy block of building from which a porch projected. The whole front was draped in ivy, with a patch clipped here and there where a window or a coat of arms broke through the dark veil. From this central block rose the twin towers, ancient, crenellated, and pierced with many loopholes. To right and left of the turrets were more modern wings of black granite. A dull light shone through heavy mullioned windows, and from the high chimneys which rose from the steep, high angled roof there sprang a single black column of smoke.

Above: *The Dark Walk. In his diaries Fr Gerard SJ mentions that Bandy was sometimes played here.*

Baskerville Hall, with some modifications, is really Stonyhurst; for between 1869 and 1875 Sir Arthur Conan Doyle was a pupil at the College; and although he researched and set *The Hound of the Baskervilles* in the West Country, he also drew on many schoolboy memories. The Dark Walk with its Gazebo and opening half way along is similar to the place (also a yew alley) where Sir Charles Baskerville met his dreadful end; Longridge Fell has been transposed into Baskerville Moor; and there is even an oblique reference to the Observatory in the person of Mr Frankland and his telescope.

Other stories, too, bear the Stonyhurst stamp. Its classical and mathematical education undoubtedly prepared the way for 'The Science of Deduction' and

Left: *The 'Fronts' in 1858, one of several pictures of Stonyhurst and its district taken by the great Victorian photographer Roger Fenton shortly after he returned from the Crimean War. Note the completion of the façade.*

Facing page: *The 'Fronts' today viewed from beside the Mill Pond.*

'We were a patriotic crowd, and our little pulse beat time with the heart of the nation.' Doyle with his class in 1873. He stands directly in front of the window.

the subsequent modelling of Sherlock Holmes himself on the celebrated Dr Bell of Edinburgh University. Similarly the Stonyhurst Museum and the exploits of Charles Waterton in South America may have stimulated Conan Doyle's taste for exotic objects and nostrums from far-away places. Two of his Stonyhurst contemporaries had the name Moriarty, one of whom won mathematics prizes. In *The Final Problem* the master criminal is described as 'a man of good birth and excellent education, endowed by nature with phenomenal mathematical ability'.

Another and very different picture of the College at this time emerges from the Tichborne trial. Roger Tichborne, scion of one of the oldest landed families in England, came to Stonyhurst as a Secular or Gentleman Philosopher in 1845. The department, which hitherto had led a rather shadowy existence since its inception at Liège, had just been moved to new quarters in St Mary's Hall and enjoyed much greater consequence. Numbers, which had obstinately remained in single figures during previous decades, rose to 16 in 1848 and peaked at 50 in 1880, making it the largest 'university' department of its kind in the English Catholic world. The fees, fixed first at 100 and later 120 guineas a year, were a most welcome increment to the College finances. One reason for its growth was Stonyhurst's affiliation with London University in 1840. For the first time since the Reformation Catholics could take degrees at an English university. More significant perhaps was the arrival of several often very distinguished sprigs of European nobility, who treated the place as a sort of finishing school. As a result the curriculum, from the 1847 prospectus, presented a most curious amalgam:

> This Establishment is set apart – first, for students of Philosophy; secondly for those who intend, with the privileges of private rooms, a separate table, and particular attendence, to follow the University course; and thirdly, for those who, to supply the deficiency of their earlier education, find it necessary to direct their attention, with the advantage of private assistance, to any particular branch of science, literature, Ancient or Modern Language as taught at the College.

Coming from France, where he had been educated by a succession of private tutors under the eye of his foolish but devoted mother, Roger clearly fell into the third category. Whether he really made much progress it is difficult to say for, as the prospectus puts it, 'No other means will be resorted to for their management than those of persuasion and verbal admonition. Should such means prove ineffectual their Superiors will immediately resign the care of their education into the hands of their parents or appointed guardians.' Certainly, in marked contrast with the rest of the school, Roger would have enjoyed a very free and easy lifestyle. His contemporary Percy Fitzgerald describes how:

Right: The Philosophers' Drawing Room, formerly the 'Duke's Room' (after the 8th Duke of Norfolk) and now the Staff Common Room, and, far right, the Philosophers' Dining Room.

You had all the comfort and luxuries of such a station, and then there were no cares, no anxieties, nothing to do but to look forward to a round of amusements, of 'Rector's Days', of great dinners in the refectory with the masters, in full dress, of coursing [the Philosophers kept their own pack of foxhounds], of long walks, and finally of Christmas and its long-anticipated long-sustained whirl of plays, scenery, feasting and gaiety.

In 1848 Roger left Stonyhurst and was shortly afterwards gazetted as a cornet in the Carabineers. But his military career was not a success; nor were amorous advances towards his cousin Catherine Doughty much appreciated by her family. So, in 1853 he set out for South America. On his return the following year he sailed from Rio de Janeiro in the *Bella*. She was never seen again.

The story now shifts to Australia where the Dowager Lady Tichborne, who had never reconciled herself to her loss, had advertised for her son. In 1865 one Thomas Castro, a bankrupt butcher from Wagga Wagga, claimed to be the missing heir. Amazingly the claimant, whose real name was Arthur Orton, was 'recognised' by the Dowager and the case was on.

In the actual trials, first to establish his identity, secondly to try him for perjury, Castro's counsel ingeniously tried to show that a Stonyhurst education was by no means incompatible with the life of a corpulent illiterate from the Australian bush. According to Mr Kenealy James Tichborne sent his son:

> To a place where . . . no attention of any kind was given to the mental education of the boys. He sent him to a place where he was allowed to do whatsoever he pleased . . . His French habits and his foreign gibberish made him a sort of butt with everybody; . . . he lived very much alone and passed the greater portion of his time in smoking . . . He frequently resorted to Preston and was known there in certain places to which vestal virgins do not belong.

To substantiate this picture several of Roger's contemporaries were summoned to give testimony. Some, like Walter Strickland Mannock, responded in a most gratifying manner:

> Dr Kenealy: 'Am I right in supposing that you philosophers were allowed pretty well to do as you pleased?' A. 'Pretty well.' Q. 'To learn or not as you pleased?' A. 'We were supposed to learn.' Q. 'But you never carried this supposition into practice.' A. 'We did, occasionally.' Q. 'What did you learn, may I ask?' A. 'I cannot say, it was so long ago.'

Later, in the same cross examination:

> Lord Chief Justice: 'Did you never learn any Latin?' A. 'No.' Dr Kenealy: 'Did you ever cross the Pons Asinorum?' A. 'I believe not.' Q. 'Did you ever hear of it?' A. 'I remember hearing of it.' Q. 'Where did you hear it?' A. 'At school, always.' Q. 'Tell me the meaning?' A. 'I know nothing of it.' Q. 'You have not the least notion what it refers to?' A. 'Not the slightest.' Ld C. J.: 'Did you learn any mathematics?' A. 'I did not.'

Nonetheless, in spite of these unpromising answers the period 1829–48 was one of progress. The Great Church, dedicated to St Peter, was completed in 1835; and three years later the Old Observatory or Weather Station was built – the first step towards establishing Stonyhurst's reputation as an astronomical and

'Baronet or Butcher?' The Tichborne claimant. Cartoon by 'Ape', Vanity Fair, 10 June 1871.

Meet of the Pendle Hunt, 1908.

meteorological centre. At about the same time, in accordance with the provisions of his will, Lord Arundell's library of over 5,000 books was presented to the college by his widow. Next, in 1842–3, the old coach-houses were converted into the Infirmary; Fr Wright's North Wing was torn down in 1843 and replaced by the present wing; a new Corn Mill was erected in 1840 by the Ponds and in 1846 a new gasworks was opened in Loach Field Wood.

Academically, the picture was more mixed. In 1832 the revised *Ratio Studiorum* required Provincials to promote the study of vernacular languages, history, geography, mathematics, and science. Stonyhurst's affiliation with London University gave an added boost. In the fervour of the moment separate professors were appointed to the Poetry and Rhetoric classes; first for Latin, Greek and Mathematics; later for French, History and other subjects. The experiment was only partially successful, perhaps because the College had not yet fully recovered from the effects of the migrations and resettlements. Matriculations to London that decade ranged from nine in 1844 to only one in 1849; and, although the assertion that Stonyhurst for a time ceased to send up candidates is untrue, the constant tinkering with the system certainly betokens a crisis of confidence. Only one of these changes, the creation of separate Mathematics classes by Fr McCann in 1841, proved to be of lasting value.

The late 1840s were also a period of indiscipline, a problem that had never been entirely eradicated since the troubles of 1817–21. Certainly there were more outside influences. The London Matriculation was one; the rapid spread of railways another. In 1847 it was even planned to have a line outside Hurst Green. There were also growing numbers of books, periodicals and newspapers to be censored. In 1846 the Minister's Journal records that 'Fr Rector reminded the Community that no book is to be put into the hands of any scholar without the sanction and knowledge of the Prefect of Studies nor without the College mark.'

This was also an age of liberal revolutions abroad, Chartist agitation at home and a wave of unrest in many a public school. In the circumstances any attempt at maintaining a Continental system minutely regimenting every aspect of a boy's life proved increasingly untenable. Numerous petty restrictions combined with the harsh rigour of Stonyhurst life to give endless opportunities for challenge. A typical 'dare' would be to climb over the Playground wall and range through the forbidden territory of the gardens. Another would be to parade down the Avenue in full view of the College windows to dinner in the Shireburn Arms. Smoking and snuff taking were rife; and the 'scraping' of iron-shod shoes in the Study Place frequently drove masters to distraction.

In 1844 the trouble came to a head. Percy Fitzgerald recalled the arrival of 'a number of insubordinate and tumultuous spirits who about this time came to the College. They brought with them a sort of Land League insolence and wantonness and were soon defying all authority'; and, as the quotation implies, the Irish were at the centre of many a disturbance. That very year members of Syntax and Poetry 'barred' the Prefects from the First Playroom. However, when suppertime approached; some of the occupants decided they were too hungry to continue and tore down the barricade. Next year came the 'Brick Riots'. Percy Fitzgerald describes how:

> The occasion, if not the cause, was the disappearance one day of the religious books which were read out at meals. This daring and profane act filling everyone with awe and alarm. The authorities having obtained some

Facing page: Exterior of St Peter's consecrated by Bishop John Briggs on 23 June 1835. The Minister's Journal for 7 January 1839 reported 'a most terrific storm . . . five pinnacles were blown down on the SW side of the church, and took with them a good part of the coping-stones. The notable cross over the grand entrance rocked about most fearfully, but did not turn round this time (referring to damage in a similar storm of 31 December 1833).'

Interior of St Peter's church.

information as to the individual culprits, announced that the entire class should be deprived of 'recreation' until the books were restored. This almost led to open rebellion. A barbarous chorus used to be abruptly intoned on the smallest provocation, and 'who stole the books?' was yelled at the top pitch of a hundred voices.

These events split the school; 'Bricks,' or those who defied authority, being ranged against 'Clats' or sneaks. A 'Brick' passing a 'Clat' would mutter 'From Clats and telltales good Lord deliver us'. Graffiti, usually in the form of WSTB ('Who Stole the Books?'), appeared on desks, walls and doors in every part of the school. The response was savage. In 1847, after another surge of disorder, the *Preston Guardian* reported:

> We have learnt, with some surprise, that the practice of flogging is carried on in a College not far from this town with a severity, which calls loudly for reprobation. No fewer than six youths were very recently subjected to this degrading punishment in one day. One of the youths has preserved his blood-stained linen to exhibit to his parents. Another took refuge in the

house of a gentleman in this neighbourhood, having found an opportunity to escape from his tormentors. It is not the rod, but the *cat* to which we allude; nor are those subjected to the lash children, but youths, verging on manhood.

But all was to no avail. The authorities seemed helpless. Frequent changes of personnel at the top cannot have helped either. They may even have been symptomatic of a paralysis of will; the Rector Andrew Barrow (1841–5) being replaced successively by Richard Norris (1845), Henry Walmesley (1846) and Richard Sumner (1847). Equally significant, perhaps, was the fact that Thomas Speakman, who in 1845 had been re-appointed First Prefect to tighten up discipline, stayed for only two years. Several boys were expelled. Others were withdrawn by their parents. For example, the Minister's Journal on 15 October 1847 records how 'Fr William Lomax came this afternoon to take away Edward Middleton, in consequence of his and his brother's letters describing barrings out and riotous behaviour towards Mr Booker. Mrs Middleton thought that the College was in the greatest state of disorder and that Edward was sure to be ruined.'

The hapless Mr Booker was immediately relegated to the post of supply prefect and the following year left for America. His colleagues were less fortunate. On 15 May 1848 'in consequence of recreation not being granted today much excitement was observed among the scholars. A few hisses and groans were occasionally heard and at the end of the afternoon recreation, they gave a public demonstration of their feelings by refusing to obey the signal for coming in and staying at their benches until the Prefect on duty summoned them by name. They then came on, though sulkily. And there ended the demonstration.'

For this act of insubordination two boys were expelled and another two 'confined' in the Infirmary.

This then was the situation confronting the new Rector, Fr Francis Clough, in September 1848. He, too, could be tough. For instance in 1855, when the boys habitually harassed the deer in the Park, he slaughtered the entire herd; if smoking took place behind hedges and manholes then the hedges were razed and 'The Flue' filled in. However the Philosophers, now summoned from St Mary's Hall to quarters on the top storey of the Front Quadrangle, were allowed to smoke, thereby depriving the practice of much of its point. For the rest it was different. The *Stonyhurst Examiner and Times* recalled how 'during these years of tyranny, no sooner was an unfortunate youth suspected of having any communication whatsoever with tobacco or snuff, the existence of the latter article being usually discovered by a most minute and diligent examination among the pocket handkerchiefs, than he was immediately summoned to attend the Prefect in the Study Place and then commenced a most strict scrutiny of the culprit's desk.' With other more minor offences experiments were made with fines; while the ferula, a short strip of gutta-percha applied to the palm of the hand, remained the regular stand-by. On 4 July 1850 the Minister's Journal reported that, for striking and abusing a servant in the Refectory 'Master M was sentenced to receive twice nine ferulas and to kneel in the middle of the Refectory during the Scholars' dinner. As the servant had done more then merely defend himself, he was forbidden again to serve in the Refectory.'

Equally startling were the measures deployed to deal with trouble among the London Matriculation students. In 1858 the Minister's Journal records how 'Master Robert Peard . . . was telegraphed for from London for unsatisfactory

Fr Francis Clough SJ, Rector of Stonyhurst (1848–61), Superior and Vice-Rector of St Francis Xavier's Liverpool (1862–4) and Rector of Beaumont (1867–71).

Drill in the Ambulacrum.

conduct' and 'returned looking very miserable'. In 1861 special skill was shown by his handling of St Patrick's Day, always a potential source of trouble. The Minister's Journal records that after dinner he 'invited the Irish to the Parlour to drown the shamrock'.

Nevertheless, Fr Clough was shrewd enough to realise that, while efficacious in themselves, these methods did not strike at the root of the problem. The key to the situation was the quality of life. His rectorate was therefore characterised by much renovation and building activity. His first step in 1850 was to dam up a stream in the Park and, by building a row of wooden cots beside it, create the first bathing-place. Later, because of the coldness of the water, this was shifted to Hodder Roughs where the remains of the stone bathing-cots still be seen. Next year further steps were taken to improve the boys' cleanliness. The old primitive washing-place was abandoned in favour of new facilities in what is now the Do Room below the Top Refectory. More improvements followed in 1857. A four-inch iron-pipe brought water from a nearby reservoir, basins of Clitheroe marble were installed and separate brush and soap boxes allocated to each boy. Similarly the insanitary old toilets were replaced by the present Common Place. Needless to say the boys, with all the conservatism of youth, objected to the change. John Gerard, a future Prefect of Studies, records one typical piece of graffiti:

> I don't like these new water closets at all
> The seats are too high and the holes are too small.

To which the reply was:

> I think, Sir, your conduct provokes a retort,
> Your bum is too fat and your legs are too short.

The Ambulacrum itself, built in 1851, was one answer to the problems posed by the damp Lancashire climate. Recognising the pent-up frustrations of those cooped up in the Playrooms Fr Clough in effect created one of the first indoor school sports halls of its kind. On its earthen floor Seniors played Bandy – a Stonyhurst version of hockey. Juniors had to content themselves with 'Ambulacrum Football'.

Another photograph by Fenton, this time of Hodder Roughs. Note the regulation fur cap worn by boys at this time.

At the same time significant improvements were made to the Playrooms themselves. Wooden boards replaced cold flagstones; new – fixed – playroom tables were substituted for old movable ones, now relegated to the Ambulacrum for service as Christmas boxes. Billiards was introduced in 1858. To encourage greater sobriety, especially in the Study Place, Fr Clough insisted that boys coming in from the Playground change into house shoes in Shoe Places specially constructed for the purpose. In 1855, with the departure of the noviciate to Beaumont, Hodder preparatory school was expanded allowing him to redistribute the Playrooms. Thus the Second and Third Playrooms were merged into one for use by the remaining Juniors, Poetry received the newly converted Rhetoric Classroom and Rhetoric were left sole occupants of the First Playroom.

Finally, in 1856–7 Fr Clough brought his building programme to an impressive conclusion by the completion of the Great Quadrangle. The site was first cleared by the demolition of Sparrow's Hall and its associated buildings. At the same time the Shireburn Steps leading up to the Refectory were removed to their present site in the Gardens. The new building, designed by Fr Richard Vaughan, linked the 1844 North Front to the specially extended Refectory. It contained Lord Arundell's recently presented library, a 'School Chapel' (equivalent to the present Boys' Chapel), the Community and the Philosophers' Refectories. The building was further extended in 1856–9 by the construction of the Sodality Chapel.

Meantime, on the academic front, the setbacks of the 1840s were retrieved by the reforms of Fr Gallwey (Prefect of Studies from 1857 to 1859). These involved a conscious return to the principles of the *Ratio Studiorum*. The quantity of reading matter was greatly reduced to ensure greater accuracy; the system of separate subject masters was abandoned in favour of the old 'Classmaster' system; the practice of dividing classes into rival teams of 'Romans and Carthaginians' was revived and for a short time Concertatios took place in the Refectory – just as in the old days at St Omers. There was even a brief revival of the class names used in the Walloon College – Syntax, Grammar and Rudiments being replaced by Higher, Middle and Lower Grammar. The number of prizes was increased from 77 in 1848 to 123 in 1865, the revived classical emphasis being highlighted by this subject's enlarged share of the rewards – 46 and 111 being the relevant figures. For the ablest boys a special 'Classical Honours' course, examination and prizes were instituted.

Fr Peter Gallwey SJ. Prefect of Studies (1857–9) and Provincial (1873–6).

The Chapel 1858–87.

Old buildings in the Back Court, demolished in 1856 when the Top Refectory was extended. Note the medieval 'chip' entry.

These efforts were rewarded by improved performances in University of London examinations. Already, by 1852 these had reached a peak of 14 passes. Thereafter, numbers fell back to about six or seven a year; but in 1858 this was more than compensated for by five Special Honours, which were taken separately. In the next five years up to 1864, when Special Honours were abolished, Stonyhurst candidates regularly came first in the Classical Honours list. Testifying before the Taunton Commission on 15 March 1865 Dr W Smith observed: 'I heard from my colleague, Mr Murcham, that the candidates they sent up for examination came very ill prepared, so much so that they were frequently rejected. They were withdrawn for a year or two, and after a lapse of time there were some exceedingly well prepared, so well prepared that I do not believe any of the boys from the sixth form of our public schools have a better education given to them than Stonyhurst gives.'

The net effect of Fr Clough's reforms then was a transformation in morale and performance at every level of the College. Numbers rose from 156 in 1844 to 192 twenty years later. The latter figure does not include the 36 who attended the prep school at Hodder. Living conditions continued to improve. One of Fr Clough's last acts was the appointment of a resident physician; his successor, Fr Joseph Johnson (1861–9) in 1862 built a new kitchen in the Shireburn Quadrangle, refloored the Refectory

with Sicilian marble and substituted iron-railings for the stone wall separating the Playground from the gardens. Further afield, new towers were added to the Preparatory School at Hodder where, between 1866 and 1915, a gentle but imaginative regime was established by Fr Francis Cassidy, who was appointed Superior there in 1875. Similarly, in the main College, as the authorities recovered their nerve, a more relaxed approach to discipline was adopted. New societies and occupations sprang up on every side. Skating on the Ponds became a popular pastime; in 1850, as a response to the public outcry over the restoration of the Catholic hierarchy, a debating society was founded; the following year two rival magazines began to circulate in Higher Line; a Junior Sodality, dedicated to St Aloysius, was set up in 1852 and Fr Clough personally presided over the establishment of the Stonyhurst Cricket Club in 1860. Excursions, treats and other exciting events supplemented the traditional but now more closely supervised country walks. Thus, on 20 July 1850 (Rector's Day), 25 scholars went to Parlick Pike to see the devastation made by a waterspout. At the same time another party would have visited Sawley Abbey but for the rain. On 21 July 1852 Donkey Races took place on the Great Stonyhurst Field after dinner; while on 24 September the Minister's Journal records that 'a large fire balloon was sent up successfully from the Playground after bread and beer [the nineteenth-century Stonyhurst equivalent of Tea]'. On 12 December 1854 the same source declared:

News arrived about 9.45 of the Immaculate Conception having been defined, on the 8th, to be an article of faith; a cannon shot was fired, the schools were at once ended, and a great shout raised, at the announcement of this glorious event. Wine for the Community and Philosophers. Punch for the B.B. [lay brothers] . . . The *Te Deum* was sung in the Church as soon as possible after the glorious intelligence.

Nonetheless, there is no doubt that Fr Clough's act proved a difficult one to follow. Many of the societies inaugurated during his rectorate collapsed, including the school magazines and Debating Society. Numbers, too, temporarily declined to 162 in 1874, though this figure does not include the 52 studying at Hodder. His successor, Fr Joseph Johnson, although himself an ex-Prefect of Discipline, had his work cut out keeping order. On 17 March 1866, the Minister's Journal records:

St Patrick. About 54 Irish boys had Punch . . . Later, some 5 or 6 of them for riotous conduct were taken to the Study Place. On the whole the Irish performance this year was a little more respectable and orderly, though not altogether free from the Fenian element. During the boys' supper, the

The Top Refectory in 1858. To discourage conversation during readings from the Martyrologium boys were seated on one side of the tables only. Photograph by R Fenton.

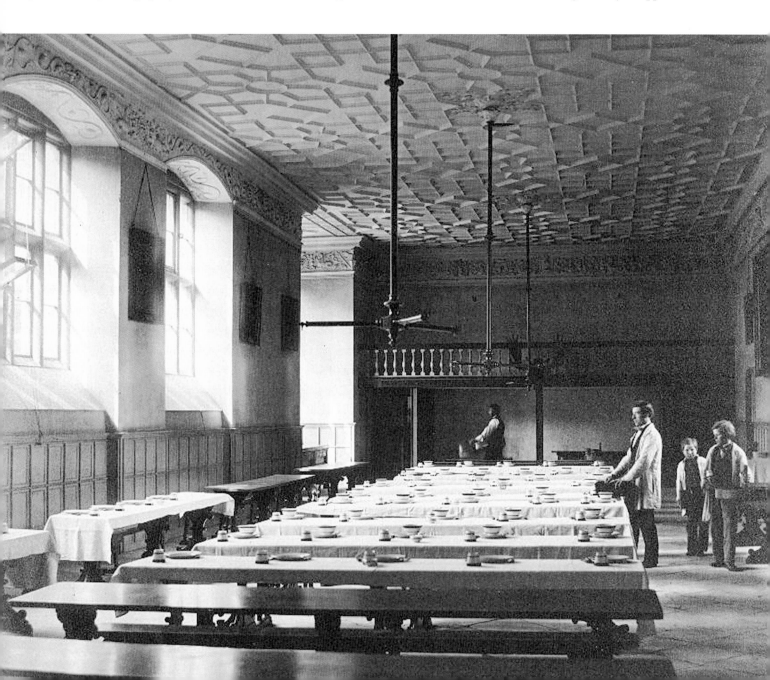

Philosophers' Band played a few pieces – the playing was more noisy than musical and NOT TO BE REPEATED.

However, progress continued to be made on this front. Between 1869 and 1887 the position of First Prefect was held by the redoubtable Fr Thomas Kay. From the 1870s it became accepted that at least one of the Prefects of Discipline should be a priest. The problems caused by placing inexperienced scholastics in these difficult but highly responsible positions were at last beginning to be recognised.

Similar developments took place on the academic front. There was a slight lapse in the London Examination results in the late 1860s; but, on the whole, standards were well maintained by Fr Kingdon, Prefect of Studies between 1864 and 1878. They were brought to a peak by his successor Fr John Gerard (1879–93). In 1885 166 prizes were given, of which 112 were for Classics; and if Poetry's composition marks, perhaps the best indicators of performance at this time, fell from 81.5% in 1865 to 52% in 1885 they soon recovered to a respectable 82% by 1895.

It might be inferred from this that Stonyhurst, by concentrating on Classics, stunted the development of the scientific side of its curriculum. It is true that, until the middle of the century, the Chemistry laboratory was available only to the Philosophers. Moreover, no candidates were put forward when the University of London introduced a BSc degree in 1860. However, the following year a new laboratory and lecture theatre were added; and at the same time the existing facilities were converted into an instrument room for all the old apparatus that hitherto had been laid out in the Academy Room. By the 1870s it seems that Syntax, Poetry and Rhetoric were attending weekly lectures in science as part of their preparation for matriculation; while some lay Philosophers pursued a more extended course for their BA degree. In 1897, following the arrival of a Mr A F Fryer, who was a layman, this was reorganised and extended downwards to include Grammar as part of the adjustments necessary for fitting in with the Oxford and Cambridge examinations. Perhaps as a result of this in 1900 a Biology room was opened on the ground floor of Shirk; and two years later another room was converted to form a new Physics laboratory. All told, by the beginning of the new century, the College had six science rooms in service.

Meanwhile, the Philosophers were at last stirred from their hedonistic sloth by the arrival of Fr William Eyre, Prefect between 1871 and 1879. In 1874 a new scheme of studies was unveiled. All those not preparing for a university examination were to attend nine compulsory classes in branches of Philosophy, Science, Maths and English supplemented by three optional courses in French, German and Italian. By 1879 Stonyhurst was advertising in the *Catholic Directory*:

> Lectures . . . in the subjects required for Examinations of the London University, for the Competitive Examinations for Woolwich, Sandhurst and the Indian Civil Service; as well as in the studies necessary for the Medical Profession . . . There are also Resident Professors of English, French, Italian, Spanish, German, Hindustani and Sanskrit, including composition and literature.

As might have been expected, such offerings were not always appreciated. For instance, as late as 6 July, 1907 the Philosophers Log reported that the entire body were not freed from classes because they 'would not give a promise that "They would never fool again during the Philosophy lecture" (Bullets thrown about & ducks alive imported') Nonetheless, despite such obstacles, academic standards were raised, as shown by some of the results in the London University examinations. True, after the reorganisation of the syllabus in 1864, Stonyhurst did less well at Matriculation; but, under a new system inaugurated in 1882, Philosophers obtained 30 passes each at Intermediate and Final Honours levels in the next decade – no mean achievement for a body of only 30 to 50 members, many of whom had other academic irons in the fire.

Even so, the limitations of such achievements should be recognised. Throughout this period Stonyhurst remained a 'bottom heavy' school; only a small proportion of which ever made it to Rhetoric, let alone Philosophy. Moreover, compared with Oxford and Cambridge, London was generally reckoned to be a much less demanding university at this time. It is therefore pertinent to close with the judicious remarks made by Mr Bryce visiting the school on behalf of the Taunton Commission in 1865:

> The avowed object of the teaching is to bring every boy up to a certain level rather than raise a few to a very high pitch of excellence. In most great schools every class, except the highest, has its tail – boys who, sometimes from dullness, more often from idleness, are far below those at the head of the class . . . The Stonyhurst system seeks to destroy this tail, and seems, from all that I can ascertain, to succeed in doing so. Of course something is lost. There are far fewer ignorant boys, but there are also fewer brilliant ones.

Likewise, a similar ambivalence appears when looking at the disciplinary system. At this time other public schools were evolving House systems with the assistance of boy prefects; but at Stonyhurst the Prefects of Discipline were masters. While this greatly reduced the amount of bullying and other abuses commonly associated with the House system, at the time it might have seemed to be unduly oppressive. As Mr Bryce put it:

> The most peculiar feature in the disciplinary system is the superintendence so unremittingly maintained at all hours. In the Playground, two prefects walk up and down in the midst while games go on; during the preparation of lessons a prefect sits in a pulpit looking over the room full of boys and enforcing the strictest silence; and at night, when the boys have gone to bed, prefects pass at intervals through the dormitories, to see that all is quiet and that no boy leaves his compartment . . . The authorities of the college consider surveillance indispensable to good order when numbers are so great, and assured me that their relationships with the boys are of so intimate and cordial a nature that their open presence during play, and their possible though unseen presence in the dormitories, was not felt to be a check but rather a pleasure.

Facing page: The Old Infirmary, converted from the old coach houses in 1842–43. Repairs in the 1980s disclosed a considerable network of underground channels among the foundations.

Below: The winter of 1857–8. On such occasions the Ponds rang to the swirl of skates. Photograph by R Fenton.

Old Alma Mater, here's to thee!
Stonyhurst! Old Stonyhurst!
Long life and all prosperity!
Stonyhurst! Old Stonyhurst!
While generations come and go,
While boyhood doth to manhood grow,
Be aye the same we used to know,
Stonyhurst! Old Stonyhurst!

The Stonyhurst Chorus: introduced in the late nineteenth century and
sung to the tune known as 'Tannenbaum' which is better
known to the public as 'The Red Flag'.

SPORTS AND PASTIMES

O LD STONYHURST SPORTS are like the parable of the sower: some fell by the wayside; others fell on stony ground, flourished quickly, but because they had no roots, withered in the sun; while a few, falling on rich soil, 'grew tall and strong, produced crop and yielded thirty, sixty, even a hundred fold'. For although these games had been preserved in isolation at St Omers they were not dried-up rusks, but living organisms, capable of producing numerous offshoots and branches to suit their new environment. Thus, in a general sense the early history of many sports can be inferred backwards from nineteenth-century Stonyhurst practice; but any suggestion that it is cast-iron evidence for Tudor or Stuart habits must be treated with some caution.

Of the games that fell by the wayside the most important were 'Top' and 'Trap Ball'. Of 'Top' little is known. 'Trap' got its name from the pivoting wooden slipper which, when struck by a bat, catapulted a ball at the other end into the air. The ball then had to be struck before it hit the ground.

Some games were weeded out. The 'Scholars Rules' for instance, dating from about 1795, discountenanced 'the trifling games of Tip-Cat, Marbles, Pitching Half-pence Odd and Even, especially for money'. They also forbade 'all Games in recreation rooms, except Drafts and Chess and [other activities] of that nature'.

One game not mentioned in the Scholars Rules, perhaps because the wall had yet to be built, was Handball, played between Whitsun and the Long Vacation. This was a hardy perennial, but it suffered from the fact that there were only three Handballs in the Playground – hence the practice of 'Touching In' for places; though in Lower Line the authorities tried to regulate this on the basis of positions earned in Compositions.

An important offshoot from Handball, played by teams of four a side, and well adapted to the summer months, was 'Second Bounce'. As the name implies the ball could only be played after it had bounced twice on the ground after hitting the wall. It therefore had to be both hard and elastic. The size of a golf ball, it consisted of an inner core of India rubber, wound round with strips of the same material, and covered with kid-leather sewn on with silk. These balls were so fragile, and lost their essential properties so quickly, that sets of six, 'snowy white, glistening, smooth as eggs', as Percy Fitzgerald put it, were only made immediately before a match; and throughout the contest someone always had to stand by, armed with needle and thread, ready to make running repairs.

Facing page: 'Saluting the Flag', one of the many rituals associated with the Grand Matches. The number of players shown is almost certainly too small. Watercolour by F P Barraud dating from 1890.

Above: *The Stonyhurst Cricketer. This photograph probably dates from the 1880s and is almost certainly staged, since the old uniform had disappeared by the 1850s. Note the portable cricket stone and Handball in the background.*

Above right: *Bats, balls and other accoutrements associated with Stonyhurst Cricket. The white balls are survivors from 'Second Bounce'.*

The most vigorous transplants were Stonyhurst Cricket and Stonyhurst Football. The former was probably derived from 'Cat' – not to be confused with 'Tip-Cat' – which survived at the College until the 1830s and was played between Shrovetide and Easter. Stonyhurst Cricket proper was played between Easter and Whitsun, after which Handball took over. On the eve of Ash Wednesday 'Matches' boys, subdivided into teams of five, were organised and assigned to their respective cricket stones ranged in a line twenty yards from the back of the garden wall. Bats, three feet in length tapering to an oval head 4½ in in width, were made by villagers in the winter months. Some consisted entirely of ash, but most had an alder-head spliced on to an ash-handle. Balls, which had a core of cork – sometimes with India rubber at the centre – were covered with worsted, soaked in glue and baked before the fire by the boys. They were then taken to the shoemakers for casing with two hemispheres of hard leather sewn to form a thick seam around the ball. Pitches were dominated by the single-wicket stone; 27 yards away stood the 'running-in' stone, placed at a slightly oblique angle to give a clear path for the striker. The 'running mark', from which the bowler released the ball underarm and with the seam, was a further three yards away. 'Play' was called for the first ball, but thereafter 'the bowler is at perfect liberty to bowl as quickly as he likes, and if the batsman be not ready, need allow no time'. At the wicket he was assisted by a 'second bowler' and three 'faggers' or fielders. Amongst other things the second bowler was required 'to have the cricket-stone free from all books, bats etc, which may in any way prevent him striking the stone with the ball'. The batsman, who retired after 21 balls, was obliged, from the nature of his implement, to slog. The hard surface of the Playground was well adapted for this and 'greeners' could be dispatched 100 yards across its length into the gardens beyond the Penance Walk. Runs were scored by racing to and from the running-in stone and, on the final ball, counted double.

At the end of the cricket season two stones were carried to the centre of the Playground for 'Double Puffing', played by unlimited sides using large soft balls.

During the season proper those excluded from matches had to make do with 'Common Innings' and 'Tip and Run'.

Stonyhurst Football commenced at the end of the Grand Vacation. Like Double Puffing it was for teams of unlimited size, especially since the Community and visiting Old Boys often took part. The pitch, according to a late set of rules copied in 1921, was 70 ft. long, but no width is specified. Goal posts were 7 ft. apart, 25 ft. high and without a crossbar. Except when the ball was in the area no one apart from the 'guarder' could stand within a semicircle of 8 yards radius about the goal posts. 'Second guarders' patrolled the perimeter against incursions by 'poachers'. The rest of the pitch was quartered by 'players up', while on the fringes smaller boys kept the ball in or out of play as the fortunes of each side dictated. The oval ball had a diameter ranging from 22 to 23 in. at its narrowest and widest points. Smaller balls though were often used and on one occasion, in 1819, one with a 25 in. diameter was introduced. It could be kicked, boxed or stopped with the hand provided it was then immediately placed on the ground. A player in possession of the ball could only be tackled by someone approaching from more than three yards in front. If it ricocheted out of play from two opposing players the one who touched it down first got the throw in. Revivals in the early 1990s suggest that the shape of the ball, and the small size of the pitch, produced an end-to-end game; so goals could be scored from almost any quarter. Because the rules were ill-defined and not well understood – they were only displayed once a year – the air resounded with cries of 'Call the Ball'. Temperatures were further raised by the stipulation that the first goal only counted half. The most dramatic moments came with the 'squash', which took place when a defender knocked the ball into touch near his own goal post. At this point the eight-yard rule was suspended and the ball precipitated into a flailing mass of bodies whose primary object was to drive or prevent the ball from being shoved over the goal line by main force.

Grand Matches, fought on Shrove Tuesday and the Thursday and Monday beforehand, were the climax of the season. To assemble the teams Heads of the Line organised trial matches, after which came the 'Match for the Name' the winners and losers taking the titles – and sporting badges to match – of 'English' and 'French'. Other names were sometimes used, 'York' and 'Lancaster' being an early example. During the Crimean War the 'English' fought the 'Russians', while minor games were contested between 'Pipes' and 'Windows' after the gas piping and windows on either side of the Study Place.

Grand Matches were accompanied by much ceremony. On the eve much 'speechifying', poetic declamation and cheering took place in the Playrooms. On the day itself the proceedings were announced by the brass band, formed between 1832 and 1836 under the rectorate of Fr Parker. At a given signal, which before 1856 was the tolling of the Bread Room bell, boys tumbled into the Playground, flags were broken out at each end, and a salvo of artillery – presented by Admiral Manners in 1845 – brought the two sides into line. Another salvo and the ball was kicked into play. Further discharges signalled the progress of every half-hour, while the 'fortunes of war' could readily be determined by seeing which side had its flag at half-mast. At the conclusion each team gathered round its flagpost to cheer, and roar out 'La Marseillaise' or 'Rule Britannia'. Final results were determined from the number of matches won, or, if there had been a draw, the number of goals scored.

In its heyday the sheer pulsating excitement was terrific; and there is no better way to catch this than to quote from the diary of B E James, written in 1866–7:

Feb 25th Monday . . . Played for the Name in the morning. O'Reilly won it.

Feb 26th Tuesday. Schools. Flagposts set up in the Playground. Bought a pair of gloves for the coming struggle.

Feb 27th Wednesday. Schools. All talking of the morrow. Consultation at 8. Hy Parker first mounted the French rostrum. Advice was all he gave. Mr Edwards [the First Prefect] was next and gave very capital advice and instruction. Mr Gerard [then Poetry classmaster] followed him with a first-class oration and was loudly cheered at the conclusion.

Feb 28th Thursday. 1st Grand Match day. Flags hoisted, 8 yrds marked etc. and the 'artillery' ready by 9.30. Gun fired just as clock striking. Fr Hartell obtained the first goal (which only counts half) for the English, but C. Clarke took another for the French and Mr Lane following suit placed us a goal and a half above them. This was the result of the first day's fight. A jolly mutton dinner and good beer . . . very weary.

March 1st. Friday. School. Stiff and hoarse with shouting. Schools very dull.

March 3rd. Sunday . . . Match at 9.30. French victorious again by one goal. O'Reilly passing wrath. Lemonade at one p.m. Innumerable songs sung; 'Polly Perkins' and 'A Bunch of Watercresses', being amongst the number . . . very, very tired. Consultation. Loud cheering on account of our late victory. A hard fight expected tomorrow.

March 5th. Tuesday. Match commenced at 9. Tremendous engagements at the commencement. The steady play of the French and the very superior tactics of our leader Henry Parker, again triumphed over the rashness and impetuosity of the English Captain P. O'Reilly. Your humble servant had the honour to take the last goal. French side obtained 4 goals, English 1. Total of 3 days French 8, English 2½. French victorious by 5½ goals. Hurrah! Hurrah! Hurrah! O'Reilly's skill as general loudly condemned and censured by all: he is a thorough humbug. Strangers' lemonade. The plays much better tonight.

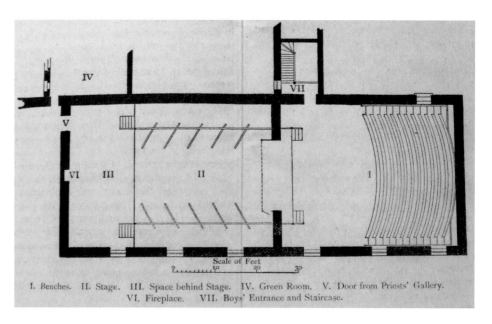

Plan of the old Academy or 'Mathematical' Room, drawn by A Parkinson for The Stonyhurst Magazine *in 1888. The projections half-way down mark the point where it could be divided by sliding doors.*

Scale of Feet

I. Benches. II. Stage. III. Space behind Stage. IV. Green Room. V. Door from Priests' Gallery. VI. Fireplace. VII. Boys' Entrance and Staircase.

The plays referred to were the Shrovetide plays, at that time produced by Grammar; for until 1872, when a longer three week vacation was introduced, the most important dramatic performances took place over Christmas. As with the Grand Matches, and especially after the construction of a new stage in 1837, the proceedings became highly formalised. On 8 December the actors, by immemorial custom limited to 21, were selected by the Poetry and Rhetoric Classmasters. For the Green Room two more boys were supplied by the master of Syntax. Since the object was as much to foster oratory as to entertain, the plays, though now in English, had to conform with certain requirements. The most bizarre of these, the excising of all female parts, often produced most curious results. Lady Macbeth, for instance, on one occasion became Macbeth's son Donald. Another ritual was the custom of keeping the identity of the play secret from the rest of the school. For this purpose actors often concealed their parts in specially designed pockets within their waistcoats.

At 4.30 or 5.00 on Boxing Day the whole school assembled in the Academy Room to hear the first performance of the 'Comedy' given by Poetry. It was always preceded by the Prologue, describing the scrapes and shifts by which the cast had tried to conceal the name of the play from the vulgar herd. In 1850 it concluded:

> Your patience tried, now let us ease her,
> and say at once the play is *Julius Caesar.*

A second performance of the comedy was given the following night, after which the next two evenings were given over to the 'Tragedy', enacted by Rhetoric. However, as the case of *Julius Caesar* shows, the definition of what constituted a comedy or a tragedy was given considerable latitude.

From 1841 onwards the Philosophers also produced a play, usually of a light burlesque character: one of these – *Castle in Andalusia* – was quoted to startling effect during the Tichborne trial:

> Mr Hawkins: 'We have not arrived at the fact of there being any love play enacted at Stonyhurst.'
>
> Dr Kenealy: 'There is plenty of it in the *Castle of Andalusia* –
> "Gad, I'll court a lady fair
> How I'll prattle, tattle, chat,
> How I'll kiss her and all that
> All amongst the leaves so green, O!
> How d'ye do! How are you! Why so coy! Let us toy!
> Hey down. Ho Down. Derry, derry down.
> All amongst the leaves so green, O!"
>
> That is a good preparation for bush life in Australia.'

Plays were not the only highlight of the Christmas season. In 1858, recalling the decorations that festooned the Higher Line Playroom 38 years before, a contributor to *The Stonyhurst Magazine* described how 'the plainest of all possible plain rooms [was] . . . for a time converted into something between a shrubbery and an oriental pagoda: the iron pillars had become columns of holly; ropes of holly drooped across the ceiling and round the walls; lanterns red green and orange glowed overhead, and transparencies gleamed in the corners.' Christmas Day itself of course was celebrated with 'a grand High Mass and solemn Vespers, followed later in the evening by a concert of a very orthodox character'. Christmas

Macbeth in 1921. One of several pictures taken in the Great Quadrangle of this highly successful 'Shrovetide' production.

'A Rub of The Green'. Highland cattle were introduced to the golf course by the Procurator, Fr Pedro Gordon SJ. From The Stonyhurst Magazine, *April 1909.*

boxes also appeared that day. Meanwhile outside, as winter deepened, skating became all the rage. On 6 January 1861 the Minister's Journal reported 'Skating by torchlight until 6.00pm. The Hurst Green Band played. A fire was lighted on the ice and the boys had spiced ale and cake.'

Summer, by contrast, was a lazy season. Boys lounged about the Seminary Wood or 'Jungle', rooted around for pig-nuts in the Park, or set about exploiting the local fisheries. 'Brook Fishing' and 'Rogging' for eels were popular pastimes. In the former a team of boys would dam up a stream, leaving a gap in the middle for the nets. One boy stayed there while the rest worked down towards him in line turning up every stone and poking into every crevice along the banks. Rogging, practised in the Hodder, was somewhat similar. According to Gerard nets were placed upstream of a large stone; then, while some stood on either side making as much noise as possible to discourage the quarry from going in their direction, others prized it up with a crowbar. 'The nets were then quickly whipped up to secure what might have entered.'

As the century wore on the pattern of activity began to change. New pastimes, blown in from outside, challenged the indigenous growth. Traditions were further undermined by the reshaping of the Playground and the programme of massive reconstruction that followed. The effects, as we shall see, were manifold. In 1860, after many false starts, the First Prefect, Thomas Welsby, inaugurated the Stonyhurst Cricket Club. Not to be outdone, the Philosophers organised their own 'Aighton Manor Cricket Club'. A year later, on 18 July, the College won its first outmatch against the Britannia Club from Blackburn. On this occasion, according to Gerard, 'the Eleven burst upon an astonished world in a uniform, secretly prepared, of white flannel trousers and pink shirts'. As the pitch, located on Parker's Field, was only 30 yards square fielders had to stand in the tall grass – a situation that was not remedied till 1865 when it was expanded to form the Oval. Between 1861 and 1894 144 matches were played, 82 of which were won, 52 lost and a further 10 drawn.

The new game at once killed off Second Bounce. Handball followed suit two decades later, its demise expedited by the construction of Racquets courts in 1883. Stonyhurst Cricket held on rather longer. In the 1870s it produced one last rather degenerate offshoot – Wicket Cricket, so called because a stump was substituted for the bat, being played with some vigour around the old cricket stones. However, the introduction of Association football fatally limited the amount of time in which the old game could be played. In 1885 bats and balls were ordered for the last time; by 1893 the game was effectively dead.

Cricket on the Oval: a contemporary view.

Association football, originally intended to cover the period between Shrovetide and Easter, was first put on a proper footing by the Second Prefect, Fr Baldwin, in 1884. Quickly, pitches were laid out in the Avenue; the following year the club had the temerity to challenge a team from Preston North End. They lost by five goals to seven. Nonetheless, under the enthusiastic patronage of Fr Robinson – appointed First Prefect in 1888 – the game continued to grow. In 1891 the first sod of the Philosophers field was cut; more ominously, in 1899 the first note of compulsion appeared in the Minister's Journal: 'Thurs Dec 12th Match against Bohemians. Kick off 2.35 . . . Boys won 2–0 – all went to see the match.'

Under these pressures Stonyhurst football steadily wilted. In 1889, at the last shot of the Grand Matches, one of the cannon burst. The remaining pieces were then relegated to ceremonial duties in the main quadrangle. The old goal posts were cut up in 1901.

Cross-country in the 1950s.

Meanwhile, a whole range of new pastimes supplanted the last vestiges of the old. In 1881 that terrifying symbol of Victorian athleticism – a gym – was opened in the basement of the New South Front; 33 years later the present purpose-built building appeared. Fencing was introduced; while on the front lawns Philosophers played tennis. In the Park, from 1894, they could take exercise on one of the first golf courses to be laid out in an English public school. Here it is worth remarking that G H Walker, founder of the Walker Cup competition, was a Philosopher between 1892 and 1894. Athletics, as one might expect, was vigorously promoted. Originating with an Amateur Athletics Club formed in 1866, after a period of desuetude it was revived on a more formal basis from 1887 onwards. In 1897 new cups were presented by J P Aspinall. Entries for Easter Monday in the Prefect's Journal show the steady growth of a grimly efficient atmosphere:

> 1896 Sun. April 7th 3.30 Sports in Avenue. (1) Three-legged race. (2) Egg and Ladle Race. (3) Wheelbarrow Race. (4) Tug of War between schools beginning with Elements and Figures the victors tugging against the next class. (5) Kicking Football. (6) Sack Race. (7) Obstacle Race.
> 1907 440, ½ mile, hurdles, steeple chase, sack race, tug of war.

In 1900 these developments were capped by the introduction of a Cadet Training Corps or CTC. After the Crimean War, an attempt had been made to form the 'Stonyhurst Volunteers'; but this had proved stillborn, though 'Drill' did become a permanent feature of the punishment system. Now, during the Boer War, the attempt was renewed. Initially under the command of a boy, in 1908 it was reorganised and renamed the OTC with a much greater degree of adult control. Before long it had become a vast empire. Training for the whole school took place on Monday and Thursday afternoons; while General Inspection and Camp were among the highlights of the school year. Lavishly equipped, it took part in many a religious ceremony – and with special effect on Easter Sunday and in the Corpus Christi celebrations. The Fife Band and pantomime concerts became an established tradition. It had its own system of discipline. It was a state within a state.

An early Athletics team. The shield modelled on a design by Benvenuto Cellini, now hangs in the Top Refectory.

The OTC Band in 1906, featuring Drum-Sergeant Taylor

The implications of all this were profound. In the first place masters had always taken a prominent part in sporting activities; but this was now carried to an unprecedented degree. Games were being used to keep boys occupied; they were a means of social control.

But, paradoxically, this led to a weakening of the Jesuit influence; for some of the staff who ran these sports were lay professionals brought in from outside. Nonetheless, because they were responsible to him, these changes also enhanced the authority of the First Prefect *vis-à-vis* the Prefect of Studies. Hitherto, the Playroom staff had been of inferior status; but now they could demand equality – sometimes even precedence – in the treatment accorded to them by the Rector. Passages from Fr White's Journal make this abundantly clear:

> Wed Jan 16th 1907 the Rector ruled:
> (1) My position in house identical with that of Fr Robinson and Fr Kay i.e. when boys out of schools I am responsible to the Rector for them and *nobody* could dispose of or arrange to take or send or anything else without leave from the Rector . . .
> (2) He would never allow any Prefect of Studies to take boys from games etc against my wish.
> Sunday Jan 21st
> N.B. 1st Prefect (i.e. the Prefect of Discipline) settles who goes to [the academic] lectures – not *Pref Stud*. Fr Davis tried to claim it but Fr Brown said no – the old custom not to be changed.

In fact the 'old custom' only dated from the 1860s.

The introduction of nationally recognised games also brought Stonyhurst into closer contact with the outside world. Helped by the spread of railways the College could now compete directly with other public schools and, in so doing, become recognised as one of their number. Other developments enhanced the process. In 1879, like other schools, Stonyhurst formed its Old Boys Association. Two years later there appeared *The Stonyhurst Magazine* and the Stonyhurst Union Debating Society – or SUDS for short. These changes fitted in with the desire of many wealthier Catholics to be recognised in the professional and political

spheres from which they had been excluded since the Reformation. However, progress in this direction was slow. In 1874 the first cricket match against Rossall provoked violent reactions from *The Rock*:

> How the Rossall pupils could have desired, or the Rossall masters could have sanctioned any match of the kind we are entirely at a loss to conceive. However it is some comfort to know that the Protestant youths were thoroughly well beaten, as they richly deserved to be. But have the Rossall masters never read the Bible ? or have they forgotten the consequence – as recorded in its pages – of allowing Israelites to mingle with Moabite games and dances? All these comminglings with Papists act as so many enticements to idolatry, and the masters who do not see this are unfit to manage a Protestant school. We would advise parents who have sons at Rossall to keep a sharp look out.

For this reason, and perhaps also because there were fewer schools to play against in the North, most outmatches were played against adult teams. Indeed, between 1884 and 1913 matches with other schools were totally suspended. However, any disparity of age was compensated for by the presence of Philosophers and, even under these restrictions, each contest could not fail to broaden horizons.

But the greatest alteration of all was heralded by the formation of the OTC. Hitherto Catholics, as potential traitors, had been discouraged from joining the armed forces; but the Crimean War changed all that. Now, by investing so much in its cadet force, Stonyhurst was sending out a new signal. The Catholic Church was the ally and supporter of the nation, not its enemy. Thus, on the Chapel Landing, the Boer War Memorial still recalls 'a great company of old Stonyhurst boys who in the same campaign left for all time an example of Catholic loyalty and service worthy of the traditions of the College'.

The changes to Stonyhurst sport, then, show the degree to which an isolated particularist plantation became an integral part of the social fabric. In 1900 the Rector was invited to attend the Headmasters' Conference; ten years later a contingent from the OTC took part in the Coronation ceremonies staged at Windsor. A century before such developments would have been unthinkable.

Excursus: Music for the Church

St Cecilia, patron saint of music – detail from a stained glass window in The Angels' Chapel, Stonyhurst.

On August 30th, 1794, one day after the first boys had entered Stonyhurst, the Minster's Journal stated that a *Te Deum* was 'sung for our happy arrival'. Thus, a musical tradition going back to St Omers was immediately reasserted; and during the ensuing centuries it became a principal means by which the College promoted the Catholic faith, both to itself and to a wider world. In the process it exerted a significant impact on the development of Catholic music in England.

With the church as the focal point, a formidable nexus of overlapping ensembles was developed. In addition to the main choir there was a Vesper Choir and a 'Congregational' Choir; the Jesuit community at St Mary's Hall provided additional singers and the same is true for the Sodality. Until the 1950s the main choir was a mixture of boys and Jesuits, the latter mainly responsible for the lower parts, the former usually employed as trebles. At times the sheer quantity of material must have been crippling. In 1935, for instance, *The Stonyhurst Magazine* estimated that the choir sang for twenty hours during Holy Week. The Choir 'Good Day', usually granted towards the end of the summer term, was thus a well-earned privilege. Traditionally, this took the form of an extended, and somewhat haphazard, picnic.

Outdoor processions were accompanied by the College Band; and it seems that the Guild Band from Hurst Green (later known as the Hurst Green Silver Band) may have played a part too. Indoors, surviving nineteenth-century manuscript scores show that instruments were occasionally deployed alongside the organ. The latter was of primary importance, creating a fundamental division between the choirmaster, who until the 1960s was almost invariably a Jesuit, and the organist, who was usually a lay professional. The first organ, a second-hand gift from Thomas Weld, was weak and unreliable. However, in 1835 it was replaced by one built by John Davis of Preston. In 1883 this was rebuilt and expanded, so much so that the bellows had to be driven by a Duncan Hydraulic Cylinder Engine using water from the Stonyhurst reservoir. In turn, this was replaced by the Willis organ of 1927, although even here much of the old piping was retained. This instrument, after some subsequent modifications, was completely rebuilt by John Corkhill in 1991.

Stonyhurst's choral tradition evolved through several distinct phases. The first is signalled by a copy of Vincent Novello's *A Collection of Sacred Music*, published in 1811. Almost certainly this is the first surviving volume of new music to be acquired. It also marks the beginnings of the Novello publishing company, the largest musical interest of its kind in nineteenth-century Britain. The subscription list shows that not only were several copies ordered by the Stonyhurst community, but also by members of the Catholic aristocracy, including Thomas Weld. This suggests a triangle of musical interests between such Catholic families, the embassy chapels they attended when in London, and Stonyhurst, where their children were educated. The impression is confirmed by Novello's next publication, his *Twelve Easy Masses*, published in 1816, copies of which survive at Stonyhurst. This is dedicated to Lord Arundell, donor of the Arundell library. Moreover, in the 1840s and 1880s two of Stonyhurst's organists – John Beresford and Henry McArdle – were recruited from the Arundell chapel at Wardour Castle, which was served by the Society.

The next phase was signalled by the opening of St Peter's church in 1835. Immediately this produced a much more elaborate liturgical regime. Pride of place

The Organ, St Peter's Church, Stonyhurst, installed in 1927

was given to the Holy Week Celebrations; but there were also major festivities on such occasions as the Feast of St Ignatius, when priests were ordained. As a result, more music was required, much of which was in the Classical Viennese style. For example, to celebrate its opening, the College commissioned a *Mass in D* from Salvatore Meluzzi, director of music at St Peter's, Rome. In the process some standardisation of the repertoire occurred. Thus, up till the 1950s, Francis De Vico's Antiphons and Responsories, original manuscript copies of which still survive in the archives, were always performed during Holy Week.

Vico and Meluzzi's compositions were symptomatic of an emerging Papal slant, also epitomised by the first signs of interest in Renaissance Polyphony. However, the most important effect was an increased emphasis on Plainchant, as shown by the acquisition of several Plainchant liturgical books and manuals. Of particular interest was the arrival during the 1840s of a manuscript copy of John Francis Wade's *Cantus Diversi* of 1751, containing one of the earliest known versions of *Adeste Fideles*. Note that this was not the Solesmes style chant known today, but the slower, heavy, measured chant developed during Renaissance times associated with 'Roman' composers such as Palestrina, Guidetti, Anerio and Soriano. Such Plainchant was increasingly tied in with Ultramontanism, or the claim for Papal primacy; but it was not always popular. For instance, on Jan 17th, 1869 John Gerard reported:

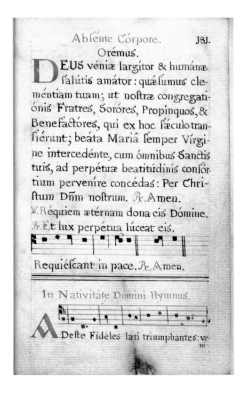

Wade's version of Adeste Fideles, *as presented in his* Cantus Diversi, *copied in 1751. The flyleaf is signed by James King, who was at Stonyhurst between 1805 and 1811, and Francis Muth, who obtained the volume in 1826. Muth was an ex-Paccanarist who became a Jesuit in 1815 and worked at Old Hall Green between 1810 and 1836. He then taught at St Mary's Hall and was buried at St Ignatius Church, Preston in 1841. This is a good example of 'measured' plainchant organised on a 4:2:1 ratio. The basic pulse is supplied by the squares, squares with tails or a dot are twice as long, 'diamonds' are twice as short. This produces a quite different rhythmic pattern to the melody as it is now known.*

Vespers tonight celebrated in a new and prodigious fashion – another move of the high and mighty party which at present rules our musical state. Ye choir in ye sanctuary in surplices – singing such tones: pure Gregorian I believe but to the uninitiated very awful. Fr Splaine remarks that it will deprive ye Office of ye dead of its unique solemnity. Fr Kingdon that he wonders how the singers know what note to put next, as one would do as well as another.

As a result of this and other similar mishaps the choirmaster, one John Rigby SJ, was despatched to Bombay. However, this did not stop his successor, Edwin Sircom SJ, from compiling an enormous manuscript set of full organ accompaniments for Vespers the following year.

In 1903 a new phase was inaugurated with the promulgation of Pius X's motu proprio decree *Tra Le Sollectudini*. This asserted the primacy in church music of Plainchant and, next to it, Renaissance Polyphony as epitomised by the compositions of Palestrina. Conversely, the Classical Viennese style and more modern music, especially if it had secular and operatic overtones, was excoriated. In addition the use of orchestral instruments in church was banned, except with special permission from the local bishop. In Stonyhurst's case this was Louis Casartelli, who applied considerable pressure on the College to comply with its provisions. It is perhaps significant that, from this time onwards, regular detailed accounts of what was performed were published in *The Stonyhurst Magazine*. At the same time the College switched from measured chant to the plainchant style promoted by Solesmes through the medium of the Vatican Typical editions.

Plainchant was often associated with campaigns to promote congregational participation; and this was further developed through vernacular hymnody and music for Benediction. Indeed, a considerable amount of Benediction music was composed by James Farmer, William Maher and Francis M De Zulueta, who had all been students at St Mary's Hall. With hymnody a crucial step was the adoption of *Arundel Hymns*, shortly after its full publication in 1901. This included material collected at Stonyhurst by its editor, Charles Gatty. In 1920 and again in 1936 it was replaced by a *Stonyhurst Cantionale* prepared by John Driscoll SJ, although with the latter an organ edition did not appear till 1940. These were part of a series of publications produced for all the major Jesuit establishments in England. They have three major features. First, contrary to the practice espoused by Richard Terry in *The Westminster Hymnal*, Driscoll was quite prepared to use non-Catholic tunes and texts. Consequently, Stonyhurst tapped into the rich Protestant hymn-singing repertory. In addition there are 59 tunes by William Bowyer, the College organist. Bowyer also contributed several items to the companion Benediction Book prepared at about the same time. Second, Driscoll provided a large number of Latin hymns, which meant that the *Cantionale* could be used by the congregation at Mass (where English texts were forbidden). Third, he established a balance between items solely for the use of the choir and those that could be used by choir and congregation singly or in combination.

By the 1950s, Renaissance Polyphony had come to predominate; and music of this type continued to be sung on major feasts during the 1960s, 1970s and 1980s, despite trends in favour of contemporary popular styles. Yet, at the same time, there were the first signs of real change. The starting point was the shake-up caused by the Second World War. In the first place, between 1942 and 1945 the boys ceased to stay for Holy Week and Easter, forcing a curtailment of the usual ceremonies. These were reinstated with full vigour in 1946. However, ten years later, the introduction of a new Order of Holy Week forced the choir to learn a substantially new repertoire, and from 1967 the boys ceased to attend. Instead, right into the 1980s, the choir and orchestra performed substantial extracts from Handel's *Messiah* and – more frequently – Bach's *Matthew Passion* during a Passion service held at the end of the Easter term. With the latter work the chorales were sung by the congregation. Secondly, according to the Minister's Journal, from 1942 the Carol service emerged as a distinct entity, although originally it seems to be have been simply a series of carols bolted on to the rendition of the Rosary, Benediction and *Te Deum* on the last Sunday evening of the Christmas term. During the 1950s this grew steadily in importance; and, once thrown open to the general public in the early 1970s, it became a major musical showcase for the College. Thirdly, as early as 1935 (in other words, before the War) the College made its first public broadcast from the church. This was repeated in 1941, 1949, 1957 and on a number of subsequent occasions, including the first TV broadcast in 1969.

The other great catalyst for change was the Second Vatican Council and the introduction of the vernacular liturgy. Initially, this was slow to take effect. Undoubtedly, one factor was the formal processional nature of the building. Moreover, 'Folk' hymnody never gained a foothold and instead was sung in the more informal circumstances of the Playroom Mass. Nevertheless, some modern Masses, including settings by Britten, Seiber and Peeters, were added to the choral repertoire, and in 1968 the first English Mass was sung, composed by Colin Atkinson, the ex-director of music at Beaumont. During the 1980s a notable supplement was the regular congregational performance of William Matthias's *Gloria*, whose last composition, a setting of *AMDG* for choir and organ, was commissioned for the 1993 Centenary celebrations.

Two other factors compounded the effects of Vatican II. One was the general shift in musical education among Independent schools during the late 1960s from a choral religious emphasis to a secular instrumental orientation, from which Stonyhurst was not immune; the other was the establishment of SMH as a separate preparatory school. The latter dealt a body blow to the supply of upper voices for the choir, especially after the transfer of Rudiments I, and then the rest of that year, in 1956 and 1963 respectively. However, on special occasions determined efforts were made to combine the resources of both establishments. Perhaps then the greatest achievement of the 1970s and 1980s was the further development of Stonyhurst's congregational singing tradition to truly terrific proportions. This was the 'Magnum Opus' of Anthony John, Director of Music between 1973 and 1993. Every week, virtually single-handed, he rehearsed the entire school using a microphone attached to the Organ console; and it was he who masterminded the production of the justly prized *Stonyhurst Cantionale* of 1976 and its revision of 1988. Currently a new version, due in 2006, is being prepared.

Otherwise, the most recent developments have been triggered by the arrival of girls. Initially, the opportunity was taken to attain greater variety through the alternation of girls and boys choirs at different services – and indeed within them. However, eventually the two bodies were merged to form the 'Chapel Choir', thereby restoring the balance of voices, and with a fuller tone than is usually possible with boy trebles. This body continues to sing Mass every Sunday with an eclectic mix of 'ancient' and modern motets or anthems at communion. Indeed, between 1998 and 2004, original composing traditions were revived through the regular performance of several Mass settings by the then Director of Music, Robin Highcock. At the same time past traditions have been maintained. Plainchant is performed by choir and congregation every first Sunday of the month and on feast days. An unusual feature of the 2003 Carol Service was the rendition of a Christmas Psalm setting from the magnificent set of six eighteenth-century Graduals formerly belonging to the Spanish Royal Chapel in Granada. Obtained by the Duke of Wellington during the Peninsula War, these had been donated by one of his descendants to the College in 1954. Nor has Renaissance Polyphony been forgotten, especially in the repertoire of the recently formed Schola Cantorum, which sings at Mass twice a term.

THE GREAT REBUILDING

IN THE LATE 1870s the College embarked on a massive programme of building and renewal. The Plunge and Boys' Chapel were constructed, the façade backing on to the Long Room rebuilt, the Sodality Chapel extended and, further afield, new wings added to St Mary's Hall. But it is the South Front, 560 ft. long, composed of a powerful central block flanked by two projecting wings, that catches the eye. Arguably it is the largest single scholastic façade in England; and the exuberant free Renaissance style, encapsulating the driving vision of its creators, makes it a marvellous advertisement for the College.

The records are especially plentiful. In addition to the plans and contract notes, there are numerous reports, photographs, subscription lists and an enormous correspondence between the architect and Fr Colley, Rector between 1885 and 1891. Most interesting of all, because they tell us exactly how the building was put up, are two volumes of estimates. They show that many of the techniques, such as the cast-iron pillars in the Playrooms, were borrowed from contemporary mill design – rather an alarming thought for an educational establishment! Mortar was 'composed of the best burnt stone lime and clear river sand or chicken ashes [!] in proportion of *1 to 3 ground in a steam mortar mill*'. Similarly plaster was made up from 'the best white stone lime pure two years before being used and clear sharp river sand in the *proportion of 3 to 1* well mixed with the proper quantity of

'We daily behold the monster rising which is utterly and entirely to demolish those familiar walls.' So wrote The Stonyhurst Magazine in May 1881 describing the destruction of the South Front seen here.

Below: *Two views of the South Front.*

'He wears his cassock and a sort of unbecoming sleeveless gown; grey socks and slippers made his humanity easy and close . . .' so wrote Edward Benson, the future Archbishop of Canterbury, of Fr Ignatius Purbrick SJ after his visit to Stonyhurst in a letter to Joseph Lightfoot of 1872. All three had been schoolfriends at King Edward's Birmingham in the 1830s. Fr Purbrick went on to become the English Provincial (1880–8) and, later still, Provincial of New York and Maryland (1897–1902).

the best cow hair'. The stone was local, quarried at Kemple End; but the timbers came from opposite ends of the globe. Red Memel was used for the carpenters' work, American pitch-pine for the ceiling boards and joinery, while the floor-boards themselves were cut from the 'best St Petersburg Red Battens . . . stacked on the premises *three months before being laid down.*' In a very physical sense the isolation characteristic of the school's earlier history was being broken down.

Why was this vast work undertaken? The obvious answer at first appears to be numbers. In the Appeal the authorities desired to secure 'additional accommodation, the want of which has long been pressing'. But the trouble is that the evidence on this point is very ambiguous. Take the size of the school, for example. In 1864–5 there were 228 pupils aged between eight and eighteen, 192 of whom actually lived in the building; but ten years later the figures had fallen to 214 and 162. This suggests that the College hoped to expand as a result of the building and not the other way round – a very courageous decision one might say. But the evidence again proves to be uncertain. The original plans, drafted between 1872 and 1875, made provision for only 225 beds; though the architects optimistically asserted that 100 more could be placed down the centre of the three dormitories. The final plans, adopted in 1876, present a similar story. The Washing Place had 226 marble basins and individual lockers; while the Study Place, where each boy was assigned to his own desk, was planned on a similar scale. Numbers, then, do not seem to have been a compelling argument.

More convincing perhaps was the need to keep up with the competition. All over England lavish new facilities were springing up to meet burgeoning demands for a public-school education. So the Appeal referred to the 'improved character of the accommodation, so as to leave nothing to be desired in respect of size and ventilation of rooms, provision for health and reasonable comfort, and appliances for the advancement of studies'.

But even this appears to have been insufficient. With two architects on the staff and numerous amateur experts years were wasted tinkering around with various schemes. What was needed was a catalyst. It was supplied by the discovery that the existing South Front was in imminent danger of collapse. As the Appeal put it 'The work . . . now begun, is not a matter of choice, but of sheer necessity.'

Planning began in the 1850s. In an article for *The Stonyhurst Magazine* 50 years later Fr Purbrick recalled how 'Fr Clough and his minister, Fr Henry, used to spend long hours together at night discussing the future of the College buildings'. The result was a plan drawn up by Fr Postlewhite and Fr Richard Vaughan which, according to Fr Purbrick, 'looked not unlike some of the forbidding and hideous armories which adorn(?) New York'. The next rector, Fr Johnson, did not like the scheme either; and preferred to concentrate on piecemeal reforms, the substitution of iron-railings for the stone wall around the Playground being one example. So it was left to his successor Fr Henry to pick up the threads; but within 15 months of his inauguration he was dead. All that had been achieved was the laying out of the kitchen garden and the decision to extend Hodder by adding an east front overlooking Paradise. Fr Purbrick then became the man of destiny. In 1872, three years after his appointment, two rival schemes were presented. The first, prepared by Fr Francis Scoles SJ, consisted of a powerful central block built around a court. The second, presented by Messrs Dunn and Hansom of Newcastle, envisaged a shallower central block 470 ft. long crowned by dormer windows of 'Jacobean' design. By opening up the Bayley Room 360 ft. long corridors could be driven down its axis. Shirk would be demolished; and in its place would emerge a new Boys'

Chapel: while at the other end an east wing, projecting out into the Playground to shelter it from the wind, would contain the Academy Room and a large dormitory. The central block, dominated by twin towers, would have schoolrooms on the ground floor, masters' accommodation on either side of the Study Place on the first and second floors, and at its west end the Higher Line dormitory. Behind it the Shireburn Quadrangle was to be substantially rebuilt with a tower over the present entrance; opposite would be the latrine; while facing the kitchens would be a range containing three playrooms on the ground floor and a dormitory for Lower Line above. Alongside the Ambulacrum, on the site of the present power-station, the Plunge and a Racquets court were planned.

This scheme, especially those parts involving the Shireburn Quadrangle, aroused a lot of opposition. For one thing Fr Johnson's kitchen block took up too much space. Others disliked the way the Playrooms faced into the court; while the building committee 'apprehended some nuisance from the neighbourhood of the latrines'.

Nonetheless, despite such objections, this plan was eventually adopted by the building committee late in 1875. However, shortly afterwards, there was a radical change. The chief limitation on the site was the Seminary Pond. If this was removed then the South Front could be extended eastwards obviating any need to reorganise the Shireburn Quadrangle. The solution was produced not by the architects but by Fr Purbrick. At a cost of £300, one-tenth of the original estimate, an enormous drain 30 ft. deep was driven under the pond, through the gardens and out near Woodfields. To quote Fr Purbrick 'on the day of its opening the well under the Church dried up, and a steady stream of spring water was set running through the drainpipe so that the whole morass became quickly solid ground fit to sustain the weight of the lofty pile'.

Meanwhile, energetic steps were taken to raise the necessary finance, fixed at £105,160.8s.1d, according to the contract notes. Fr Henry had done much to reduce the College debt; now Fr Purbrick, after selling several outlying farms, launched a subscription in 1878. This was supplemented by a special appeal (repeated in 1885) for the Boys' Chapel. Potential donors were reminded that 'the College numbers . . . in its community more than twenty priests and sixty non-priests. Each of the latter is bound to say special prayers and a Rosary every week for the Benefactors

Higher Line Playroom in 1907. Today it is occupied by Grammar!

The newly completed West Wing. Note the entrance to the Old South Front on the right. This dates the picture to between 1879 and 1881.

131

Fr William Eyre SJ, Prefect of the Philosophers, (1871–9) and Rector (1879–85).

of the College; and weekly and monthly Masses to the number of more than four hundred a year will be said for the same intention'. The Plunge, appropriately enough, was funded by £4,500 from Blackburn town council as compensation for building a reservoir in the Dunsop valley injurious to Stonyhurst's fishing-rights. On top of this Fr Eyre, who succeeded Fr Purbrick in 1879, was left £60,000 by his father in 1881. Despite the violent protests of his brother, the Archbishop of Glasgow, a substantial proportion of this went towards the new buildings.

As for the work itself, this was done in stages. To lower the structure to the same level as the old mansion the Playground was levelled and extended. With his flair for a cheap job Fr Purbrick opened the proceedings in a most unconventional way. In his words 'On the 2nd of August 1876, Fr Rector in the afternoon of that, the Great Academy Day, announced to the boys in the Playground that they were at liberty to demolish the Eastern boundary wall of the Playground. At once goal- posts were employed as battering rams, and in ten minutes time the wall for its whole length lay flat on the ground.' Two hundred navvies then shifted 30,000 cubic tons of earth from the west to the eastern end of the site.

Next, starting in June 1877, work commenced on the West Wing. Here again the accounts show Fr Purbrick's cost-cutting proclivities. By eliminating several ornamental features and substituting flagstones for the mosaic floor he saved £10,107. 16s. 0d. from the original estimate of £61,361. At the corner, carved on the turret staircase, is a Gothic presentment of an otter hound, commemorating the death of Squire Lomax, who had contributed £2,000 to the Boys' Chapel. In earlier days his otter pack had been a frequent sight about the area; and he often used to invite Philosophers and boys to participate in his favourite sport. It was he who laid the foundation stone for the East Wing in August 1878. Unlike its counterpart, which served the Community, this was devoted to the needs of the boys. In the basement was a gym, music and drawing-rooms; the ground floor held three large and spacious Playrooms; next, on the first floor, were classrooms and the Academy Room, notable for its elaborate stucco ceiling. Above were dormitories and storerooms. The first Academy in the new building was held on 2 August 1881, when ladies were admitted for the first time since 1796. Their exclusion had been justified on the ground that there was a 'lack of room'; in reality a flighty Miss Gandolfi had disgraced herself by joining in the boys' 'display of dancing'.

A truly daunting prospect, whichever way you look at it! Two views of the Study Place, c.1907.

Two views of the Academy Room before the First World War. Note the absence of the Proscenium Arch.

The East and West Wings had been built without interfering with the old front; but now the moment of truth had come. After the boys had been decanted to the newly completed wings the whole structure was demolished, but not without at least one 'unpleasant disadvantage', as *The Stonyhurst Magazine* put it: 'A quantity of rats and mice, that formerly gambolled in security beneath the time-worn boards of Rhetoric and Poetry school-rooms, have been unearthed, and are thrown on the world . . . to continue their vagaries in whatsoever part of the new building their fancy or enterprise may lead them to.'

In its place was erected the central block. At its entrance there stands a statue of St Aloysius designed by John Francis Bentley, the architect of Westminster Cathedral. To right and left of the glass doors were specially designed shoe-places. On the ground floor were located classrooms, offices and the Higher Line Library; above were more classrooms and the magnificent Study Place. On the top floor were dormitories.

The Study Place had several notable features. It had three doors, each with a separate lock, to prevent boys paralysing the proceedings by filching the keys. Within, active steps were taken to preserve the mahogany desks from vandalism. Each boy had his name inscribed on a brass plate screwed to the top; and since the desk could be removed from its supporting iron-frame, it could be transferred with the boy as he progressed up the school. Moreover, to give the duty master a clear view of the student, the two desk-flaps opened out sideways. The only trouble was that they could make a considerable din when 'accidentally' slapped shut.

Linking the central block with the West Wing was a range containing two important rooms. On the ground floor was the Washing Place, built in 1884–5. Each basin had a separate locker with a mirror secreted within. As plugs were not supplied boys used to bring down pennies to prevent the water from draining out. To cope with the plumbing special taps were designed by Fr Richard Vaughan; but unfortunately they never worked very efficiently. Above was the Boys' Chapel, reached by a staircase embellished with a statue of St Joseph by Meyers of Munich at its base. The steps consist of metal grids into which are let 30,240 wooden

The Lady Statue and shrine in what is now the Pieta Gallery. Behind the curtain on the left was the Sodality, occupying what is now the Bayley Room. In 1889 the statue was moved to Hodder.

Above: *'Blessed Virgin, compared to the air we breathe' by Hopkins should have been written with this in mind. Erected in 1882, it is in fact a replica of the statue put up in Rome by Pius IX in honour of the Immaculate Conception 28 years before.*

Above right: *Exterior of the Boys' Chapel, one of several pictures taken in 1888.*

Facing page: *The Playground, with the statue of Regulus in the foreground. The Handballs, two of which still stand, are probably unique. Two other examples are known to have existed at Tonbridge, but were demolished in 1893. These though were designed for 'Bat Fives' and accordingly were fitted with buttresses.*

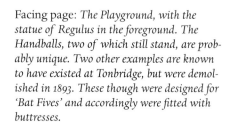

cubes. The design, known as the 'Hawksley Patent Step', proved so durable that, when restoration work was attempted in the 1950s, the College found that the firm, J Westwood of Bow Street, East London, had gone bankrupt because it had received too few orders for replacements. However in 1991–2 George Dewhurst & Co successfully carried out a complete restoration. Half way up the flight stands another statue, this time of the Sacred Heart, presented by admiring pupils in memory of Fr Kay. This was originally located on the Grammar staircase but moved to its present position in 1892. Far more curious are the carvings on the newel posts, each beast grasping a shield emblazoned with the symbols of the different classes. Some have a rather macabre touch. Rhetoric for instance is symbolised by St Catherine – a broken wheel; Grammar, appropriately enough, by a cannon – the emblem of St Barbara; while Preparatory, dedicated to St John Berchmans, possesses a rule-book, a crucifix and a rosary.

No expense was spared on the Boys' Chapel. For this reason, although the shell was ready by 1888, it was not completely furnished until 1900. Outside there is a wealth of statuary since – fond hope – Hansom intended to remove the seemingly permanent 'Shirk'. High up on the wall opposite the windows are four oriels, originally inserted to allow the Community, who then lived in the West Wing, to move to their devotions without disturbing or, more likely, being upset by the worshippers below. Beneath their feet – a surprisingly modern touch this – was Geary's patent 'Pennine' system of wood-block flooring. Above, masking the rubberoid roofing, flourishes the splendid neo-perpendicular ceiling, but built of wood, not stone! Glowing over the altar stands the enormous reredos, depicting scenes from the life of St Aloysius. This, together with all the other fittings except the tabernacle, designed by Fr Vaughan, was planned as a complete ensemble by Hansom. In 1988, thanks to a generous gift from Joseph Fattorini OS, the Chapel was completely re-cleaned.

The last portion of the South Front, completed in 1889, was the south side of the Priests' Quadrangle. Here were the Philosophers' lecture room and the

The School Chapel after its conversion into a museum and library in 1887.

Choir Room. The Pieta Gallery behind it was converted to hold the great plaster cast by Achtermann bought at the Great Exhibition of 1862 in memory of Fr Clough. Formerly it had stood in the lobby of the Sodality Chapel; but when this was extended it was moved to its present position. The Lady Statue that had stood there before was given to Hodder and a new 'Lady Gallery' opened on the Chapel Landing.

As may be surmised, the erection of the South Front prompted much other activity. The old Washing Place was converted into the 'Do Room', the old Boys' Chapel started a new life as the College Museum, while in 1884 the Stonyhurst Association opened a boys' carpentry shop. Elsewhere Edmund Kirby of Liverpool designed the Cricket Pavilion on the Oval and the gargantuan altar in St Peter's. The most important event though was the opening of the Plunge in 1880: 60 ft. by 20 ft., with a depth ranging from 5½ ft. to 3 ft., its 20,000 cubic tons of water were heated by hot pipes passed under the gratings at its base. It was one of the first indoor-heated swimming pools to be built in a school.

With the completion of the South Front the Jesuits at last got what they had always wanted: modern purpose-built facilities incorporating the latest educational devices of the day. But there is a limit to the size of any building that can be conveniently managed; for it is one thing to build, quite another to maintain. Henceforth they would have to wrestle with the far trickier problems of renovation and renewal. Moreover, by producing what was essentially an enlarged version of the old South Front, they committed themselves irrevocably to the Playroom system; and at precisely this time the Benedictines, led by Downside, began to move over to the House system. Whatever its educational merits the Playroom system imposes a strait jacket on numerical expansion; for once numbers in a year rise significantly above a hundred it has to be cut in half – thus in effect creating two 'Houses'. By contrast a House system can be infinitely expanded. As numbers rise all a headmaster has to do is build another house.

But the new South Front concealed an even more insidious danger. If you have the perfect building there is nothing left to do. The temptation is to sit back, rest on the laurels of the past, and simply keep the machine 'ticking over'. Long ago Northcote Parkinson posited a connection between the completion of a great headquarters and the decay of the organisation it served. In the first half of the twentieth century it is arguable that this was what happened to Stonyhurst. But we should also remember that the world does not stand still and that, as Toynbee suggested, challenges invite responses. The new century was to give Stonyhurst plenty of opportunities to show what it was really made of.

The Plunge, shortly after its extension in 1907. In July 1880, when it was first opened, Squire Lomax 'pulled out sovereign after sovereign to offer as prizes for various feats of speed and daring'. Camillo Paloma 'stimulated by the friendly hand of a companion' was the first to jump in – with his clothes on! (The Stonyhurst Magazine, July 1906).

THE WIDER WORLD

NINETEENTH-CENTURY STONYHURST was more than a school. Like its predecessors it was a part, and for a time the centre, of the English Province. So this chapter will start by examining the impact it had on the immediate neighbourhood; then, by analysing its relationship with the Society, we will see what role it played in the development of the Catholic community; lastly, as a kind of excursus, something will be said about the Observatories.

The purchases of 1812, 1828 and 1837 made Stonyhurst a great landowner; and in the succeeding decades this position was strengthened by several smaller acquisitions. Of these the most important were Fairfields and the Shireburn Arms, bought in 1866 from some Dominican nuns when they decided to leave for the Isle of Wight, the Bayley Arms with its surrounding fields in 1899, and Grimshaws' farm in 1914. All in all the College ended up with an estate of about 4,000 acres.

Partly because of this the College became a major employer, especially after the decay of the village textile industry. A striking feature among many College servants was their length of service, which often gave them a peculiar status as they became living legends. Thus we hear of 'Jack Tipping' the gasman, 'Owd Till' the gamekeeper, or the two Rawcliffe sisters who sold tarts to the boys on Tuesday and Thursday afternoons. These were numbered: '3' denoted cranberries, '2' were damsons and those with no numeral contained apples. 'Owd Till' or William Wilkinson was the third of three gamekeepers who between them notched up 130 years' service on the estate. A poacher turned gamekeeper, he was also a notable fisherman. Shortly after his appointment in 1867 he started breeding pheasants and, not without danger to himself, he used to take Philosophers out on shooting-parties. On these occasions he usually wore three waistcoats to safeguard his person. Once a Belgian Philosopher hit him below the waistline whereupon, rushing up to his victim, the offender with profuse apologies proffered half a crown. The response was typical. 'Thankye, Yo can keep yor hayfe creawn. Ah values ma thickside at more'n hayfe a creawn!' He died in 1921, aged 88.

As a great landowner the College inherited social and religious obligations left by the Shireburn and Weld families. From 1837 till 1900, a representative of the Rector presided over the manorial court. The College also took responsibility for the Shireburn almshouses at Kemple End and the village school. In the 1850s

Two views of Corpus Christi during the First World War. Note the splendid vestments and the OTC.

this was relocated in new premises known as 'Walker's Castle', after the local missioner, Fr James Walker, who was one of the Stonyhurst Community. In 1794, just before the arrival of the College, a 'Society of Good Friendship', later known as St Peter's Guild, was instituted. On its feast day members still process down the Avenue accompanied by the martial tones of a band. It is the oldest Catholic guild of its kind in the country.

The most notable occasion for philanthropy came in 1826. Writing to Fr Hughes on 12 April Fr Sewall reported that 'the distress of the country is beyond description, no one knows whom to trust . . . the crowds of poor people coming everyday to Stonyhurst for food would astonish anyone'. In a remarkable deal Fr Wright lent £500 to the local workhouse at Overhacking, set up a cotton manufactory there and, by the time the loan had been repaid in 1828, had not only relieved much local unemployment but saved the College and Mr Weld's tenants some £300 to £500 in poor rates.

As Lancashire was still a very Catholic county the College had good opportunities for evangelisation. In his 99-year lease of 1797 Mr Weld stipulated that the Society had to maintain a missioner, or priest responsible for the local community. St Peter's then is not just the boys' place of worship; it was in effect a parish church. Before its construction villagers used to hear Mass in the Bayley Chapel, then they attended the converted stables next to Shirk, and after that they went to 'Fairclough Square' on the site of the Infirmary. Later, in 1859–60, a chapel of ease, St Joseph's, rose alongside the village school.

From this base the Community quickly spread its wings. Through Fr Dunn and Fr Sewall there were already close ties with Catholic Preston. Then in 1796 they began sending a priest to Clitheroe. By 1850 it was possible to open a new church, St Michael and St John's, capable of holding 900 people. The opening service, conducted by Fr Clough, was attended by Bishop Brown, the Provincial and, according to the *Preston Guardian,* 'a tribe of young levites and ecclesiastical students from Stonyhurst College'. Elsewhere members of the College said Mass and catechised congregations at Billington, Chaigley, Chipping, Dutton Lee, Sabden and the Almshouses.

Catholic devotion was reinforced in the great festivals held by the College at various times during the year. In his diary John O'Neill, a poor Clitheroe weaver, gave a detailed description of the Corpus Christi celebrations of 14 July 1857. This

St Mary's Hall Chapel c.1906.

Gerard Manley Hopkins SJ (1844–89) studied philosophy at St Mary's Hall in 1870–2, returned briefly in the summer of 1878 and taught the Gentlemen Philosophers classics in 1882–4.

was attended by 8,000 people. The procession, headed by children from the village school, included the St Peter's Guild with its own band, 200 boys from the College carrying lighted candles, also accompanied by a band, 40 priests in surplices and a further 37 wearing full canonicals. At the centre, preceded by three boys with baskets scattering flowers before them, was the Host 'carried by an old priest under a beautiful canopy carried by eight students'. It was, he concluded, 'a beautiful sight, the finest I ever seen'.

These functions also attracted parents, Old Boys and local gentry. Naturally the College was keen to entertain, and above all advertise its achievements. Thus the Easter Retreat was balanced by the Past vs. Present match held after Mass on Easter Sunday. At Grand Matches or on Great Academies of course the blend was different. During the latter, before the main display, boys lined up in the Long Room could be put through their paces by anyone who cared to examine them.

In the earliest days perhaps the most important aspect though was underlined by the editor of the *Yorkshire and Blackburn Mail*. Writing in 1824 he referred to 'a regular intercourse of the most friendly disposition . . . between the neighbouring Protestant gentry, clergy and others, and members of Stonyhurst College, which tends to remove those confounded suspicions and jealousies which it is the object of interested parties to increase.'

Having examined Stonyhurst's connections with the neighbourhood we must now look at its relationship with the Society. As stated earlier, until the middle of the century in fact, if not in name, the College was the centre of the English Province. Partly this was due to Fr Strickland's negotiations with the then ex-Jesuits. In 1784 they had decided that, as old priests died off, new ones would be trained by the College to replace them. The result was that all Province investments tended to flow towards Stonyhurst; a factor further emphasised by Fr Sewall's decision to buy land. Thus, although there was a London Office, until the opening of Farm Street in 1849 most business was transacted from the College. A glance at the 1843 plans confirms this; for, on the site of the Stuart Parlour, there was an office suite for the Provincial and his Socius or advisor.

Even after 1849 Stonyhurst remained a dominant force. The 1851 Catalogue shows that 65 out of 182 Jesuits in the Province lived on the site. Of these, ten were based at St Mary's Hall, where Philosophy and Theology were taught, and a further 21 attended the noviciate at Hodder. In effect Stonyhurst was the main training centre for the English Jesuits. At St Mary's Hall the course included the study of Logic, Pure and Applied Mathematics, Psychology, Ethics, Metaphysics and Cosmology. Lectures were delivered in Latin. Three times a week, in an exercise known as the 'Circle', a student was required to give a summary of the day's lectures and defend its contents against two others. The other students joined the discussion and assessed the quality of their arguments.

Another point to notice is the way senior posts were filled. In the earliest days the posts of Provincial and Rector were combined. Even after their separation there seems to have been a constant interchange of personnel, not unlike a game of musical chairs. Thus in 1817, when Fr Plowden became Rector and Provincial, his predecessor Fr Stone took the subordinate position of Minister. Later we find Fr Joseph Johnson, a mere classmaster in 1850, catapulted upward to become Provincial in 1853, but still continuing with some teaching in St Mary's Hall. Seven years later he relinquished the post to become Rector.

Gradually, a definite pattern of appointments evolved. Fr Reginald Colley is a good example of this. Sent to Hodder in 1858 he progressed up the school, winning many prizes in the process, before taking his London University degree. After his noviciate at Roehampton he became Master of Rhetoric in 1874. Six years later he began his Theology. In 1885 he was ordained and became Rector; but due to poor health in 1891 he had to be transferred to Grahamstown in South Africa. From there he returned to do a further stint, this time as Prefect of Studies between 1894 and 1901, when he finally became Provincial. He died in 1904.

The system had manifold effects on both the school and the Province. It meant that the latter was dominated by men bred at Stonyhurst. During the century there were only two Provincials who were not Old Boys and one of them, Fr Purbrick, had anyway been Rector at the College before his appointment. Moreover, although the Society recruited from every walk of life, the men at the top were usually classroom academics, and had little experience of parish, playroom or administrative work. On top of that the 'man in the hot seat', whether Rector or Provincial, was surrounded by others who had done the job before. The system was therefore tremendously inbred; and what is remarkable is not how conservative, but how innovative many of its leaders were.

Given that for a long time Stonyhurst was the only fully-fledged Jesuit College in the country the Society was excessively dependent on it for a regular supply of recruits. Failure here meant not just the collapse of the school but the disintegration of the whole Province. Not surprisingly the Society paid great attention to this side of the College's work, using methods very similar to those that had been employed on the Continent. From the beginning there were Church scholarships, though inevitably many of the holders proved unworthy. Fr Plowden supplies an early instance of this. On 19 May 1818 he wrote to Fr Sewall complaining of the ignorance of seven candidates recently sent to Hodder. As for those at the College, several had been retained 'long after they had solicited their dismission and clearly proved themselves to be blockheads, idle, insolent and even vicious'.

Another time-worn device was the Sodality, many of whose members went on to hold the highest positions in the Province. For a long time it operated on much the same lines as at St Omers. A new record book, issued in 1838, shows that it was dedicated to the Immaculate Conception; and in 1852 a Junior Sodality, dedicated to the 'Queen of Angels and St Aloysius', came into existence. Both were run by the Spiritual Father; and since he held no disciplinary powers, in theory at least he was a neutral figure whom boys could approach to sort out their personal problems. One weakness though was that the post was often given as a kind of retirement job to some old Jesuit.

The Spiritual Father had two other responsibilities: the teaching of religious doctrine – usually the catechism – on Sundays after Mass, and the organisation of the massive three-day school retreats held at the beginning of each academic year. The religious tone was further reinforced by the numerous sacred objects scattered about the building. Worshippers at St Peter's, for instance, would be confronted by the impressive High Altar, the gift of an anonymous donor in 1893; on either side, towering above the side altars, are frescoes of St Francis Xavier and St Ignatius with his companions executed by Herr Worms and Herr Fischer, using pigments specially brought over from Munich; around the walls are a fine set of Stations of the Cross, while the windows depict the stylised features of many a saint and martyr. From the pulpit, which used to stand looming over

The tabernacle, St Peter's.

One of the splendid Stations of the Cross in St Peter's.

*The Chapel Landing. This shrine replaced
the one formerly used in the Pièta Gallery.
'May Verses' used to be exhibited there.
Hopkin's* May Magnificat *though was
rejected. 'She, wild web, wondrous robe,
mantles the guilty globe.'*

the body of the nave, the famous Lenten Sermons or a panegyric to St Aloysius
might be declaimed; behind, the powerful organ added to the sense of power and
beauty that permeated and still pervades the whole.

Now all this suggests a very mechanical and calculated approach towards
religious education; and so in a sense it was. But this ignores the genuine faith
and devotion that informed the whole. Jesuits worked until they dropped; and
the example they set could not fail to make a deep impression on their charges.

During the late nineteenth century these patterns substantially changed.
Although the 1895 Catalogue shows that, with 62 scholastics at SMH, the
Stonyhurst Community had expanded to 131; as the Province now numbered
698 its share had contracted from one-third to one-sixth. Whereas in 1851 Jesuit
education and training had largely been concentrated on one site, by 1895 this
had become widely dispersed as the Province had grown. As early as 1849 the
theologate had been transferred to St Beuno's in North Wales; the noviciate
followed suit in 1854, starting a new life at Beaumont Lodge and afterwards, in
1861, moved to Roehampton, which was then just outside London. The same
thing happened with boys' education. From 1842 a string of new colleges began
to appear.

Mount St Mary's, Derbyshire (1842)	Malta (1877)
Liverpool (1843)	Georgetown, Guyana (1880)
Glasgow (1859)	Wimbledon (1892)
Beaumont, Old Windsor (1861)	Stamford Hill (1894)
Preston (1865)	Bulawayo (1896)
Grahamstown, South Africa (1876)	Leeds (1905)

Strictly speaking, these Colleges were founded by the Province; but in a very real
sense it is not surprising that the earliest among them maintained a recognisable
Stonyhurst stamp until they had found time to establish an ethos of their own.
For several years Mount St Mary's and Beaumont sent their Rhetoricians to
Stonyhurst; the staff, especially at the beginning, were led by hardened veterans
from Stonyhurst. Fr Clough, for instance, after his rectorate at Stonyhurst, held
identical posts at Liverpool and Beaumont; and in the latter case virtually his
entire teaching community had been educated at Stonyhurst. Naturally, they
brought the old customs with them. Beaumont was organised by playrooms,
taught a classical curriculum, played Stonyhurst Football, and counted among its
buildings an Ambulacrum and a Plunge. Nonetheless, in the long run there could
not fail to be divergences. As many of the Colleges catered for a lower-middle
or working-class clientele Classics came to be challenged by more practical and
scientific subjects; and when they got into their stride they too supplied their
quota of Jesuit novices. No longer was Stonyhurst so vital for the life of the
Province.

Even more momentous was the spread of the missions. Overseas, English Jesuits
worked as far afield as Bombay, Calcutta, Barbados, Jamaica, British Honduras,
British Guyana, Malta, South Africa and Rhodesia. Some of the most celebrated
names, like Archbishop Porter of Bombay or Bishops Etheridge and Butler in
Guyana, were Old Boys. Many maintained their connections with Stonyhurst. Fr
Francis Scoles, for instance, in October 1869 sent from Guyana several dehydrated
insects, the skulls of two monkeys and the tail of a rattlesnake! Archbishop
Goodier left his pallium, silver crozier and a magnificent collection of Mogul
miniatures. But the sheer distances involved meant that they could no longer be

controlled by a Provincial based at Stonyhurst; and, in a different way, the same was true of missions in this country. As we have seen, at the beginning of the century, they were directly run from Stonyhurst; but all that gradually changed after the opening of Farm Street. Even missions like Clitheroe and Accrington were run by the 'College' of St Aloysius under a local Superior answerable to the Provincial. More significantly still, with the arrival of the Irish, there was a shift from countryside to town, from the landowning to the urban classes. Situated in the country, Stonyhurst was being bypassed by this development.

This, in turn, affected relations with the bishops. In the beginning, as Fr Plowden's difficulties show, they were still dominated by bitter memories from the past. In 1815, for instance, Fr Plowden's brother Robert was expelled from Bristol for refusing to read out Bishop Collingridge's Lenten pastoral. He claimed that it was heretical! Equally absurd were the quarrels at Wigan three years later. Here rival factions each had separate church buildings on the same site; the secular priest, Fr Thompson, claimed that the bishop would expel his Stonyhurst rival; in retaliation an open letter castigated 'his speech at an Inn, amidst the roar of toasts and the tinkling of bottles and glasses!'

These quarrels continued long after 1829. Between 1830 and 1843 Bristol witnessed Bishop Baines's long campaign to eject the Provincial's nominee from Trenchard Street; and this within months of securing Papal recognition for the Society in England. Indeed, he even went so far as to purchase St Mary's On The Quay from the Catholic Apostolic Body, or Irvingites, and open it as a rival church. Thus a situation emerged that was not unlike what had already occurred at Wigan.

The bishops in London also proved to be equally implacable. In 1834 plans to open a new church at St John's Wood were aborted; and two years later a school at Marylebone Park House was shut down. Their efforts to prevent the establishment of Farm Street however proved to be unavailing.

Nonetheless, despite appearances, the issues were different. To evangelise the towns bishops had to mobilise scarce resources. A rural recusant system was of no use to them, since Catholic gentlemen stood in the way of clerical redeployment. Even when clergy got to the towns there was still a danger that congregations could play off bishops against regulars to get the man they wanted. Likewise bishops hoped to centralise the training of priests in their own diocesan seminaries. That was why Bishops Gibson and Baines tried to take over Stonyhurst and Downside. In short the Jesuits in general and Stonyhurst in particular symbolised many of the things that some of the bishops abhorred. It was rural, tied to the gentry and deployed its members without much reference to episcopal authority. The only solution was to adopt an Ultramontane position; to use the Pope's insistence on his authority to overcome the particularist obstacles that stood in their way. It was ironic that English Jesuits, despite their special oath of obedience to the Pope, appeared to be on the opposite side.

Not all bishops, though, took this view; and merely to concentrate on the sources of conflict does not do justice to the genuine spirit of goodwill and the desire to serve a higher cause that informed both sides. What is remarkable is not how much conflict there was but how little. Had things been otherwise it is difficult to see how the English Catholic Church could have made such strides during the course of the century. Besides, many of the bishops came from the Catholic aristocracy; thus, they were unlikely to dispense entirely with the attitudes of their class. It is significant too that Cardinal Manning, the supreme

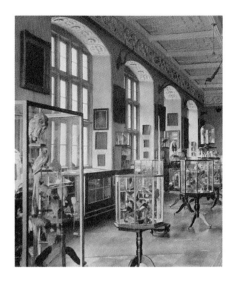

The Long Room containing Charles Waterton's collection of preserved birds and animals. As a taxidermist Waterton used his special, but highly effective, techniques. These exhibits were handed over to Wakefield Museum in the 1960s. The room is now a display area and art gallery in the heart of the school.

Fr Bernard Vaughan SJ.

Ultramontane, was a convert. Cardinal Vaughan though is a different matter. Through him we can see the tensions in their most exquisite form. A scion of the Catholic aristocracy, he was closely related to the Welds and Cliffords, many of whom were bishops. At the age of nine Herbert was sent to Stonyhurst, but in 1847, six years later, he was transferred to a school in Belgium, where he acquired the epithet 'Milord Roast Beef'. His uncle, Fr Richard Vaughan, worked at Stonyhurst, playing a prominent role in the building programme there; and his brother, Fr Bernard Vaughan, was the most celebrated Jesuit preacher of his age. Yet, during his theological studies in Rome, he became a protégé of Manning – a bond strengthened by the fact that his brother Kenelm for a time acted as secretary for the Cardinal. Under his direction *The Tablet* and the *Dublin Review* were turned into vehicles for the Ultramontane position. As Bishop of Salford, within which diocese lay his old school, typically Ultramontane concerns showed themselves: 40 new parishes were created, a pastoral centre for new priests about to undertake their first ministry was set up and in 1886 the Catholic Rescue Society was founded, not simply to care for the destitute, but ensure that they were saved from Protestant temptations in the workhouse. Similarly, he was concerned about the future of Catholic education, inaugurating the Voluntary Schools Association to ensure that Catholic schools got an equal share of government funding. As Archbishop of Westminster he continued on the same lines: Social Union Clubs were founded as recreation centres for the working classes, the 1902 Education Act triumphantly realised the aims of the Voluntary Schools Association and, after the closure of St Thomas's Hammersmith, the seminaries of the Southern and Western Districts were merged at Oscott.

No wonder, then, that he sometimes looked askance at the Society. In 1875, three years after his arrival in Manchester, he shut down a newly opened Jesuit school on the grounds that the Provincial, Fr Gallwey, had opened it without his permission. Vaughan felt so strongly about this that he took the case right up to Rome and threatened to resign. In the event his stand was vindicated for, after two meetings between the Jesuit General, Fr Beckx, and himself, poor Fr Gallwey was ordered to close the school. To rub the point home Vaughan immediately afterwards set up a new school, dedicated to St Bede, staffed by diocesan priests.

But, unlike Manning, he did not take his views to an extreme conclusion. Shortly after the Manchester episode he made a retreat at Stonyhurst; three years later he blessed the foundation stone of the East Wing; and at the centenary celebrations of 1894, as President of the Stonyhurst Association, he donated £550 towards the costs.

Nonetheless, as a result of the quarrel, Rome at last acted to remove the causes of dissension once and for all. Under the brief *Romanos Pontifices* all parish work, including the subdivision of units and appointments to them, were subordinated to the bishop; though in the latter case Provincials did have the right to appeal to Rome after the event. Moreover, no houses, schools, colleges or churches could be opened without positive episcopal approval. Thus, by the end of the century, the Catholic world was very different from what it had been at the beginning. Jesuits could no longer be distributed about the country at the whim of a Provincial based at Stonyhurst; the College itself was only one among many Jesuit establishments; and, although numerically it was still the most important of them, it was not *the* centre from which the Society's operations were conducted.

Excursus: The Stonyhurst Observatories

1838–1992

In an earlier chapter reference was made to the building of an observatory in 1838. This, the first step in Stonyhurst's long and distinguished history as an astronomical and meteorological centre, was thought by Fr Gerard to have been the brainchild of Fr Charles Irvine, Prefect of Studies between 1832 and 1836. But between 1836 and 1842 Fr Irvine was stationed at the St Helens mission. So, despite the fact that he visited the College in 1838, it is more likely, though by no means certain, that the real driving force was supplied by Fr Henry McCann, Professor of Natural Philosophy, Mathematics and Chemistry from July 1839 and the first person to be named as Director of the Observatory in 1842.

Fr McCann's work was developed by three great directors. The first of these, an Old Boy, was Fr Alfred Weld, director between 1847 and 1851 and 1856 and 1860. It was he who, at the suggestion of General Sabine, began the study of terrestrial magnetism. However, this work was neither regular nor systematic and his successor Mr Stephen Perry continued the astronomical and meteorological work. It was therefore under another Old Boy, Mr Walter Sidgreaves (he was not ordained till 1871), that terrestrial magnetism became a regular area of study at Stonyhurst. In 1866, three years after his appointment, self-recording instruments were purchased with the aid of a grant from the Royal Society; and, as one of seven official meteorological stations in Britain, Stonyhurst became eligible for grants from the Board of Trade. A year later the College acquired an 8-inch telescope. Since the iron pillar on which it stood interfered with the self-recording instruments these were placed in a specially constructed underground magnetic chamber below the building and a new Dome Observatory built to house the telescope.

The third great director, who returned in 1868 after completing his studies for the priesthood, was Fr Stephen Perry. Initially, he also concentrated on terrestrial magnetism, conducting three great surveys, or a 'scientific overhauling of the Continent', as Gerard called them, in France and Belgium between 1868 and 1871. However, in 1870 his work took a different turn when the government commissioned him to observe a solar eclipse at Cadiz. Three more eclipses followed; one at the West Indian island of Carriacou in 1886, another at Pogost on the Volga in 1887 and a third at the Île du Salut – Devil's Island – in 1889 where he died of dysentery complicated by gangrene picked up from one of the convicts. Two other expeditions were made to observe the transit of Venus; one to Kerguelen – or Desolation Island – in 1874, the other to Madagascar in 1882. From the latter he brought back the first ring-tailed lemur, or 'Perry's cat'. His observations enabled him to calculate the Earth's mean distance from the Sun at 92,890,000 plus or minus 150,000 miles. (Modern calculations suggest 92,951,000 miles.)

In the process Perry pioneered the art of stellar photography. With the able assistance of Br McKeon he combined this with almost daily drawings of sun spots and magnetic storms using a technique first developed by the seventeenth-century Jesuit Fr Scheiner. In 1924, at the invitation of the Royal Society, these were a focal point of attraction in an exhibit sent by the Observatory to the Empire Exhibition at Wembley.

Fr Perry also studied the 'Upper Glows' caused by the eruption of Krakatoa; in 1886 he confirmed the hypothesis that meteors were the debris from

Above: *A most kindly, gentle and amiable character, distinguished by great sympathy and charity for all who came into contact with him'* (The Stonyhurst Magazine, *July 1919*). Fr Walter Sidgreaves SJ (1837–1919).

Below: *Stonyhurst's greatest astronomer, Fr Stephen Perry SJ (1833–89).*

disintegrating comets, and he measured the incidence of Lancashire's rainfall. Here he 'proved' that, whatever the layman might think, it compares very favourably with other parts of the country, including the South. A by-product from this was the examination of 'black rain', caused by the clouds of carbon belched into the atmosphere by Lancashire's 'dark satanic mills'. A bottle of this obnoxious mixture, dated 26 April 1884, can still be seen at the College.

Perry was a great publicist; and his lectures, one at Wigan in December 1887 being attended by 3,000 people, put Stonyhurst firmly on the astronomical map. Twice, in 1883 and 1887, the College was host for the annual gathering of the British Association for the Advancement of Science. His death then came as a great shock. At a public meeting, chaired by Sir Edward Watkin after Great Academies, Bishop Herbert Vaughan proposed a subscription for the Perry Memorial. This, a 15-inch lens made by Sir Howard Grubb, was fitted to the telescope on 6 November 1893.

Using the new equipment Fr Sidgreaves, in his second term as director, continued Perry's researches. His camera, fixed to an equatorial mounting beneath a canvas shed in the garden, consisted of an old snuff-box mounted on the original 4-inch telescope of 1838 fitted with an objective prism. In 1892 and 1901 new stars were identified; and at the St Louis Exhibition of 1904 he was awarded a gold medal for work on the Beta Lyrae star. He died in 1919.

Thereafter, the story is one of relative decline. His former assistant Fr Aloysius Cortie was director until 1925. Already he had observed solar eclipses at Vinaroc in Spain (1905), the Tonga Islands (1911) and Hermosand in Sweden (1914). On the first of these he was helped by John Aidan Liddell, the future VC, then aged 17. In 1922 the Observatory was recognised as an international centre for visual observations of the solar surface; and shortly afterwards the Royal Society presented an up-to-date Milne-Shaw seismograph. This replaced an instrument loaned by the Royal Geographical Society in 1909, which had been used by Captain Scott on HMS Discovery in Antarctica during 1904. But, although standards were being maintained, Stonyhurst, especially after the discontinuation of government grants in 1882, lacked the resources to keep up with the competition. Fr Cortie therefore turned to lecturing and, despite some early setbacks, gleefully recorded by Fr Gerard in the 1880s, became very good at it. His tours took him as far afield as Toronto and Detroit.

Work continued after his death. Fr Edward O'Connor made elaborate preparations for Stonyhurst's own solar eclipse in 1927, but they were marred by the appearance of a tiresome cloud at the critical moment. When he became Rector in 1932 his place was taken by Fr James Rowland, who initiated the publication of weather forecasts in the local press – a practice discontinued at the outbreak of war for security reasons. At the end of 1947 he retired, the Observatory was closed as an official professional station and the equipment transferred to the science laboratories. Nonetheless, Fr Lawrence continued to supply the Air Ministry with weather reports and in 1957, the International Geomagnetic Year, reopened the magnetic station, where readings were taken until 1977. Such records, reaching back to 1845, constitute an important source of local data about global warming. However, during this twilight period, little astronomy was done and the telescope was sold in 1966.

Revival began with the establishment of the Astronomical and Space Research Society in 1976 under the aegis of Fintan O'Reilly. Three years later the East Lancashire Astronomical Society offered to restore the Observatory. A 7⅓-inch lens made by the great American telescope-maker Alvan Clark was unearthed and on 1 June 1980 Fr Henry Macklin, who had worked at the Observatory before the war, triumphantly reopened the building. Ten years later the College, regretting its past folly, grasped the opportunity to recover the Perry Memorial. Once again the boys have an unrivalled opportunity to study the wonders of the night sky. For example on 7 May, 2003 some observed the transit of Mercury across the Sun. Thus, as the inscription unveiled in 1980 proclaims, 'The Heavens Declare the Glory of God'.

Comet Hale-Bopp over Stonyhurst, on Easter Sunday 1997. Photograph by F O'Reilly.

The Dome Observatory, photographed by F O'Reilly on 14 December 1981.

PRAY FOR THE ETERNAL WELFARE OF
THE STONYHURST MEN WHO DIED FOR
THEIR COUNTRY IN THE GREAT WAR OF
1914 - 1919.
MAY THEY REST IN PEACE.

THE TWENTIETH-
CENTURY CHALLENGE

IN RETROSPECT THE 1894 centenary celebrations looked like a triumphant affirmation of Stonyhurst's achievements to date. Certainly the national press thought so. The *Pall Mall Gazette*, for instance, declared that 'the foundation of Stonyhurst marks an epoch in the history of Catholic emancipation, and the completion of its hundredth year of existence naturally sets English Catholics thinking of days gone by, pleasantly recalling past difficulties and persecutions, and contemplating with satisfaction their present happy condition.'

Preparations were vast, far outdoing those surrounding the tercentenary two years before; for at that time it was erroneously supposed that St Omers had been founded in 1592. To accommodate 300 guests the Infirmary, schoolrooms, St Mary's Hall, the Higher Line dormitory and the Philosophers' rooms were all commandeered. The 15 bishops and archbishops slept in the West Wing, forcing the Community to camp out in the Observatory and science laboratories. Every guest received a card identifying the place and number of his room, the table he belonged to at meals and listing the times of carriages and trains. To obviate confusion luggage was assembled at prearranged points and from thence carried to the appropriate room. Extra drafts of servants supplemented those taken from the gardens, tailors', shoemakers' and other departments. The laundry was converted into a temporary kitchen, while spiritual needs were met by setting up 29 altars in the College and a further 11 in St Mary's Hall. All of them were alphabetically numbered. Elaborate decorations appeared before the main entrance, the South Front and in the Ambulacrum – the latter crowned by the curious inscription 'Iam Cornicibus Omnibus Superstes'.[1] In the Academy Room an extra gallery, capable of holding 200 persons, was constructed. Musical entertainment was supplied outdoors by the Hurst Green Band, indoors by the 18-man Haslingden Orchestra specially hired for the occasion.

As for the festivities themselves, these opened on the night of Monday 23 July with a blaze of fireworks. Over the next three days there followed a riot of entertainment, religious ceremonial and academic and sporting displays. Special features included the Past vs. Present cricket match, won by Past; a Philosophy defension and presentation of prizes, the Great Academy itself and 'An Historical Harmony' – *Oliver Cromwell and his Table* – devised by Fr Gerard. With music

Bernard Patridge's invitation card for the 1894 celebrations.

---

[1] Translated as 'Now you outlive all the crows', i.e. 90 years old. It is also a play on the word 'crows', a nickname given to members of the Society.

Facing page: *The War Memorial at the far end of the Schoolroom Gallery.*

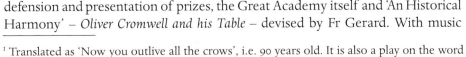

The Centenary Celebrations in the Ambulacrum, Wednesday 25 July 1894.

The Stonyhurst '350' taken on 14 November 1912, just after the school roll had risen above this psychological barrier. Boys were woken from a long sleep' at 6.30 by the tones of the OTC Bugle Band. A Requiem for Old Boys was followed by a 'Good Breakfast', after which the OTC were pitted against Infantry and Artillery drawn from the Preston garrison. The assured figure in the front row (tenth from the right) is the Archduke Franz Karl, grandson of the Austrian emperor.

pillaged from Gilbert and Sullivan operettas it recounted the various imaginary mishaps suffered by the Lord Protector and his Ironsides when they rashly decided to spend the night at Stonyhurst on their way to the battle of Preston. On a more serious note Abbot Burge of Ampleforth celebrated a pontifical high Mass, incorporating a *Te Deum* specially composed for the occasion by Fr De Zulueta. The Wednesday following saw a requiem for the Old Boys of the College. Since the day was the feast of St James a special Papal dispensation was obtained. In the afternoon 606 persons sat down to a centenary dinner lasting for almost four hours. The Duke of Norfolk requested, and got, three whole holidays, while Lord Herries proposed what *The Stonyhurst Magazine* was pleased to call 'the toast of the day' – 'PROSPERITY TO STONYHURST'.

In the years after it at first seemed that the promise would be amply fulfilled. After a brief pause numbers rose rapidly, necessitating the creation of Fourth Playroom in 1917. Academies prize lists show that in July 1894 there were 180–200 boys living in the building. By August 1905 the figure was at 209; but by November 1914 it stood at 309. Four years later it had reached 358; adding boys in Hodder the statistics are 252, 246, 382 and 419 respectively.

Equally impressive is the evidence supplied by the *Stonyhurst War Record*. In the First World War there were three VCs, 393 other honours, 85 of which were foreign, and a further 348 mentioned in despatches. Sadly, the casualties and suffering involved were equally great. Of the 1,012 OS serving in the armed forces 207 died, 143 of whom were killed, died of wounds or went missing in action. 228 others were wounded and a further 28 became prisoners of war. Consequently, when the War ended, a magnificent memorial was unveiled at the end of the Schoolroom Gallery. In addition, as part of the appeal, new Physics laboratories were opened over the Gym while the old laboratories next to the Ambulacrum were converted for Chemistry.

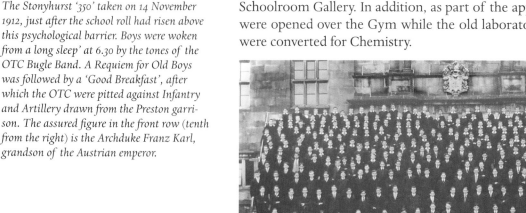

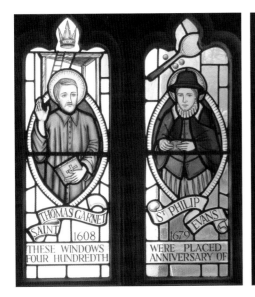

The War Memorial at the far end of the Schoolroom Gallery: detail of the stained glass windows, designed by Pat Feeny (OS 1919–28), and installed in 1993 to commemorate the foundation of the College. They feature four of the St Omers Martyrs.

However, beneath the impressive façade a number of cracks were beginning to show. Numbers, after reaching a peak in 1918, began to fall. By June 1925 there were 379 boys in all, 319 of whom lived in the College. There were many reasons for this. Undoubtedly, one difficulty was the building. Its very completeness engendered a feeling of complacency; its sheer size precluded further extensions and, as the authorities were soon to discover, renovation could prove to be a complicated and expensive business. Moreover, precisely at the time when Ampleforth, by switching to a House system, was growing, the design trapped Stonyhurst within the numerical constraints imposed by what some regard as the educationally superior Playroom organisation.

A second factor was the growing exclusiveness of Stonyhurst. As it became more of a public school, and as the Society built more secondary schools in the cities, so the College found that its pool of potential pupils was gradually shrinking. This was especially true with boys from the neighbourhood, who in the early days had constituted a significant presence. Moreover, as Catholicism broke out of its northern heartlands in the 1920s, its centre of gravity moved southwards and eastwards, giving an advantage to Stonyhurst's southern competitors.

Third, there was the matter of school fees. In 1918 these stood at £65 a year, which was very favourable when compared with the £120 charged by Downside or the 140 guineas required by Eton. But by 1926 Stonyhurst's fees had risen to £142. This was due to the closure of the Lay Philosophy department in 1916. Whether this could have survived is open to debate. Numbers before the War were falling and the opening of Oxford and Cambridge to Catholics in 1894 destroyed much of its *raison d'être*. However, the fact was that the College, by charging each Philosopher 120 guineas, had been able to make good any deficiency in its school fees.

With the Philosophers went a certain social cachet; and it is interesting to observe how members of the old Catholic families began to appear in larger numbers on the rolls of Stonyhurst's competitors. On top of that the Society ceased to send the high-calibre staff needed to run a 'University department' and who had contributed so much to the high intellectual tone of the place as a whole. This point was further accentuated by the decision in 1926 to merge St Mary's Hall and St Beuno's into one seminary of Philosophy and Theology at Heythrop in Oxfordshire. This drastically cut the Stonyhurst community from 134 in 1924

The Gym interior, opened in 1914. After the War, physics laboratories were built directly above.

to 47 ten years later. As with the closure of the Lay Philosophy department this did not directly affect the staff-pupil ratio within the school, but it did remove another body of men who in all sorts of ways had added to the extracurricular and specialist sides of the school. In any case, with the development of the new secondary schools, the Province was having to share its best available teachers between them and the old foundations. Put very simply, Stonyhurst was not at the top of its order of priorities.

So, by the 1920s, although there were still some very good teachers, the overall quality was rather mediocre, especially in Lower Line. Already, before the War, there had been complaints about the insidious effects of extracurricular activities. For instance, Fr Davis's memorandum of 1 January 1907 declared:

> It is agreed on all sides that Studies do not hold the place of honour which is their due. There are several reasons for this:
>
> (1) The following always take precedence over studies or penances for studies:
>
>> Gymnastics after supper
>> Boxing during Maths schools
>> Cadet Corps after dinner
>> Music practice at 5.00 and after dinner
>> Choir practice after supper
>> Orchestra practice on Sundays
>> The Parlour: the dentist . . .
>
> (2) The treatment of the Eleven . . . and the treatment of the Choir . . . make it clear that *it is better* to be in the Eleven than to succeed in Studies.

Thus Stonyhurst, by responding to pressure from its clientele and by becoming more of a public school, was in effect undermining its academic standing. Yet, the importance of this must not be exaggerated. Stonyhurst actually had quite a sizeable presence at Oxford, and only a minority wanted to go to university anyway. Those who did saw it mainly as a passport to a professional or political career; and besides you might anyway get in by means of your sporting prowess. And what was true of Stonyhurst applied to virtually every public school in the land, the prevailing attitude being summed up by Fr Charles Macadam SJ, who came to the College in 1918. Asked 'how much importance was attached to academic work compared with today (i.e. 4 March 1983)' his reply was unequivocal:

> Far less. Not everybody went to University . . . and well you could get in because your father had been to New College or something or because you played Rugger well . . . and only chaps who were doing a profession which required it – doctors – were all that keen on the work and the rest of us – nobody pushed me. I sort of sailed through life, in my case not giving a thought to what I would do when I left the school.

The Top Refectory between the Wars. Note the revised layout of the seats.

But, in fact, the academic challenge was potentially more dangerous than ever before. Once Stonyhurst had decided to send pupils to Oxford or Cambridge it had to switch from London Matriculation to Higher and Lower Certificate. In this way, almost without realising it, the College abandoned the academic curriculum laid down by the *Ratio Studiorum* and started to compete directly with the major public schools. Jesuits found that they had tied themselves to the chariot wheels of government educational policy.

Low academic expectations were matched by uninspiring routines. In the mornings, boys were jolted out of bed at 6.00 by the ear-splitting tones of the rattle (In 1893 and 1920 this was pushed forward to 6.30 and 7.00). Bleary-eyed they trooped down to the Washing Place – 'a frigid barn of a place with endless rows of basins' as H C Flory (OS 1919–28) described it. 'The food', according to Fr Frederick Turner (OS 1922–9), 'was no doubt wholesome but it was often badly cooked and prepared with little imagination.' Virtually all of it was still grown on the farm; for Stonyhurst was still a very isolated place. There were few cars and the first 'talkies' – *Northern Lights* and *The Doomed Battalion* – did not appear till 12 February 1936. Discipline remained tight, the obituary of Fr James Robinson recalling that 'the merest glimpse of that stark black-a-vised figure in the distance was sufficient to quell incipient pogrom and send the little Bolsheviks scuttling like frogs before a heron'.

But the picture can be overdrawn; and there is a danger in comparing Stonyhurst then with Stonyhurst now. Most other schools had similar characteristics – the same blend of strict discipline with rather basic facilities. So people accepted this way of life as the norm. Moreover, Stonyhurst suffered little from the bullying and other defects generally associated with House systems. Many of the negative impressions come from Old Boys like Macdonald Hastings (OS 1917–27) who never got to Higher Line. Those who entered Poetry and Rhetoric were treated in a much more grown-up way. 'Thus', wrote Fr Turner, 'those who reached the top of the school . . . often remembered Stonyhurst not only with affection but with a sense of indebtedness.'

The Society also still maintained a vigorous religious ethic, made all the stronger by its fusion with the public-school ideal of service; and this was developing in a number of new and interesting directions. As early as 1905, in an address to the Congress of Catholic Colleges, the Rector, Fr Joseph Browne, had urged the need to develop a 'social sense' in Catholic secondary schools and impress on the boys 'the conviction that there is a great and increasing amount of social work for them to do in the world'. One result was the foundation in 1911 of the St Francis Xavier Boys' Brigade Club by Philip Watson OS in Liverpool. Stonyhurst was soon affiliated with this. Then, after the War, young OS proceeded to finance and set up Stonyhurst's own club in the East End. Nor should we forget Fr Charles Plater (OS 1887–94), organiser of the Catholic Social Guild (CSG), which promoted adult education among the lower classes. It was he who encouraged Stonyhurst to form a branch of the Catholic Evidence Guild, something that was being taken up by many other schools up and down the country. Here the idea was to train Catholics to argue effectively about religious and social issues at public meetings. For this purpose boys, before going out into the cities, were 'grilled' at a viva and heckled at assemblies held in the Ambulacrum or Playground on Sunday evenings.

So, although Stonyhurst faced many difficulties, as the 1920s opened it still had a lot going for it. The question was whether it had enough drive to meet

Left: *Interior of the Boys' Chapel,* and above, *detail of the mural behind the altar.*

the challenge. Here the key figure was Fr Edward O'Connor, Rector between 1916 and 1924 and again from 1932 to 1938. As an astronomer and musician his background was very different from that of his predecessors; and it was under his aegis that most of the improvements between the Wars took place.

One of his most important acts was to modernise the lighting and heating systems. This had become a matter of urgency, for the College still depended on its original gas plant. In 1888 electricity had been tried out in the Ambulacrum, but this was not followed up. Instead, in 1906 the authorities experimented with acetylene gas, only to find that it was too expensive; so in 1908 a Loco Vapour gas plant was installed in the Priests' Quadrangle. Within a year it had burnt to the ground in spectacular fashion. So Fr O'Connor returned to electricity. At the same time he took the opportunity to add a row of hot baths to the Plunge, installed a fully automatic Silverlite gas-plant – the largest of its day – to supply the kitchens and laboratories, and redeveloped the Shireburn Quadrangle and other areas adjoining the Ambulacrum to hold a new laundry, better servants' quarters, the Orderly Room and a miniature rifle range.

The technology was most ingenious. Steam, generated by two 'Lancashire' boilers 30 ft. by 7 ft., was passed through two turbines and a calorifier. The turbines, rotating 15,000 times a minute, generated 220-volt direct current, which was then stored in two large batteries. The calorifier, an iron-case containing 160 brass tubes, supplied the central heating, laundry and hot water for the Plunge. Thus two-thirds of the fuel needed to heat the College was reused to supply the lighting. Moreover, by concentrating the generation of heat in two large central boilers instead of in five smaller ones scattered about the building, Fr O'Connor effected further savings in the consumption of coal. Before its installation the College consumed 2,342 tons a year; afterwards this fell to 850.

The system, then, represented a considerable technological achievement; for at that time it was not really feasible to link up with one of the big towns. That was only achieved in 1932 when Stonyhurst was partially connected to the National Grid. Under this system the College bought national power during the day but at night switched over to its own form of lighting. Although, by our standards, this was dim in those days it was considered more than satisfactory, especially since electric light did not reach most rural areas until the late 1940s. Certainly it improved the boys' cleanliness. Fr Turner remarked that 'Boys who previously could only have four hot baths a term could now have as many as they wanted to though many chose not to and stuck to the bare minimum [once a week in the 1940s]!'

Improvement of facilities was one thing; the reform of academic, sporting and disciplinary routines quite another. On the academic side active steps had already been taken even before the War. For instance, in 1898 the time spent on exams was cut by reducing the school year from four terms to three. In 1905 the number of Blandykes, Month Days and holidays for religious feasts was drastically pruned; in compensation the Easter holidays were extended by two weeks. The most far-reaching change though was introduced by Fr Vignaux, the Prefect of Studies, in 1911. Hitherto, boys had almost automatically been moved up a class every year. Under the 'Remove system' they would be promoted (or left where they were) on the basis of the termly exams. In this way the disjunction between a boy's playroom and his class was widened, the classic example being Higher Line Grammar – 'a catch-all for those whose physical development had outrun their intellectual attainment', as H C Flory put it. Since many Rudiments boys were promoted at the end of their second term another result was the gradual appearance of 'Lower Grammar' between this class and Grammar itself.

During the last two years of his prefecture (1911–20) Fr Vignaux also encouraged the formation of societies, examples being Popinjay – devoted to English Literature, and Photographic, Natural History and even Ratting societies. His successor, known as 'Boolah', continued his work. Fr Bellanti, an immensely vigorous but excitable Maltese, began his prefecture by reorganising the prize list and syllabus, bringing it into line with the recently reformed School and Higher Certificate examinations. He also appointed a number of capable lay staff, examples being Christopher Hollis and Percy Haddock. The result was an impressive increase in the number of Higher Certificates taken. In 1920 there were just two; ten years later there were 30.

These reforms were accompanied by attempts to humanise the disciplinary system. One of the first steps was taken by Fr 'Paddy' Ireland, Prefect of Discipline between 1915 and 1922. Starting with the class walks he transferred their supervision from masters to senior boys and from that basis inaugurated a corps of boy prefects, known as the Committee, in 1921. Before long there was a Committee in every Playroom. The process was completed in 1942 when Fr Rooney in a similar fashion transformed the Church Monitors into a corps of junior prefects. At the same time the job description of the Prefects of Discipline began to alter. In 1938 they were renamed Playroom Masters. This was more than a cosmetic change; it represented a move beyond the merely punitive side of the job; and furthermore steps were taken to break down the division between those who taught and those who supervised the boys. Henceforth, every master was expected to do his bit in both spheres.

Fr Edward O'Connor SJ Rector 1916–24 and 1932–8. Photographed outside the Observatory.

Opening of the school power station.

The First XI in 1920–1. Rugby became the main winter sport the following year.

On the games front the most important changes arose from the experiences of war. In the first place, the school's war record underscored the compatibility between the values of the Catholic Church and those of the patriot; so great attention was paid to the OTC. Under Col Louis Robertson it became one of the most efficient cadet forces in the country. War also drew attention to the fact that most public schools played Rugby rather than soccer, and a considerable correspondence in *The Stonyhurst Magazine* ensued. In 1921 therefore the College switched over to Rugby, partially justifying this on the ground that it was more akin to Stonyhurst Football, which had undergone a brief revival. The effect was to expand the fixture list considerably. At its peak in 1901 the first XI had played 10 away matches; but by 1937 the first XV was playing 20; and, unlike in the old days, these were against schools rather than professional clubs. Similarly other public-school sports, notably boxing, fives, squash, hockey, athletics and cross-country, were adopted or expanded.

In turn, these developments affected school organisation and routine. To compete in away matches half-holidays were moved from Tuesdays to Wednesdays; likewise the time available for sport was increased by extending the afternoon recreation from 3.30 to 4.15. Most important of all, in 1922 Fr Wilson, the new Prefect of Discipline, reorganised the system of internal competitive games by dividing the whole school into 'Lines' – Shireburn, Campion, Weld and St Omers. Partly this was a bid to mobilise the full games potential of the school, but it was also intended to encourage 'House spirit', especially since senior boys played an organising role. In this way, as with the Committee system, Stonyhurst tried to benefit from some of the virtues of a boy-run society characteristic of most public schools.

How successful were these reforms? First, on the debit side it has to be said that numbers remained stagnant. In 1935, for instance, there were 340 boys, 279 of whom lived in the College. However, by June 1939, with 348 boys, 286 of whom lived in the College, there were some small signs of recovery. Games results show a similar pattern. As a soccer school Stonyhurst's performance had been undistinguished. Of the 170 outmatches played between 1884 and 1920 the XI won 80, drew 21 and lost 69. What will surprise many though is that, except between 1929 and 1931, Rugby was no better. 360 matches were played in the years from 1921 to 1944; and of these the XV won 168, drew 14 and lost no less than 178. However, with the arrival of Mr Colin Fairservice performances dramatically improved. Between 1941 and 1944 the team won 42 out of the 52 matches played; and in the process Stonyhurst's reputation as a Rugby school was firmly secured.

As for academic work, it has to be said that results were only partially satisfactory. By 1935 many of the clubs founded by Fr Vignaux were defunct. At the same time, because of their deleterious effects on 'class spirit' – though the Lines were equally to blame – the Remove system was abandoned.

Nonetheless, during the 1940s the revised system proved to be extraordinarily resilient; and for this some at least of the credit should go to the Rector, Fr Leo Belton, who was appointed in 1938. An exceptionally sensitive man, much of whose life had been dogged by ill-health, he was sustained by a strong sense of duty combined with a meticulous attention to detail. These qualities had already become apparent during his long and highly successful period as Superior of Hodder; now they were made manifest in the College itself. To be sure, there were some breakdowns: transport difficulties disrupted boys' travel arrangements; consequently, from 1942 till the end of the War, they no longer stayed up for Easter. Coal was sometimes difficult to obtain; and in April 1944 shortages nearly brought the College to a standstill. There were also cases of indiscipline and inefficiency. For instance, in September 1942 a shortage of clothing coupons crippled the Rugby arrangements on which the whole afternoon routine depended; as a result, many boys were asked to work on the farm. Lower Line's attempts to till the Playground though merely produced a crop of broken hoes. The very isolation of the College proved to be an advantage. It still generated its own electricity and grew most of its food. Never was the farm so productive. Just before the War, using stone taken from the old gas-works, a modern milking-shed had been erected alongside the Shireburn Barn; now, the Procurator set about planting 12,000 trees a year and put large acreages, including Parkfield, the golf course and parts of the Avenue under the plough. During the holidays many boys worked in lumbering camps or on a farm in Hampshire. Towards the end of the War a major scheme brought proper supplies of water to 1,000 acres of farmland and their attached cottages.

During the war the OTC, now renamed the Junior Training Corps (JTC), took a new direction. Under Captain or Major Tobin, depending on which organisation one refers to, it was integrated with the local Home Guard. Much of its former ceremonial was abandoned for exercises of a more warlike nature. Particularly realistic was the waterborne assault across the Infirmary Pond in February 1943. Live ammunition was used, *The Stonyhurst Magazine* commenting that 'under such realistic conditions there is not only a marked readiness, but even anxiety to obey instructions to the letter'.

However, the best tribute to Stonyhurst's achievement can be found by referring to the *Stonyhurst War Record 1939–45* and the War Service lists published by *The Stonyhurst Magazine*. The evidence here is not quite complete; but as far as one can tell 1,164 OS served in the forces: 78 of the 107 who died were killed in action, died of wounds or went missing on the battlefield; 59 others were wounded and a further 49 became prisoners of war. Obviously, when set against the First World War, the casualties were lower. Nonetheless, the details show that the College had lost nothing of its capacity to produce men of exceptional calibre. Two points stand out. The first is the sheer variety of jobs Old Boys were engaged in; for instance Lieut.-General Vernon Walters of the US army (OS 1928–31) eventually became, amongst other things, Deputy Director of the CIA. The second is the presence of a small but significant group of people engaged in SOE, intelligence or commando-type operations. The unsung hero here is Major F A Suttill DSO (OS 1919–26). In 1942 he organised the largest French Resistance circuit, code-named 'Prosper'. At its peak in April 1943 his groups carried out 63 operations against the enemy. Betrayed in June, he was shot by the Germans at Sachsenhausen camp three months before the end of the War. His career, and those of others like him, gives the lie to those who argue that the Jesuit system at Stonyhurst stifled individual initiative. On the contrary, as Fr William Hewett (OS 1941–50) said, 'the best thing Stonyhurst does is plant time-bombs in its pupils, and that gives hope to slow-developers like me'.

17 September 1938. Fr Leo Belton SJ (Rector 1938–45) with Queen Mary. During her visit she saw the Stuart portraits, Mary Queen of Scots' Book of Hours, the St Cuthbert Gospel and the vestments woven by Catherine of Aragon and her ladies while in retirement in Kimbleton.

The Stonyhurst VCs

EDMUND WILLIAM COSTELLO (1873–1949)
Won his VC in the Malakand Campaign 1897.

PAUL ALOYSIUS KENNA (1862–1915)
Won his VC at the battle of Omdurman 1898.
Killed at Gallipoli.

MAURICE JAMES DEASE (1889–1914)
Won his VC at the battle of Mons 1914. He was
the first VC of the First World War.

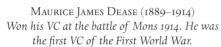

JOHN AIDAN LIDDELL (1888–1915)
Won his VC in aerial combat over northern
France and Belgium.

GABRIEL GEORGE COURY (1896–1956)
Won his VC in the battle of the Somme 1916.

HAROLD MARCUS ERVINE ANDREWS (1911–95)
Won his VC at Dunkirk 1940.

JAMES JOSEPH JACKMAN (1916–41)
Won his VC at Tobruk 1941.

POST-WAR CHANGE AND DEVELOPMENT

Fr Francis Vavasour SJ: Rector 1952–8.

DURING THE WAR Fr Belton had been determined that the Stonyhurst that emerged would be as similar as possible to the institution that he had known and loved in the 1930s; and for a time it really did seem that his intention would be realised. But in the late 1960s everything seemed to change – numbers, staffing, organisation, curriculum and even the buildings. Few things remained unquestioned; and a new sense of urgency was injected into the whole. It was a revolutionary age.

Little of this was apparent in the late 1940s. Fr Bernard Swindells – known as 'Shaggy' behind his back – replaced an exhausted Fr Belton as Rector in 1944. In the 1920s he had organised the Science laboratories, taught Higher Certificate Mathematics and been a pillar of the Catholic Evidence Guild. A notable pianist, his oboe and double-bass swelled the distinctive tones of the school orchestra. From 1933 to 1943 he was Prefect of Studies; and in 1938 he helped to organise the Playroom system. As Rector he was fortunate to enjoy the efficient support of such men as Fr F X Rogers as Minister, Fr Frank Roberts as First Prefect and Fr Francis Vavasour as Procurator.

'Business as usual' seems to have been the motto. It was the natural reaction to the upheavals of war, a certain shortage of cash and the prevailing mood in the country. The Bleasdale Beagles continued to meet; while the duck shoot took its annual toll of the local birdlife. On these occasions dozens of the half-tame creatures were transported to Longridge Fell. They were then required to fly back to the Ponds running the gauntlet of the OS and local gentry below. Great Academies remained an afternoon event; a traditional sequence of academic entertainment, prize-giving and tea on the Bowling Green followed by a gymnastic display and presentation of trophies. Once more the boys were required to attend the school at Holy Week and Easter; 70 or 80 OS regularly came to the Easter Retreats; and panegyrics continued to be delivered on the feasts of St Aloysius and St Ignatius. In 1964 the latter was given by Fr Basil Hume, then Abbot of Ampleforth. As before the work of the Sodality was supplemented by a revived Catholic Evidence Guild and the Barat Club for boys and girls. This was based at 128a Lancaster Rd, Ladbroke Grove and financed by proceeds from the annual Stonyhurst-Roehampton Ball.

Nearer to home social causes were supported by Open Days. In 1949 1,702 visitors contributed some £182 to the Queen's Institute of District Nursing.

Facing page: St Mary's Hall. Fr West's block is in the centre, flanked by the east and west wings erected in 1880–81.

Older customs, like the May Verses or the Corpus Christi procession, were also maintained. Here, the presence of the Corps, reorganised on traditional lines by Colonel Robertson, continued to be felt. Indeed, there is a suspicion that some old habits were becoming more deeply ingrained. Routine, if anything, became more tightly regulated, following the installation of bells automatically controlled by a 'synchronome' in the physics laboratories. The College remained only partially connected to the National Grid; the laundry, contracted out in the 1930s, was revived in 1953; and a year later Stonyhurst's landed independence was consolidated by the acquisition of the Winckley estate.

But this does not mean that the period was devoid of achievement. Numbers, which in those days included those receiving preparatory education, remained buoyant, rising to 417 in September 1947 – 'the highest ever' exulted *The Stonyhurst Magazine*. Next year there were 460. Staff like Fr Rea or Fr Keegan provided teaching of the highest quality; in 1948 a Scouts organisation was introduced, while on the Rugby field Mr Fairservice continued to produce spectacular results. In the Public School Sevens Stonyhurst reached the finals in 1947, won in 1949 and again reached the finals in 1951. Nor should this imply a lapse into philistinism. This was the heyday of competitions within the Playrooms, a string of societies were founded or revived and trips to performances in nearby towns were complemented by the evolution of some highly successful subscription concerts.

One of the most important developments was the foundation of St Mary's Hall (or SMH) as a Middle School between Hodder and Stonyhurst. Indeed, a 'Junior House' had existed in 1930–2 but at that time the idea had not really been carried through; and in 1939 the premises had been requisitioned by the Army. However, this visit proved only temporary, perhaps because the soldiers thought that it was the most Spartan accommodation they had encountered. So, for the rest of the War, staff and students from the exiled English College in Rome had occupied the building. One of them was John, son of J R R Tolkien, who stayed at Stonyhurst on a number of occasions and, indeed, wrote part of his *Lord of the Rings* trilogy there. This has led to speculation that elements in the geography of Middle Earth – especially The Shire – represent a transposition from scenes in the Ribble Valley. Following the departure of the English College, a squad of 12 young Jesuit volunteers from Heythrop refurbished the structure; and in September 1946 Fr Dermot Whyte opened the new school. The first boy to enter was Nicholas Gore-Ormsby. Despite occupying an adjacent site and sharing some of the College facilities SMH immediately became a separate entity. By the summer of 1949 it had its own sports day. At the same time Common Entrance was introduced 'chiefly', noted *The Stonyhurst Magazine,* 'with a view to measuring themselves against the outside world'. Alongside a strong games tradition Major P Caton-Baddeley built up an interest in drama with such home-brewed productions as *Rough Stuff in Rusticana* and *Night Train to Fairyland*. In the 1970s this was taken up by the then Deputy Head, Rory O'Brien and extended with a series of films made by the Rudiments year in the weeks after Common Entrance. At about the same time the rare breeds centre known as 'The Ark' was established. Meanwhile, during this later period, music was not neglected. In the 1980s its choir – Pueri Sanctae Mariae – became well known under the direction of Harry Duckworth. Appearances were made at the Montreux and Llangollen Festivals; several recordings were released; and in 1989 the choir represented Britain at the Loreto Festival in Italy.

The most impressive feature of SMH has been its growth. Originally intended for about 60 boys, within two years of opening numbers had grown to 86. In 1949 the Rudiments boys in Hodder were transferred; Rudiments I and the rest of the year up at the College followed suit in 1956 and 1963. By 1960 there were 137 boys on the rolls. In 1964 SMH and Hodder were placed under one head. Seven years later, the closure of Hodder brought the numbers up to 190. In 1985 the first day-pupils (other than the children of lay staff) were admitted.

Such expansion necessitated extensive building and renovation. A playground was laid out in 1949, followed by a gym in 1955 and tennis courts in 1959. In 1963, 'to the sound of previous reverend classicists turning in their alexandrines' *The Stonyhurst Magazine* reported the installation of a science laboratory. In the 1980s, under the vigorous leadership of Peter Anwyl, a new sports hall was opened in 1984. A cricket pavilion, an art and craft studio, additional tennis courts and a new playground were also provided, together with extensive improvements to the classrooms, kitchen, staff dining-rooms and accommodation.

In 1952, when Fr Vavasour took over as Rector, much of this was in the future. A New Zealander from South Island, he was also the scion of an ancient recusant family. After education at St Ignatius College, Riverview in Sydney, he returned to manage the family estate; but in 1926, he handed it over to his brother and came to England to train as a Jesuit. Ten years later he succeeded Fr 'Solid' Robinson as Procurator at Stonyhurst. Fr Robinson gave him no briefing at all. He simply cleared out his papers, leaving nothing but an empty desk and a bunch of keys. Nevertheless, although initially his work was confined to the estate, it did not take Fr Vavasour long to catch on. During the War, as we have seen, the properties were managed with imagination and verve; and it was largely due to his efforts that the College remained solvent. Soon he became a powerful force in the surrounding area, serving as Vice-Chairman on the local council and Chairman of its Finance and General Purposes Committee. In 1947, using proceeds from the Stonyhurst Open Days, he began the construction of the village hall; a year later, the Shireburn almshouses were transferred stone by stone from Kemple End to their present site in the village.

It should be apparent, then, that Fr Vavasour had virtually no classroom or playroom experience. Although unusual, this was by no means unique in Stonyhurst's history, as a glance at Fr Henry's career in the previous century will show; but it did mean that Fr Vavasour depended heavily on his subordinates for the day-to-day running of the school. Naturally, he played to his strengths. One of his most notable achievements was the Composition Fee Fund, or CFF, established in 1954. Under the scheme prospective parents were offered a reduction in fees if they agreed in advance to pay either a lump sum or a fixed number of annual instalments. The money was then managed by the Province Procurator as part of the total assets belonging to the English Province. In 1956 these were strengthened by Fr Vavasour's acquisition of a large estate near Skipton, half of which was regarded as Stonyhurst's share. So successful was the scheme that, from 1968, it contributed regularly towards the College bursaries.

Similar acumen, though on a smaller scale, was shown with the building of a new Chemistry block in 1957–8 at half the estimated cost using a grant from the Industrial Fund, which had been put together by a consortium of British firms to finance improvements in the science laboratories of independent schools. This allowed the Biologists, who since 1938 had operated in the laundry area, to move into the old Chemistry laboratories.

The Shireburn Almshouses before and after their removal from the 'Copper Sulphate Pool' near Kemple End in 1948.

Fr Vavasour SJ's iron gateway of 1955 designed by Vincent Hall (OS 1907) and Wilfrid Mangan. This was financed by a £2,000 bequest left by E C C Firth to Fr J A Firth SJ (OS 1918) one of the Stonyhurst Community.

Rhetoric Wing, under construction and after completion. It was designed by J Armes of Darlington. The foundations below the showers were built through eighto feet of quicksand.

Elsewhere, using a gift from Mrs Ruby Grumitt, Fr Vavasour laid down new hard tennis-courts in the Playground. He also found the money to redecorate St Peters, improve the kitchen and servery, and create two new squash courts. At the main entrance he installed new iron-gates and a pair of oak-doors using timber planted on the estate in the 1770s. His finest achievement though was the erection, to designs by J Armes of Darlington, of what is now known as the Rhetoric Wing. Although largely built by Fr Tranmar, the real inspiration, fund-raising and initial construction work was produced by Fr Vavasour himself. It had all the hallmarks of his style. Charles Brand OS, lent a crane, timber for the doors and panelling came from Eaton Hall in Cheshire, the stone from a bank and a Methodist chapel. The whole façade was intended to fit in with the existing buildings. In 1965 it was triumphantly opened by the Earl of Derby. It was the last hurrah of the old regime.

For by this time the demand for change was too great to be resisted. The first, and as it happened, least serious challenge came from the Labour Party, with the attack on private education, implicit in the changes brought about by the War, coming to a head in the 1960s. Far more insidious though was the shift in expectations among parents and boys. This was an era of student protest; and within schools, in an atmosphere reminiscent of the 1840s, the sap was rising. Despite the ferula Stonyhurst was not immune, as numerous breaches of discipline show. Parents, too, became more critical of the Spartan conditions prevailing in most public schools. To ensure entry into the universities they demanded higher academic and cultural standards and, perhaps as a consequence of this, they were less willing to sacrifice material prospects in the cause of religious education. In turn these attitudes affected and were influenced by the changing character of the Church. The Second Vatican Council did not just declare that Mass could be said in the vernacular or that the priest should face the people; these were but symptoms of a great liberalisation, fitting in with the increasingly middle-class tone of English Catholicism. People were better educated, and therefore more willing to reflect about things for themselves. Nor did the Church just accept this; it actively promoted it. Congregations, instead of passively absorbing some Latin mystery, now actively participated, not only in the service, but in the whole management and development of the parish as a living community.

All this was a direct challenge to the Society. Hitherto, its stress on hierarchy, Papal obedience and conversion from the top had made it a quintessentially Tridentine organisation; but in 1965 the 32nd General Congregation, while affirming the importance of education, renewed the emphasis on missions and retreat work. Unfortunately, because the Society was receiving fewer vocations, in practice that meant that there would be a withdrawal from some schools. Between 1964 and 1991 the number of Jesuits in the English Province declined from 993 to 452, and those at Stonyhurst from 31 to 14. Scholastics and lay brothers, who had played such a large part in school life, virtually disappeared from the building. But there was a positive side; for now the College could recruit more laymen. Undoubtedly they were more professional, often younger and usually had more experience of the world. It is true that their arrival required the College to make some fundamental adjustments: married staff could not be expected to work the same hours as Jesuits, those who lived in had to be given better accommodation, and in the long run the career structure would have to be overhauled. Nonetheless, it opened the way for a new partnership between Jesuits and lay people in a manner that was going on throughout the Church. The latter were now being encouraged to take on new responsibilities, and at Stonyhurst, as in the rest of the world, it was coming to be realised how much the Society's ideals could be shared with lay people. Jesuits acquired a new perception of their founder. Hitherto, they had concentrated on the older Ignatius, the man who from Rome had organised the Society in a highly bureaucratic way. Now, many people began to enthuse about 'Inigo', the wandering Basque who, as a layman, had created the *Spiritual Exercises*.

Coincidentally, there was a stronger movement to help those who were less well off. In the 1970s and 1980s, influenced by the Society's experiences in Latin America, this was misleadingly associated with 'Liberation Theology', or a 'Preferential Option for the Poor', something that was extensively debated in some issues of *The Stonyhurst Magazine*. But this was not, as some suspected, an attack on the public-school ideal; for at the heart of that ideal lies the concept of service for others, something that is fully compatible with the values behind the Catholic faith. As Fr Peter-Hans Kolvenbach, the Superior General of the Society, put it:

> The Option for the poor does not mean – sticking to the field of education – that we Jesuits should dedicate ourselves solely to the neediest boys and young men. The option is actually more comprehensive, more demanding, and requires us to train everyone – rich, poor, middle-classes – in the perspective of justice, that is to say, in the universalist, Catholic horizon of salvation history. It means, in other words, teaching the young of every social class to grow in Christ's special love for the poor.

The man called upon to meet these challenges at Stonyhurst was Fr George Earle. His background was unusual. While serving with the RAF in India he had become a Catholic; he then read history at Balliol College, Oxford, before joining the Society. Thus, when he took over in 1963, he had been a Jesuit for just 12 years and a priest for only two. Like his successors, Fr Bossy and Dr Mercer, he was in his thirties – a fact that may be of some significance. Certainly, as the first convert to be put in charge since Fr Purbrick, he could look at Stonyhurst freshly and from the outside; and if his decisions proved controversial then it must be remembered that he had very little time.

His first task was to assert himself as Headmaster. The office itself was a new one, created in 1961 by dividing the responsibilities of the Rector. The Rector himself, at that time Fr Desmond Boyle, continued to lead the Community; but the Prefect of Studies took over the general running of the school. Fr Frederick Turner, after a long and highly successful period as Prefect of Studies, therefore had the honour to be first Headmaster in Stonyhurst's history. However, as his tenure was short, it was Fr Earle who really made the office what it is now, and in so doing radically restructured the school. Thus the Procurator, First Prefect and Prefect of Studies, who all reported to the Rector, were replaced by the Bursar, the Deputy Headmaster and the Director of Studies, all of them answerable to the Headmaster. Lower down the Playrooms were realigned with classes so that every year boys moved up a Playroom and a class together. Thus Playrooms came to be named after classes – Poetry, Upper Syntax, Syntax, Grammar and Lower Grammar. In 1986, with the abolition of seventh-term entry to Oxbridge, the two Sixth Form years were reclassified as Rhetoric and Poetry. The 'express' stream was abolished and, as A-levels became the main criterion by which students were admitted to University, more and more pupils stayed on for the full five years.

Fr George Earle SJ, Headmaster 1963–72 and Provincial 1981–7, with Fr General Peter-Hans Kolvenbach SJ.

The last 'old style' rector, Fr Desmond Boyle SJ (1958–64).

Fr Freddie Turner SJ during the filming of a BBC documentary.

The Top Refectory in 1966, shortly before the opening of the present refectory.

Whereas in 1961 31 pupils took A-levels, by 1972 the figure had risen to 78. In this way Stonyhurst ceased to be a 'bottom heavy' school.

These figures tell us something else; namely, that under Fr Earle, the College had grown much larger. This was mainly due to the closure of Beaumont. The decision was announced in 1965; and, since the Province had guaranteed a place to the son of every Beaumont parent, Fr Earle had to work fast to provide for the new arrivals. The first boys began to arrive in September. Exactly a year later the remainder came into almost every level of the school; and in subsequent years many others entered Stonyhurst who had perhaps been originally intended for Beaumont. Thus, between 1963 and 1971, the number of pupils rose from 360 to 500, matched by a proportionate increase in staff from 36 to 57. In the long run the increase benefited the College, since it conferred the economies of scale. Moreover the Preparatory school at Beaumont – St John's – continued to function. From 1970 it was managed from Stonyhurst, regularly sending up about 20 pupils a year, or between a fifth and a quarter of the total intake. Initially though the closure caused great strain. Although some Jesuits and lay teachers had come up from Beaumont, at short notice Fr Earle had to recruit new members of staff. It is a tribute then to his powers of persuasion and judgement that he was able to secure such an able team. Jesuits such as Fr Michael O'Halloran, Fr Robert Styles and Fr Tony Richmond gave yeoman service as successive Deputy Headmasters; laymen such as Denis Henry or Brigadier Peter Lawson worked as Director of Studies or Bursar respectively. In the process lay people began to play a larger role in the school's management. An obvious sign of this was the establishment in 1966 of an Advisory Council. Three years later this had grown into a fully-fledged Governing Body chaired by the Rector, Fr David Hoy.

Beaumont's closure also accelerated the programme to improve buildings and facilities. As early as 1957, the Long Room had been converted into a study area. Under Fr Earle the Study Place itself was transformed into the present More Library. The old library on the Lower Gallery was then subdivided into three Syntax classrooms. Henceforth Lower Line studied in their own classrooms under the supervision of monitors while Higher Line worked in their own rooms or, occasionally, shared the Long Room with Syntax. To meet demands for more science laboratories and Sixth Form teaching facilities the 'new classroom block' was run up, allowing the old Biology and Geography areas to be turned into Art and Technical-Drawing rooms.

Living arrangements, too, had to be improved. The Community, now rather smaller than before, moved into Shirk, making the West Wing available for Syntax. At last, in 1966, the arrival of a rectifier enabled the College to switch over entirely to the National Grid. A massive programme of rewiring and relighting then followed, complemented by the installation of new automatic clocks, bells and a proper fire-alarm system. Damp and cold meanwhile were attacked by a new oil-fired boiler, especially designed by Fr Noel Wilson, which replaced the old 'Lancashire' boilers.

1966 also saw the removal of the farm and estate from direct College control. This did not mean, as some have supposed, that Stonyhurst was deprived of its endowment. For a start, the Province made available a large grant that was gradually repaid from the revenues generated by the estate. Later the whole property was integrated with the assets belonging to the Stonyhurst Charitable Fund. What it did do though was to alter the feeding arrangements. As with electricity Stonyhurst was no longer even partially self-sufficient. One sign of this was the appointment of a catering manager. At the same time the Top Refectory ceased to be the main place where meals were eaten. It was too small, costly and inefficient, for all the food had to be brought up on a lift and served out to the boys at table. Instead Fr Earle set up a cafeteria system in the old Philosophers' Refectory, which was greatly extended, and refurbished the kitchens. 'Whether', speculated a sceptical *Stonyhurst Magazine,* 'this will affect the quality of the food remains yet to be seen.'

As in the days of Fr Clough, advances in the quality of life were accompanied by the growth of more liberal attitudes. For instance compulsory membership of the Corps was abolished for all except those in Grammar; its regular meetings were reduced to Thursday afternoons and its independent authority to punish curtailed. The same point applied to discipline in general. The Committee's privileges were cut down, excessive employment of the ferula discouraged and runs used to deal with petty offenders. In addition, the first steps were taken to deploy lay staff in Playroom teams to assist the overdriven Playroom masters.

At the same time more positive initiatives were encouraged. Music is a case in point. Not since the days of Fr Schondonch had so much effort been put into this department, albeit with a greater emphasis on music outside the church. Music scholarships were set up, Wilfrid Usher took the Chamber Orchestra on tour and every boy was expected to learn a musical instrument in his first year. Elsewhere 'Project Weeks' were introduced at the end of the summer term and the work of societies expanded. The fullest efflorescence of this occurred at the massive three-day Great Academies – Stonyhurst's Fourth of June – where parents could meet staff and combine business with pleasure. At a more low-key level they were invited to the parents' weekends held by each Playroom at various times during the school year.

Liberalisation was also apparent in religious worship. Gone was compulsory daily Mass before breakfast; gone too were the huge three-day retreats held at the beginning of the school year. Instead boys could go to voluntary Mass at 12.35. (Later this was shifted to 5.35pm; and some time after that an additional service was offered at 7.20am) Class and Playroom Masses were held weekly; while Retreats were given on a Playroom-by-Playroom basis, sometimes, but not always, by teams of outsiders.

The extent of these changes is quite bewildering. Wherever one turns something new was being done. Together they amounted to a complete reorientation of the whole school. The spirit was aptly summed up by Fr Earle's own manifesto:

> Stonyhurst College is a community of boys, parents, Jesuits, lay staff and friends. The partners in this growing family are working together to discern and develop religious, moral, intellectual, artistic and bodily talents. They then wish to put their talents at the disposal of the Church and of mankind.

These themes, especially the emphasis on pastoral care, were carried forward by his successor, Fr Michael Bossy. Educated in the Jesuit College at Stamford Hill, he had read Classics at Oxford and acquired much of his teaching experience at Stonyhurst. His background, then, was rather different from that of Fr Earle. He was also a very different man. Instead of a large, bluff, outward-going presence, ready to take decisions at short notice, here was someone who was sensitive, considerate, and very concerned to get things right. These were precisely the qualities need to develop Fr Earle's vision to the full. His forte lay in meeting people one to one; for, like Fr Earle, he seemed to know everything about each boy or member of staff, his exceptional understanding enabling him to appreciate

The More Library after its conversion from the Study Place, and below, *the statue of St Thomas More which stands in the bay window of the library.*

and take delight in discovering their 'growing points'. On public occasions he was a highly effective speaker, not least because of his idiomatic and highly characteristic mode of utterance. Nor did he lack originality, as anyone who was witness to his thought can testify. Nonetheless, his 14-year headmastership was essentially a period of consolidation and development, a necessary antidote for sensibilities that had been ruffled by the headlong changes brought about by his predecessor. The key concept was that of the 'Stonyhurst family', a term originally used by Fr Earle, and the way its constituent members could help and support one another.

One of the best aspects of this was the growth of the school charities. Like so much else this had deep roots. The old Barat Club had faded away; but in the early 1960s Fr Worthy and 'Cos' (short for Cosmas) Watson founded the Voluntary Service. This was followed in 1963 by the beginning of the Stonyhurst pilgrimage to Lourdes. The real breakthrough, though, came a decade later with the formation of the Higher Line Handicapped Children's Trust by Raymond Turner. Every year the HLHCT (now known as The Stonyhurst Children's Holiday Trust or SCHT) gave (and still gives) a holiday for children with mental and physical disabilities at SMH; and later this was supplemented by the Learning to Care and Shireburn Trusts providing aid to the Third World and financial assistance for handicapped students. Funds were generated by such means as conducted tours of the College, Open Days, bring and buy sales, the Lower Grammar Minifair, the Stonyhurst Marathon and the Poetry Banquet.

Meanwhile, the system of Playroom teams inaugurated by Fr Earle was brought to fruition, reinforced by the work done by the boys' personal tutors. This was most apparent in the upper part of the school, where considerable attention was devoted to the provision of proper careers and university advice. More important, their work brought tutors into more informal contact with their charges.

The same emphasis on individual care was also apparent in some aspects of the building programme carried out by Fr Bossy. In 1973, as a token of appreciation by parents for the work of Fr Earle and Fr Hoy, the Audio-Visual Room was created out of the old Philosophers' Lecture Room. The following year the Museum was converted into the present Rhetoric Common Room. This allowed the old common room to be turned into more study bedrooms. Similarly, in what is now the Sixth Form Girls wing, another common room and additional study bedrooms, known as 'Alaska', were carved out of an old dormitory and the former Philosophers' Library area. Lower down the school in the late 1970s and early 1980s proper washing facilities were provided in the Lower Grammar and Grammar dormitories and their playrooms redesigned and refurbished.

The College viewed from the direction of the golf course.

Bleary-eyed early-morning processions to the forbidding-looking Washing Place thus came to an end; and the whole area was converted into the Campion Room. Here, Fr Bossy's order of priorities could be seen in their most remarkable form. Instead of turning it into something like a science or a computer complex, which was what many other schools were doing at that time, he chose to create a History, Politics and Religious Studies centre incorporating private study desks, display cabinets and many of the features of a library.

In his last years Fr Bossy had to focus on three things: the improvement of staff living-in accommodation, the restoration of the Infirmary, helped by a grant from the Historic Buildings Council, and – yet again – improvements in the culinary and eating facilities. Here, a drastic solution was adopted; nothing less than the construction of a brand-new kitchen, a redesign of the layout in the Boys' Refectory and the conversion of the old kitchen buildings into a pleasant eating and common-room area for use by Jesuits, lay staff and visitors.

None of these achievements would have been possible without the development of the Stonyhurst Charitable Fund or SCF, backed by two Appeals in 1974 and 1981. The concept, first mooted in 1971 by, amongst others, Fr Earle, involved a massive expansion of the work hitherto done by the Composition Fee Fund. Thanks especially to the work of Fr Hoy and Tom Harrison the scheme was brought into operation during 1973. The primary purpose was to develop and expand the College bursaries and scholarships so as, in the words of the Provincial, Fr Bernard Hall, 'to defend our [i.e. the Society's] freedom to educate boys on a basis of selection other than ability to pay high fees'. Only when these liabilities had been met could grants and loans be made for other purposes. Nevertheless, during the period from 1974 to 1990, contributions amounting to some £2.5 million for College work alone came from this source, to say nothing of the boys whose parents received financial aid through bursaries. In 1990 these numbered 53. In addition Fr Bossy took the earliest opportunity to affiliate Stonyhurst with the government's Assisted Places scheme.

In comparison with earlier arrangements two other features should be noted. First, the SCF represented a consolidation of assets that had hitherto been scattered and managed in an uncoordinated way. As finally developed in 1979 these consisted of half the Skipton estate, exchanged in 1982 for a lump sum, and Crossgills farm; the Composition Fee Fund, which after 1976 took no more applications from parents and by 1990 had met all its former liabilities; other College scholarships and bursaries, the Stonyhurst estate, a sum to be paid from the proceeds of the Beaumont estate, the Appeals money and the Rectors' Treasures Fund – essentially a device to maintain the many pictures and other artistic objects held by the College.

Second, the system of management was rather different. The Composition Fee Fund had been run by the Province; but, as constituted in 1979, the SCF was put into the hands of seven administrative trustees appointed by the Province, four of whom were nominated by the Governors. Similarly, unlike the CFF, the executive officer was the Bursar and not the Province Treasurer. This meant that, to some degree, the College endowments were outside direct Province control and were in part managed by laymen. It therefore fitted in with the increasing trend towards lay management in the College generally.

By 1984, this process had reached the stage whereby the Governors could actually consider the appointment of a lay Headmaster. One of the earliest milestones had been the appointment in 1965 of Raymond Turner as the first lay

Playroom Master and R Vaughan Rigby OS as the first lay Headmaster of SMH. By the mid-1980s all the Playroom Masters and most of the academic heads of department were laymen. Similarly, in 1984 the posts of Deputy and Assistant Headmasters, which emerged as separate entities at this time, were given to Dr Anthony Dachs and Simon Andrews; the former to stand in for the Headmaster when he was away, the latter to manage school discipline. That same year another layman, Brian Duffy, was made Headmaster at St John's. Much of the credit for this development should go to Fr Bossy; and it was he, together with a new rector, Fr Michael O'Halloran, himself a former Deputy Headmaster and a highly successful Headmaster at St George's College, Harare, who managed the next transition.

The appointment of a lay Headmaster to Stonyhurst was no light matter. On the one hand there was the argument that a Jesuit would be the obvious custodian of the Jesuit tradition and ideals of the College. Such a person would be best placed to maintain, as Fr Bossy had done, the cohesion of that many-faceted community. On the other hand, as stated above, the appointment of a layman was a foreseeable extension from previous developments; it would be in line with the way that the Second Vatican Council had encouraged lay participation at all levels of the Church; and, at a time when there was a shortage of younger suitably qualified Jesuits in the Province, it widened the potential pool of talent. Such a decision did not mean that a Jesuit could not be appointed at a later date; and the Governors appreciated that the Jesuit spirit could be maintained by an active team of Spiritual Fathers, the Rector and the Jesuit Community. Jesuits would also remain active on the Governing Body, links would be maintained with the Province and, in time, lay people themselves, in their own way, would imbibe the educational implications of the *Spiritual Exercises*.

The first lay Headmaster, Dr Giles Mercer, took up office in August 1985. Educated at Austin Friars, Carlisle, he had read History at Cambridge before taking an Oxford doctorate in Italian Renaissance Education. He had then been Head of History at Charterhouse and Director of Studies at Sherborne. His perspective then was that of an academic teacher, a Catholic from outside Stonyhurst, a married man and a parent.

His first priority, naturally, was to get to know the boys and to win general support so that the essential spirit of Stonyhurst could be preserved and developed under a lay headmaster. Linked with this was the need to make the College better

Her Majesty, the Queen, Fr Rector (Michael O'Halloran SJ) and Headmaster (Dr Giles Mercer) on 18 October 1990, standing exactly where their predecessors had stood fifty-two years before. In the Square Library a piece of tartan worn by Charles Edward Stuart was presented to the Queen.

known, both locally and nationally. A high point here was the royal visit of 18 October 1990 when the Queen presented a new Guidon to the Duke of Lancaster's Own Yeomanry. This was a culmination of the process, inaugurated nearly two hundred years before, of integration with the mainstream of British society. As far as his staff were concerned, Dr Mercer, like Fr Bossy, was anxious to improve their accommodation and working conditions. He also encouraged them to take Inservice Training Courses and promoted year-long teacher exchanges with St Ignatius College, Riverview in Sydney and with Xavier College in Melbourne. Meanwhile, day-pupils began to appear for the first time and the policy of taking girls, first suggested by Fr Earle, and put into practice on a limited scale under Fr Bossy, was continued.

At the same time extracurricular activities continued to flourish. In May 1989 the shooting team won the *Country Life* trophy. Two years later three boys were selected for the England Under-18 Rugby team and the First XV toured Singapore, Australia and Fiji. Nearer to home, following a tradition going back to the 1950s, and in the 1960s closely associated with Fr Peter Low, a full programme of outward-bound courses and Duke of Edinburgh Award schemes was instituted. Soccer too, which had tentatively reappeared under Fr Bossy, enjoyed a notable expansion. Indoors Stonyhurst's dramatic capacity showed no signs of abatement. For instance, a sequence of LCOB (Larry Crouch and Rory O'Brien) productions built on the great tradition of Academies' musicals written by Melvin Morrow, Wilfrid Usher and John Mallord in the 1970s and early 1980s. Service remained an important ideal. Twelve OSs served in the First Gulf War, and in 1988 *The Stonyhurst Magazine* produced an impressive list of alumni engaged in social and community work.

Dr Mercer also paid considerable attention to building work. Here he received notable assistance first from Michael Weld and later from Laurence Muskett, who succeeded him as Bursar. A large, attractive and technically advanced swimming pool was opened in May 1987; one year later, on 27 May, Kenneth Baker, Secretary of State for Education, opened the new Design and Technology centre containing £1 million worth of equipment supplied through industrial sponsorship. Elsewhere computer facilities were expanded, classrooms refurbished and the conversion of the Shireburn Quadrangle into study bedrooms for the boys in Poetry, long contemplated under Fr Bossy, carried out. In 1991 the Centenaries Appeal was launched; and this helped finance the massive programme of improvements and renovations described in the next chapter.

1991 also marked the five-hundredth anniversary of St Ignatius's birth. At Stonyhurst this was commemorated by a series of 'Ignatian Lectures' and a major summer holiday retreat conducted by Fr Hewett. It therefore seemed a good opportunity to reassess the school's future in the light of the policy document *The Characteristics of Jesuit Education* produced by the Society. The *Mission Statement* was one attempt to address this. Then there was the academic challenge, represented by the abolition of Oxbridge seventh-term entry, the introduction of GCSE, major revisions to A-level syllabuses and the introduction of the National Curriculum. In addition there was a national trend away from single-sex boarding school education. This had implications, not just for school numbers, but for the whole ethos of a school like Stonyhurst. The next chapter will show how the Governors, Dr Mercer, his successor Adrian Aylward and indeed, the whole College community, successfully grappled with these multiple challenges.

National Distinction! Vincente Gradillas, Paul Flood, Kyran Bracken, members and captain of the 1989 England Under-18 Rugby team.

Inside the Design and Technology Centre, shortly after its opening in 1988, and below, the Swimming-Pool, shortly after its opening in 1987.

INTO THE MILLENNIUM

IN COMMON with many other independent schools, the closing decade of
the twentieth century was a period of great transformation for Stonyhurst, as
significant as at any stage in its history. During this time the desire to make more
explicit the Jesuit ethos in a lay-Jesuit partnership, the need to adapt to the changing market and the ever increasing regulatory framework were significant factors
that were to have a far reaching impact on the school and the way it was run.

The Centenaries Appeal, under the direction of Peter Anwyl, raised just
over £2.3m, which paid for a number of much-needed and ambitious building
projects: a new theatre at St Mary's Hall, a new Swimming Pool at St John's and
vast improvements to the academic teaching areas at the College. The first production in the Centenaries Theatre took place at Great Academies in 1994, with
a performance of *A Journey to Celebrate*, written by Fr Billy Hewett SJ to commemorate the two Centenaries and charting the changing fortunes of the school
over its 400-year history.

The old swimming pool at St John's was enlarged and roofed over to achieve
a constant temperature, and new changing rooms were added. The whole complex was ready for use at the beginning of the summer term 1993.

Facing page: *Stonyhurst College was
honoured when one of its pupils was
presented to Pope Benedict at High Mass
in St Peter's Basilica – 22nd April, 2006.*

Two views of the Centenaries Theatre.

The new clock tower above the walkway linking the old science buildings to the Favretto Science Building.

At the College, the Science facilities were considerably upgraded, with a major redesign and complete renovation of the 'New Teaching Block' that had been rather hastily erected behind the main building in the 1960s at the time of the closure of Beaumont. Renamed the Favretto Science Building, the whole of the ground floor was given over to Chemistry and the upper to Biology. Inviting and spacious new laboratories had segregated theory and practical areas. Significant improvements were also made to the Physics and Geology teaching areas.

Entirely new teaching rooms were introduced into other rundown areas of the school. The large building in the south-eastern corner of the Shireburn Quadrangle – the only part of the old 1810 South Front still remaining – was given over to Modern Languages and Geography and re-named The Fattorini Rooms. The Bread Room area above the old kitchen became the new English department and each academic department acquired at least one new specialist teaching room. There was a new Common Place and Laundry, and a new, sprung, beechwood floor in the Ambulacrum. A little clock tower introduced architectural interest above the covered passageway linking the two science buildings.

Special Centenaries events taking place throughout the year included a party and half-holiday on 23 November 1993 to celebrate the 400th birthday of the College. A cake with 400 candles, cut with the sword of Col Ervine Andrews VC, was distributed to the boys, whereupon all traces of the cake disappeared with remarkable rapidity. A huge garden party was hosted by the College for the residents of Hurst Green and the surrounding area as a gesture of thanks for well over two-hundred years of service, an occasion fortunately blessed with favourable weather.

In November 1993, the Academy Room saw three performances of *Hamlet*, with the Sunday performance attended by members of the cast of the 1946 production. The play was produced and directed by Peter Hardwick, who was to retire as Head of English at the end of the school year after a long and successful Stonyhurst career, spanning 39 years. Later, in 1999, the Academy Room was upgraded with a new fire-escape to comply with the latest fire regulations, making public performances possible. Outstanding productions in the years to follow included the world premiere of *Vision*, in March 2000, an entirely new musical by two former pupils Dominic Hartley and Jonathan Smith. A thoughtful reworking of the story of St Bernadette Soubirous, it was a tremendous success, not least for the exceptional number of pupils who took part.

By the mid-nineties it was clear that the three-day Great Academies, established by Fr Earle thirty years earlier, had become immensely tiring for everyone, especially those about to sit their major external examinations, so a shortened programme was followed by a week's half-term. The major elements, including a Ball for Rhetoric, were condensed into a much shorter time-period. The Academies play, the Concert of Light Music and the Prize-Giving ceremony (since reinstated as a whole-school occasion), all took place on the Friday, followed by High Mass and the Great Academies Concert on the Saturday and by 1.20pm the College was silent and almost deserted. The changes were generally felt to be a great success, although in 2004 the play was replaced with a Variety Evening, to allow more pupils an opportunity to demonstrate their talents. This freed up valuable study and revision time in the middle of an increasingly demanding public examination schedule.

During 1995–6 Dr Giles Mercer announced that, after eleven years as headmaster, he would be leaving at the end of the school year to take up the headship

The 1810 building in the Shireburn Quad.

of Prior Park, near Bath. Former Rector Fr Michael O'Halloran SJ, wrote of him in *The Stonyhurst Magazine*:

> 'Giles was determined that Stonyhurst should be evidently Catholic and firm in its Jesuit tradition; he was determined that there should be academic success through the proper and grateful development of the gifts given to each pupil and that the same should be true in the arts and in sport; he sought a talented and generous staff who would understand those ideals and help in their achievement. None of them was new, of course, but Giles identified his headmastership with them every bit as much as his Jesuit predecessors had done.'

The cast list from the 1946 production of Hamlet.

With Dr Mercer's departure, the College needed to keep moving forward. He was to be followed at this challenging time by Adrian Aylward. Educated at Worth, Oxford and King's College, London, Mr Aylward had worked in corporate finance and run a public company before turning to education. Coming from Downside where, in a short space of time, he had been Housemaster, Head of Religious Studies and a Deputy Head, he brought with him a valuable combination of boarding school experience, a dedicated commitment to the Catholic faith and important management skills which were to serve Stonyhurst well during the next ten years.

Recognizing the need to strengthen the management of the school, one of the new headmaster's first measures was to establish a Senior Management Team, which the school had never had before and which probably was to have more impact on its running than any other single change. The school also needed to move on from the times when most of the staff were Jesuits. The first College chaplain, Fr James Campbell SJ, was appointed and the establishment of a chaplaincy team was to lead to an active lay participation in the religious life of the school. Morning prayers were reintroduced and the tutor system was extended to include Lower Line, with a twice-weekly tutor period for all, providing continuity as the pupils progressed through Lower Line.

DRAMATIS PERSONÆ

CLAUDIUS, King of Denmark	J. P. HORGAN
HAMLET, Son to the late and nephew to the present King ...	P. B. JOHNSON
POLONIUS, Lord Chamberlain	M. O'DONNELL
HORATIO, Friend to Hamlet	P. G. RAYMAKERS
LAERTES, Son to Polonius	P. H. GARRY
ROSENCRANTZ }	J. R. COOPE
GUILDENSTERN } Courtiers	W. D. O'REGAN
OSRIC }	J. D. CLOUD
A PRIEST	B. G. WELLARD
MARCELLUS } Officers	C. K. MACKENZIE
BERNARDO }	W. D. O'REGAN
FRANCISCO a Soldier	P. H. BOND
REYNALDO, a Servant	P. J. ALDERSON
GHOST OF HAMLET'S FATHER	A. P. PIERSON
FIRST PLAYER	A. McDONNELL
SECOND PLAYER	P. J. ALDERSON
FIRST GRAVEDIGGER	B. E. SHINER
SECOND GRAVEDIGGER	P. J. O'BRIEN
GERTRUDE, Queen of Denmark and Mother to Hamlet	G. H. WRIGHT
OPHELIA, Daughter to Polonius	N. F. ROBERTS
PLAYER QUEEN	W. RAYMAKERS
	C. K. SHEPHERD
	A. J. EDGECOMBE
	J. R. SZCZERBO
LORDS, LADIES, SOLDIERS & ATTENDANTS ...	G. K. GRIFFIN
	D. SLATER
	M. J. ASHMAN
	R. T. PRESTWICH
	D. F. HILL

L. B. S.

Stonyhurst Children's Holiday Trust Week 1999, photographed by John Pye.

In June 1997 the Provincial announced that Fr Michael Bossy would be leaving as Father Superior. Although the community at the time was considerably smaller than it had been even ten years earlier, the nature of the Superior's role had fundamentally changed from that of Rector. The changed role embodied the Jesuit presence within the school, one for which Fr Bossy was admirably fitted. Fr Michael Flannery SJ took over as Father Superior in September 1997. He quickly became a trusted counsellor to the new headmaster during his early years. On Fr Flannery's retirement in 2003, Fr Adrian Howell SJ (an OS) was given the demanding task of holding the fort as acting Fr Superior, in addition to his roles as parish priest and chaplain to St Mary's Hall, until Fr Denis Blackledge SJ arrived in June 2004. After four terms Fr Blackledge was forced to relinquish his combined post of Jesuit Superior and College chaplain on health grounds, leaving Fr Howell once again to step in as acting Fr Superior. Fr John Twist SJ was brought in as acting College chaplain, an appointment he took up formally from September 2006.

In the face of the understandably declining Jesuit presence at the College the shouldering by the laity of responsibility for the Jesuit ethos, not just at Stonyhurst but in Jesuit schools around the world, resulted in a spiritual reanimation the impact of which cannot be underestimated. The appointment of a lay chaplaincy coordinator in 2006 was yet another step in this process. The Sodality, reformed in 2005, holds weekly meetings and in 2006 its members made their first retreat at Prinknash Abbey. At the same time, the commitment to new accommodation for the Jesuit Community signals the continuing Jesuit presence at Stonyhurst.

The introduction of married couples into the pastoral life of the school was another major change, presenting pupils with a different model of Christian life. In Stonyhurst terms this has been a revolution. A large number of married staff and their children, interacting with pupils in many different ways, has strengthened the community spirit within the College.

True to its Jesuit roots (and with Jesuit representation still on the governing body), the school continues to offer a Jesuit education in the Ignatian tradition, developing men and women for others. Important institutions such as the Holiday Week, the Voluntary Service programme, Learning to Care, the Lourdes

Pilgrimage, the Easter Retreat and the annual Poetry Banquet have continued to thrive. On Saturday, 18 March 2000 for the first time the Banquet raised more than £10,000. The record was beaten in 2003, when the total raised exceeded £11,000, and again in 2005, when no less than £16,000 was raised for the Stonyhurst Children's Holiday Trust.

In 1997, the magnificent Tudor gatehouse in the centre of the West Front received a dramatic setback when the stone eagle on the south cupola broke free during a severe storm and smashed to pieces on the cobbles of the courtyard one hundred feet below. Luckily, the incident occurred around six o'clock on a late December evening when no one was around. Water had penetrated the lead coating around the central iron bar and its expansion had split the stone. On investigation, the remaining eagle revealed similar deterioration and had to be removed. For the first time since 1712 the cupolas were without eagles and, at least for the time being, Stonyhurst was no longer the 'College of the Eagle Towers' as portrayed in *The Stonyhurst Chorus*. The gatehouse and adjacent parts of the West Front were hidden behind an impressive network of scaffolding for several years, whilst extensive restoration of much of the stonework and roof was carried out. Exact copies of the original eagles were carved out of Portland stone by John Schofield, master sculptor, at his workshop in Liverpool. The new eagles were finally fitted in 2001 as restoration work on the West Front neared completion. Meanwhile, in 1998, the gatehouse clock was completely restored and given a new quartz-crystal electrical movement. Although silenced between 10.00 pm and 7.15 am, the melodious chimes of the bells once more announced the passing hours, audible as far away as Hurst Green.

1998 turned out to be 'the year of three inspections'. The weeklong visit by the Headmasters' Conference Inspection Team during the Easter term gave a welcome confirmation of Stonyhurst's mission as a Jesuit school – academically, pastorally, spiritually and culturally and in sport and outdoor activities. A successful Social Services inspection also took place.

During the same term, at the biennial inspection of the Cadet Corps, RSM Robert Sanderson MM was presented with the Cadet Force medal for his outstanding service, whilst Major John Cobb, CO of the Cadet Corps, was awarded an MBE in the New Year Honours list in recognition of his services to the Cadet Force. Major Cobb finally retired in July 2000 after more than twenty distinguished years at the College. The biennial inspection in October 2000 was particularly significant as it celebrated the centenary of 'the Corps' at Stonyhurst.

One of the features receiving a particularly favourable response from both the HMC and the Social Services inspectors was the recently strengthened tutor system. As a result of recommendations made by the HMC inspectors, the A-level curriculum was broadened over the next few years with the introduction of ICT, Business Studies, Sports Studies and Drama & Theatre Studies.

Sadly, the growing reputation and standing of the College and St Mary's Hall was suddenly put at risk when, quite unexpectedly, at the start of the Christmas term of 1998, the Lancashire Constabulary announced the devastating news that it had commenced a lengthy investigation into various allegations concerning child abuse by certain members of staff going back as far as the 1960s. It would be two long years before the outcome of this investigation (which produced, after due process, only one short-sentence conviction) was finally resolved. This was a very unpleasant time, which made it difficult for the recently appointed

The new Eagles being fitted to the cupolas in 2001.

Major John Cobb, MBE.

headmaster to focus on and implement his ambitious policies for the development of the College. When the shadow hanging over the two schools was finally lifted, the wider Stonyhurst community was in a position to move forward once again, setting out on the long journey of reconciliation. Following a period of great pain, which had touched so many lives, the process of healing could at last begin.

As the Millennium approached, there was a strong determination to regain momentum and look to the future. One of the highlights from that time was a major concert by Stonyhurst musicians at Blackburn Cathedral on 6 March 1999, with solo performances for the violin and cello and ensemble performances by the Orchestra, the String Orchestra, the Concert Band, The Brass Group, the College Choir, the Chapel Choir and the SMH Girls' and Boys' Choirs. It was a major showcase for the two schools and the concert was repeated in March 2000, this time focussing on 'popular classics'. A year later, Stonyhurst musicians travelled down to London to give a concert in St John's, Smith Square. The College Orchestra, String Orchestra, Concert Band, Stonyhurst Choir, Chapel Choir and Schola Cantorum (a recent addition to the musical life of the school) all gave performances, as well as the Girls' and Boys' Choirs from SMH and a Brass Ensemble from St John's Beaumont. In spite of the threat of a London Underground strike, the concert went without a hitch and was an outstanding success.

Many years before, Fr Earle had wanted to introduce coeducation. Along with bursaries to open up the school's accessibility, he saw coeducation as the way forward. There had been a sprinkling of girls in the school for many years, mostly the daughters of married staff. Although the decision to admit girls into Higher Line had been publicly announced in 1989 it was a cautious approach and the number of girls in Higher Line remained small. In 1997 the Governors, under the chairmanship of John Hartley (an OS), took the decision to go fully coeducational, commencing with girls being admitted to St Mary's Hall. By 1999 the Magazine Dormitory at the College was ready to admit girl boarders into Lower Grammar. The momentous step towards full co-education had been taken, and by September 2002 the number of girls at the College had risen to well over 100, with girls in every playroom throughout the school.

During this period the development of areas of the building to accommodate the constantly changing profile of the school roll was a challenge that required creative solutions. These had also to take account of increasingly complex National Boarding Standards and Health and Safety regulations, quite apart from the restrictions imposed on a Historic Building. In 1998 Cassidy & Ashton were appointed as architects to work with a Steering Committee on long-term development plans for the two schools. An extensive and imaginative programme followed, which included the conversion of many of the dormitory areas in the

A view of Shirk from the gardens.

East Wing and central block of the South Front as well as the Old Plunge. Derelict spaces adjacent to the music rooms in the basement became girls' changing rooms and showers. Most of the top floor of the Front Quadrangle was completely renovated and converted into rooms for Higher Line girls who, by 2003, had outgrown the Old Infirmary where they had originally been accommodated, following the relocation of the Old Infirmary (or Health Centre as it was now known) to the Shireburn Quadrangle in 1996. Wherever possible, development included better staff accommodation.

The quaint 1799 building known as Shirk must be one of the oldest 'temporary' buildings in the country. Occupied by the Jesuit Community since the time of the Beaumont closure, many rooms became empty as the number of Jesuits declined. The fabric of the building is being restored and the interior improved to provide further boarding accommodation for Higher Line girls.

In 1999 Adrian Aylward had been able to announce the best set of GCSE results in the school's history as well as outlining plans to strengthen further the tutoring and monitoring systems. From the outset, he had expressed consistent views about the undue value placed on league tables, and in 2002, along with some other HMC schools, the decision was taken not to issue the Stonyhurst examination results to the media, thereby countering what was seen as 'league table obsession'. The results continued to be issued to parents and, in any case, came into the public domain when published by the Government. The examination results turned out to be exceptionally good in 2002 and so they have remained, with the 2003 A-level examination results being particularly outstanding: a record 18 Maths gold medals won in national competition, with four going through to the Olympiad; one pupil gaining the Examination Board's National Physics Prize for his coursework; and around one-tenth of the candidates being offered places at Oxford and Cambridge. In the same year three pupils were awarded scholarships at Cambridge.

Mr Aylward always recognised the importance of Information Technology and the need to further increase its profile within the school. With the appointment of a new full-time Head of IT in September 1998, the Gerard Room (formerly the Jesuit refectory) in the New Wing was converted into a Higher Line IT workshop. In the following year, Rhetoric and most of the academic departments were networked. The Gerard Room has since been completely refurbished and re-equipped and by 2003 it was one of five ICT suites, with a growing number of interactive whiteboards in use throughout the school. By 2005 the network covered the whole campus, with links between the College and St Mary's Hall finally in place. The Stonyhurst website: www.stonyhurst.ac.uk, set up in 2002, was thoroughly revised in 2005 and has been constantly updated. Available at any time to anyone anywhere in the world, it has become the initial contact for 80% of the current pupil intake with more than 100,000 hits per week.

An important feature of Stonyhurst is that it should remain a truly local, national and international school. In this, Adrian Aylward could be seen to have picked up and driven forward Fr Earle's vision and the Jesuit philosophy of accessibility to all – a philosophy now being adopted by independent schools throughout the country in the wake of changes to charitable status. At the same time Mr Aylward has always made a point of building on Stonyhurst's longstanding international reputation, by consistently promoting the school overseas. At the time of writing, of the 440 pupils at the College, 45 are from Hong Kong (and mainland China), 19 from Nigeria, 14 from Mexico and 12 from Germany, with others from Malta,

The Stonyhurst College website.

Spain, France, USA, Japan, Gibraltar, Switzerland, Austria, Israel, Tanzania, Australia and Bangladesh. More than 70% of all pupils are Catholic and a further 20% belong to other Christian denominations. The bounds of 'the Stonyhurst family' have never been wider. It is also significant that in 2004/5 some 40% of the school roll are the children of OS or are related to OS families.

The Stonyhurst Association Office has long played an important role in reaching out and strengthening the links with the wider Stonyhurst family. Measures were taken in 2000 to increase the efficiency of its operation. The impact has been felt both nationally and internationally with a growing programme of regular and well supported dinners, receptions, reunions and sporting events. In 2006 the Association contributed to a thorough restoration of the Sodality Chapel; it is expected that the work will be completed by the end of the year.

The Modern Languages Department continues to promote exchanges with foreign schools including the Colegio San Jose, near Bilbao in northern Spain, and St Blasien's in Bavaria. The former is a novel venture, funded by the Socrates Scheme via the British Council: each pupil-group produces a written report of their visit in the other group's language. There have also been extended visits by pupils and staff from Wah Yan College in Hong Kong, St Alexander Nevsky School, Moscow and St Ignatius College, Riverview in Sydney, Australia, with whom there has also been for many years a healthy annual exchange of gap-year students. With the exception of the St Alexander Nevsky School, all of the above are Jesuit schools.

As part of the drive to widen the school's influence, Stonyhurst has been increasingly opened up to the local community, successfully dispelling the impression, once commonly held, of a rather inhospitable institution having something vaguely to do with the training of Catholic priests. As well as growing numbers of day-pupils, links with the local, national and international media have become regular and frequent. Increasing numbers of visitors continue to be attracted to the College during July and August, when the buildings and grounds are open to the public. Local football teams, including those of other schools, use the all-weather pitch and Ambulacrum, Membership of the Stonyhurst Park Golf Club (formed in 1979) is now at 450 and the Stonyhurst Sports Club (established in 1987 and now with 560 members) – for swimming and squash – continues to thrive.

As remarked earlier, St Mary's Hall became fully co-educational in September 1997, beginning with an intake of 25 girls. In the following year the Archery Attic was converted into dormitory accommodation. By 1999, girl boarders could be accommodated within the school and the number of girls immediately more than doubled to over 50. At the latest count (2006) the ratio of girls to boys at SMH has finally achieved what many will consider to be the ideal ratio of 50:50.

When Michael Higgins arrived at SMH as headmaster in 1999, the school roll was well over 200, but the number of boy and girl boarders was only 69 – a sure sign of the changing times. These social trends opposing boarding education, especially for younger pupils, also impacted on the relationship between St John's Beaumont and Stonyhurst. By 2000 it was clear that it was in St John's best interests to be managed separately from Stonyhurst and the decision was taken for St John's to leave the Stonyhurst Foundation. Since then it has been run independently with its own constitution and Board of Governors, and although the number of pupils coming to Stonyhurst from St John's has fallen, family connections have remained strong, and relations between the two schools have remained close. In spite of the growing proportion of day-pupils at both St

Larry Crouch playing the oboe during a concert given by the highly successful Stonyhurst Chamber Orchestra from the 1970s, who came together for a Reunion weekend in May 2005.

The blessing and opening of Hodder House, September 2004.

John's and St Mary's Hall they nevertheless retain significant boarding facilities and traditions.

At St Mary's Hall, an important step was taken with the decision to provide accommodation and facilities for pre-Prep pupils. This led, in September 2004, to the opening of Hodder House, a superbly attractive and impressive facility for almost 80 children which won a National Building Award. Having opened with 37 children, by the following year places were almost completely filled. As these children become an established part of the school, it is hoped that a significant number will choose to begin experiencing the advantages of a boarding education.

In September 2004, Larry Crouch replaced Michael Higgins as headmaster of St Mary's Hall. Mr Crouch is an OS who has spent most of his working life teaching in his old school – for the last ten years as Head of English. In his new position, he reports directly to the headmaster of the College, and is a member of the College Senior Management Team, thereby reflecting not only the growing ties between SMH and the College, but also the fact that the two schools are now managed as one enterprise on a single campus. With Mr Crouch's profound enthusiasm for Stonyhurst, his deep commitment to the Catholic faith and to the ethos of Stonyhurst, any aloofness in the relationship between the two schools that previously may have existed is now a thing of the past.

On its return to Stonyhurst in February 2004, The Independent Schools' Inspectorate endorsed its earlier comments and further acknowledged the excellence of the school's ethos and pastoral care and the outstanding opportunities for enrichment provided by the extra-curricular life of the College. Significantly, the quality of teaching and learning were judged to be major strengths. A full Commission for Social Care Inspection (CSCI) followed shortly after. The CSCI, combining the newly formed government body and the National Boarding Standards, acknowledged amongst the school's major strengths the pleasantness of the pupils and the strength of community spirit.

The ISI inspectors, during their visit, had made a point of registering the considerable improvements in the general appearance of the grounds, noting all

The College gardens, restored in the late 1990s.

Lower Line girls wearing the Stonyhurst tartan, an exact copy of one worn by Bonnie Prince Charlie during his flight after the battle of Culloden. One of the three surviving fragments was given to Stonyhurst and is now displayed in the Arundell Library.

who beheld them to be 'struck by awe and wonder daily'. This transformation in the College gardens was the result of loving care by a dedicated staff following a decision taken some five years earlier to increase the investment in what had become rather a neglected area.

Games of all kinds continue, of course, to be a prominent feature of Stonyhurst life. The 1990s was an outstandingly successful period for Stonyhurst rugby. During the 1994/95 season, for example, the First Seven won the Mount St Mary's Sevens and the North of England Invitation Schools' Sevens; the under-16s won the Lancashire Schools 15-a-side Floodlight competition; the under-15s and under-14s each won the Ellesmere Sevens Competition for their age group and the under-14s were also finalists in the Rydal Sevens. That year James Hurst was selected for the England U19s and Iain Balshaw for the England U16s, whilst former pupil Kyran Bracken gained several more caps for England. The First Seven had further successes in the following season, winning no less than seven tournaments, including the prestigious national event at Rosslyn Park. They were 'team of the month' in the May edition of *Rugby World* and it was written of them: 'never have there been such worthy recipients'. In 1998/99 the Stonyhurst First Seven were again victorious in the Rosslyn Park Sevens Tournament as well as in the North of England Invitation Schools Sevens Tournament and our own Stonyhurst Sevens Tournament. In the following season, the First Fifteen was named team of the month in *Rugby World* and in 2002/2003 they enjoyed an unbeaten season. It was a great source of pride to all connected with Stonyhurst when three former pupils, Iain Balshaw, Kyran Bracken and Will Greenwood (who had been at St Mary's Hall although not at the College), were chosen for the magnificent squad who were World Cup winners in Australia in 2003.

At the College, girls have continued to be outnumbered by boys and their sports teams have yet to emulate this level of success. However, a highly qualified team of instructors and coaches is giving them every encouragement and seven

Hockey on the Harry Meadow all-weather pitch.

girls have already represented their county in a number of different sports. Early in 2000, following a successful Appeal, work began on a new all-weather pitch on Harry Meadow. In spite of quagmire conditions resulting from heavy rains, the pitch was ready for use later that year. Although able to be used for a variety of sports, the hockey teams in particular have found it a great asset. It has been used for training by the England Olympic hockey teams and the England Under-21 hockey team followed their training sessions with a game against the Canadian National team.

Overseas tours have become a recent feature of Stonyhurst sporting life. The rugby First XV followed their successful Easter 1999 tour of the Republic of Ireland with a summer 2004 tour of Australia, this time accompanied by the Second XV. Both teams performed well, with the First XV managing to win their first four games before being finally defeated by an exceptionally talented Riverview side. In the same year the girls' hockey team toured the Netherlands. A St Mary's Hall rugby squad toured South Africa in 2000 and Italy at Easter 2003, when the First XV won all four matches. In 2006 plans are in place for a cricket tour to Canada and a girls' netball tour to Singapore and Kuala Lumpur.

There have also been a number of pilgrimages, beginning in the Summer term 2000 with the ambitious and highly successful twelve-day pilgrimage to the birthplace of St Ignatius at Loyola, by eleven pupils and a group of adults comprising members of staff, friends of the College and former pupils. It became a pilgrimage within a pilgrimage, with members of the party cycling from Loyola to other locations which had played a significant part in the College's four-hundred year history: St Omer, Bruges and Liège. The final leg, from Hull to Stonyhurst, followed a similar route to the one taken by the very first Stonyhurst pupils during the migration from Liège in 1794.

At the beginning of the previous millennium, one of the sites to which huge numbers of pilgrims throughout Europe travelled to was the resting place

The 2006 Stonyhurst Pilgrimage to Rome.

Pupils studying a nineteenth-century silver Nuremberg salt dish in the Arundell Library.

of the bones of St James the apostle at Santiago de Compostela in Northern Spain. In October 2004, a 39-strong party of pilgrims from Stonyhurst, including 24 pupils, set off to repeat the experience. After seven days of serious walking from St Ignatius' hometown of Loyola, often in miserable weather, they reached their destination and were able to attend a traditional pilgrims' Mass in the Cathedral.

Another of the important pilgrim destinations of a thousand years earlier had been Rome, the city of the martyrdom of Saints Peter and Paul, the founders of the Christian church. In April 2006, to mark a year of three major Jesuit anniversaries, there was a family pilgrimage walking from Orvieto to Rome. The party, ranging in age from 9 to 78, included members of staff, parents, former pupils and around 90 current pupils. The group followed the ancient pilgrim route to Rome, the Via Francigena, in the company of three Jesuits and a diocesan priest who led them in Ignatian meditation and prayer at intervals along the way. After four days they entered St Peter's Square to be greeted by 90 other pilgrims from Stonyhurst who had flown straight to Rome for the occasion. High Mass on the Saturday celebrated the Jubilee anniversaries of three early Jesuits, St Ignatius Loyola, St Francis Xavier and Blessed Pierre Le Fèvre. The Stonyhurst contingent, identified by their green and white scarves were given a block of seats near the front. After the Mass, which was offered up for all those associated with Jesuit education, Father General Peter Hans Kolvenbach SJ welcomed Pope Benedict, who thanked and praised the Society of Jesus for its key role in the life of the Catholic church over the last 500 years. Speaking of the continuing importance of the role of the Jesuit apostolate in spirituality and education, he went on to welcome the friends of the Society to the celebration, mentioning Stonyhurst by name. He then personally greeted a representative group of Jesuits and friends, including Stonyhurst Rhetoric pupil Angela Page.

Other pilgrimages have been closer to home. In 2001, a group of Syntax pupils walked over one hundred miles from Whitby to Stonyhurst, an initiative of Fr Matthew Power SJ (an OS and College chaplain 1999–2004), taking in the great abbeys of Whitby, Rievaulx, Jervaulx and Ampleforth. In the following year the Syntax pilgrimage was 'In the footsteps of Edmund Campion', including Oxford and various locations in the Thames Valley where he had lived and preached, with visits to the site of the Tyburn gallows and to see the Jesuit graffiti in the dungeons of the Tower of London.

The year 2002 saw the retirement of Peter Anwyl who, for twelve years, had been headmaster of St Mary's Hall before becoming Appeal Director for the Centenaries Appeal. In 1993 he became the College's first-ever Marketing Director, focusing on all aspects of recruitment and publicity, including the first appearance of the Newsletter. His successor was Jonathan Hewat, who took over responsibility for marketing and admissions, whilst Mark Leslie was appointed Development Director, with the responsibility for long-term fundraising. In March of the following year the Stonyhurst Access 2003 appeal was launched, raising £2.5m to support the bursary fund, the Stonyhurst Collections and The More Library.

As long ago as 1997 an outline plan, developed by a library committee, for the complete refurbishment of The More Library had been approved by the governors. After further refinement by architect Michael Hartley of Cassidy & Ashton, the extensive refurbishment finally began in November 2003, which included the levelling of the floor and the installation of underfloor heating.

A view of the refurbished More Library, and above, *Paul Johnson OS opening the Library in September 2004.*

When the floor tiles were removed it was discovered that, in numerous places, the oak boards were almost worn through and the whole lot had to be replaced. The cause of this strange wear pattern was not difficult to ascertain: years of organised shuffling of gravel-encrusted, boot-clad feet during the room's study-place days, to harass the supervising Jesuit!

On Friday 10 September 2004 the library was officially reopened. More than 150 OS, parents and friends gathered for a champagne reception in the Long Room and the eminent historian, writer and journalist Paul Johnson OS unveiled a plaque in the library dedicated to the generosity of all who had responded so generously to the Access Appeal.

For some time, the unevenness of the floor of the Top Refectory had been causing concern, especially when it was discovered that this was caused by weaknesses in the supporting joists, which were also the ceiling beams of the Do Room beneath. In December 1995, these two areas had been closed off so that work on the complete replacement of the woodwork could commence. It took four years, almost to the day, for the work to be completed and the two rooms to be completely restored to their former magnificence. The Top Refectory was reopened for use on 8 December 1999, just in time for the Stonyhurst Association Dinner, attended by 180 former pupils and friends of the College. The work on the Do Room was completed a little later.

In Mr Aylward's 1997 Great Academies speech, he had commented on the important resource provided by the various College collections, including books, pictures, curiosities and Catholic memorabilia, describing these collections as 'the

Above: pupils and staff at work on the Collections in the Square Library, and *below: Glory be to God, the first publication of the reborn St Omers Press, 2003.*

GLORY BE TO GOD

A STONYHURST PRAYER BOOK

hidden heart of the College'. Once the Do Room had been returned to its former state in 1999, it was decided to use the space to tell the story of Stonyhurst. In 2001 Mrs Jan Graffius was appointed as full-time curator and one of her first tasks was the production of a magnificent display, now referred to as the 'Do Room Museum'. Since then The Long Room has been undergoing a complete restoration so that the display can be extended to illustrate Stonyhurst's Mission and its interaction with the wider world.

Under the direction of Jan Graffius, The Arundell, Square and Bay Libraries (collectively known as The House Libraries) have become much more accessible and a great deal of progress has been made with re-cataloguing and organisation. Groups of pupils from the College and St Mary's Hall have been regularly helping with the care and conservation of the objects, whilst visitor numbers have been growing annually. The role of the Collections, which include paintings and precious and sacred objects from almost every age and every corner of the universe, continues to be to educate and inspire. Many of the items can be traced back to the school's foundation at St Omer and provide tangible links with some of the most pivotal and inspirational figures in history. The Collections are increasingly used to support the curriculum and items are frequently loaned to exhibitions – exciting outside interest and further enhancing Stonyhurst's international reputation.

In January 2005 a Legacy Campaign was launched and The Thomas Weld Society established for those pledging a gift to Stonyhurst in their Will. The first annual lunch of the Society, in October, had as its guest of honour Henry Weld Stewart, the great, great, great grandson of Thomas Weld, the donor of Stonyhurst two hundred years earlier. 2005 also saw the introduction of an Annual Fund for minor development projects at the College and St Mary's Hall.

To celebrate the bi-centenary in 2003 of the restoration of the Jesuit order at Stonyhurst, there was a visit to the College by ten Jesuits, including the Provincial, Fr David Smolira. A High Mass in St Peter's Church was followed by the blessing of a commemorative plaque in the Silence Gallery after which a group of Rhetoricians performed a dramatic piece written by Rhetoric pupil Francis Brinkley, portraying the former Jesuits preparing to retake their vows and to reconstitute themselves after many years of suppression. There was also the publication of a new Stonyhurst Association prayer book by the newly-formed St Omer's Press, with some of the prayers being written by pupils at the College. Two years later, on 22 April 2005, the resurgent St Omer's Press launched a splendid new edition of *The Life of St Ignatius*, to accompany the publication of limited edition sets of illustrations made directly from original early seventeenth-century copper plates in the Stonyhurst Collections. (See illustrations in Chapter 2) These had been engraved in Antwerp and Rome after drawings believed to be by Rubens. An 'Arundell series' of publications is planned, featuring further items from the Collections.

One of the great strengths of Stonyhurst has been its ability to embrace change whilst remaining true to its Jesuit ethos. In spite of major setbacks throughout its history, the school has continued to thrive: its transition through the closing years of the old century and into the new Millennium has been no exception. In May 2005 the school hosted a visit from no less than thirty-seven Jesuit Provincials from all over Europe and at the time of writing the Old Infirmary is being converted yet again, this time to provide improved accommodation for an enlarged Jesuit Community anticipated from the end of the year.

Old Boys

The Seven VCs

See pp 158–9

Other OS

ALFRED AUSTIN

VI's encyclical *Humanae Vitae* in 1968 reaffirming the traditional Catholic Church's position on birth control.

Fr Philip Caraman sj (1911–1998): Catholic historian. Editor of *The Month*.

Charles Carroll (1737–1832): Signatory, US Declaration of Independence.

Daniel Carroll (1730–96): Helped to draft the US Constitution.

John Carroll (1735/6–1815): First Catholic bishop in the USA. First Archbishop of Baltimore.

William N Cash (b. 1940): Conservative shadow Front Bench MP.

Sir Charles Chichester (1795–1847): Brigadier-General, British Auxiliary Legion, Spain. Governor of Trinidad 1842–3.

Pratnap Chidamber Chitnis, Baron Chitnis of Ryedale Yorkshire (b. 1936). Liberal politician.

Denzil RN Clarke (1908–85): Chairman of BAT industries 1966–70.

Joseph Clarkson (b. 1957) US Rugby international.

Arthur Clifford (1778–1830): Antiquary.

Henry Clifford (1768–1813): Legal writer.

Hugh Charles Clifford 7th Baron Clifford of Chudleigh (1790–1858): Whig politician, leading advocate of Catholic Emancipation, assistant to Cardinal Consalvi at the Congress of Vienna (1814–15) on behalf of the Papal States.

Sir Cecil Clothier (b. 1919): Parliamentary Commissioner (Ombudsman) 1979–84.

Fr Chris Corbally sj (b. 1946): Astronomer, currently working at the Vatican Observatory in Tucson, Arizona.

Fr Joseph Coventry sj (1915–98): Provincial of the English Society of Jesus. Master of St Edmunds House, Cambridge. Theologian and Ecumenist

Fr Martin D'Arcy sj (1888–1976): Master of Campion Hall, Jesuit Provincial and man of letters.

Herman Francis David cbe (1905–73): Chairman of the All-England Club. Davis Cup player in 1932. Non-playing captain of the Davis Cup team between 1953 and 1958.

Patrick Devlin (1905–93): High Court Judge and Lord of Appeal in Ordinary.

William Devlin (1911–87): Actor.

Captain Sir Henry Digby-Beste (1883–1964): Chief Scout Commissioner.

Sir Arthur Conan Doyle (1850–1930): Historian, fiction writer and creator of Sherlock Holmes. His autobiography,

Memories and Adventures, contains a useful account of his days at Stonyhurst.

Nicholas J Drake-Lee (b. 1942): Rugby International. Played Rugby for England in 1966 with A Horton.

James Etheridge sj (1809–77): Bishop of Demerara 1857–77.

George Edward Thomas Eyston (1897–1979): Racing driver of the 1920s and 1930s and late 1940s. Holder of world land speed record three times at 312, 345.5 and 357.5 mph. When he visited Stonyhurst in 1933 he drove with some boys down the Avenue in his MG K3 Magnette at 80 mph, turned the corner by the stone on two wheels and performed a skid turn by the cemetery before returning with his passengers – shaken but unhurt – to the College.

Lt Col William Fee (1920–2001): Chairman and director of studies of U3A, which he helped to found. U3A, which has branches all over the country, offers further and higher education to older members of the community.

Henry Flory (1910–2002): Pioneer of transoceanic and trans-African aviation navigation during the Second World War.

Sir Henry Gage (1597–1645): Royalist Governor of Oxford during the English Civil War. Killed, battle of Culham.

Francis Gavan-Duffy (1855–1935): Chief Justice, Australian High Court.

Peter Glenville (1913–98) Actor and TV producer in Britain and the USA.

Dr Eulagio Gillow y Zavalza (1841–1922): Archbishop of Antequera (Oaxaca) in Mexico.

Dr Robin Godfrey (b. 1931): Irish Rugby international.

OLIVER ST JOHN GOGARTY (1878–1957): Surgeon, man of letters, wit, politician in the Irish Free State. Appears in James Joyce's *Ulysses* as 'Buck Mulligan'.

ALBAN GOODIER SJ (1869–1939): Archbishop of Bombay.

MAURICE GORHAM (1902–75): Journalist, Head of BBC Television Service 1946–7, Director of the BBC.

PROFESSOR MICHAEL GOUGH (1916–73): archaeologist.

ALEXANDER HILL GRAY (1837–1927): Traveller and collector. On his death, he left his entire collection – including a Tibetan trumpet made from a human thigh-bone – to the College.

WILLIAM GREENWOOD (b. 1972) English Rugby International.

COLIN CLIVE GREIG (1898–1937): Actor; films included *Journey's End*, *Frankenstein*, and *Clive of India*.

RICHARD LESTER GUILLY SJ (1905–96): Bishop Emeritus of Georgetown, Guyana.

SIR WILLIAM HACKETT (1824–77): Chief Justice in Penang and Ceylon.

DR JAMES HANRATTY (b. 1919): physician and hospice medical director.

SIR JOHN LANE HARRINGTON (1864–1927): soldier and diplomat.

BASIL MACDONALD HASTINGS (1880–1928): Playwright. Father of Douglas Macdonald Hastings.

DOUGLAS MACDONALD HASTINGS (1909–82): Author, broadcaster and journalist. His autobiography, *Jesuit Child*, describes Stonyhurst life during and just after the First World War.

DR ANDRE HELLEGERS (1929–79): Specialist in foetal physiology – mainly at Georgetown University, USA. Founder and first director of the Kennedy Institute for the study of Human Reproduction and Bioethics in 1971. Deputy Secretary-General of the Papal Commission on Population and Birth Control 1964–6. US government consultant for population and birth control. Buried at Stonyhurst.

JOHN HINE (b. 1938) Auxiliary Bishop of Southwark.

SIR MICHAEL P J HOGAN (1908–87): Chief Justice in Hong Kong.

PRINCE LOUIS ALOYS HOHENLOHE (1765–1829): Famous Counter-Revolutionary

general. Appointed Marshall of France in 1827.

CRISPIAN HOLLIS (b. 1936): Bishop of Portsmouth.

ANTHONY L HORTON (b. 1938): England Rugby international with N Drake-Lee, 1966. For his British Lions cap, awarded Stonyhurst First XV colours retrospectively in 1968!

GILES HUSSEY (1710–88): Artist.

VALENTINE IRWIN (b. 1838): Introduced Polo to the British Isles in 1865.

FR BEDE (Cyril was his christian name) JARRETT OP (1881–1934): Dominican Provincial in England. Re-established the Dominican presence in Oxford.

PAUL BEDE JOHNSON (b. 1928): Journalist and historian.

BRUCE KENT (b. 1929): Chairman of CND.

MATTHEW KEOGH (b. 1939): Chief salvage and mooring officer for the Ministry of Defence. Recovered £45 million from HMS Edinburgh, which had been sunk on the Arctic convoys during the Second World War. This was the deepest underwater recovery operation of its kind.

CHARLES LAUGHTON (1899–1962): Stage and film actor and director.

FR FRANCIS LINE SJ (1595–1675): Scientist, maker of sundials and other astronomical instruments, correspondent of Newton.

FR EMMANUEL LOBB SJ (1593–?): Received James II into the Catholic Church.

JAMES LOMAX (d. 1886): Squire of Walton and benefactor. Laid foundation stone of the 1878 buildings.

CHARLES LAUGHTON

SIR JOHN LUCIE-SMITH (1888–1969): Chief Justice in Sierra Leone.

SIR PETER MACADAM (1921–96): Chairman of BAT Industries 1976–82; Chairman of Libra Bank since 1987.

JOHN MAGUIRE (1851–1920): Archbishop of Glasgow.

NOEL MCGRATH (1909–74): Played Rugby for Ireland in the 1930s.

DR NIALL MACGINNIS (1913–77): Actor; films include *49th Parallel*, *Martin Luther* and *Anna Karenina*, in which he played Levin.

ALFONSO MERRY DEL VAL Y ALZOLA (1903–1975): Diplomat. Private secretary to Alfonso XIII of Spain in 1929.

DON CARLOS MARTINEZ DE IRUJO Y DE ALCAZAR, DUKE OF SOTOMAJOR (1846–1909): Politician. High Chamberlain and Keeper of the Seals during the regency of the Dowager Queen Christina of Spain.

PABLO (or Emmanuel) MARTINEZ DEL RIO (1850–1907): Mexican politician. Twice president of the Mexican Congress.

DR PABLO MARTINEZ DEL RIO (1892–1962): Mexican historian.

Henry McGee (1929–2006): Actor and TV comedian. Played opposite Charlie Drake in the TV series *The Worker* in the 1960s and alongside Benny Hill from 1968 onwards.

THOMAS FRANCIS MEAGHER (1823–66): Irish Revolutionary. Condemned to be hanged, drawn and quartered for his activities in 1848. Sent to Australia instead whence he escaped to the USA. Orator, General in the American Civil War and politician – mainly in the state of Montana, where he became Acting Governor. Credited with designing the Irish flag, inspired by the French Tricoleur.

PATRICK G MILLER (1927–91): Secretary to the Cabinet (New Zealand) and Clerk of the Executive Council 1973–87.

FRANCISCO MORENO Y HERRERA, CONDE DE LOS ANDES (1911–1978): Secretary of the Spanish Falange party in the early 1930s, monarchist and writer.

JAMES H F MONAHAN (1912–85): Poet, critic and Director of the Royal School of Ballet.

JOHN FRANCIS MORIARTY. (1854–1915) Attorney General for Ireland. In court he paraded his Catholicism by slamming his rosary on the table and by interrupting proceedings to say the Angelus. With Michael Moriarty, he may have been the original inspiration for Professor Moriarty in the Sherlock Holmes stories.

CHRIS MORRIS (b. 1962): Film director and TV presenter. Described in the *Observer* as 'probably the most ruthlessly intelligent prankster in Britain'.

LEONARD NEALE (1747–1817): Second Archbishop of Baltimore.

AIR-VICE-MARSHAL JOHN C NEELY (1909–90): Ophthalmic surgeon. Hon. surgeon to the Queen.

JOHN JAMES NELSON (1891–1983): Argentinian Polo player. His club, the Hurlingham, some of whose ponies were bred on his own estates, won the Argentine, Chilean, England and US Open Championships in the 1920s. Winner of the Paris (1924) and Berlin (1936) Olympic Gold Medals for Polo.

BERNARD H NEWDIGATE (1869–1944): one of the most eminent typographers of the early twentieth century. Printed the first edition of the *Complete Works of William Morris*.

TITUS OATES (1649–1705): Perjurer. Concocted the Popish Plot.

ALEJANDRO OBREGON (1921–80): Colombian artist. Dean of Fine Arts at Bogotá University. Exhibited in Paris, Washington and New York during the 1950s.

DR MAURICIO T OBREGON (b. 1930): Director of Colombian Civil Aviation 1947–8, President of Colombian Civil Aviation (1964). Vice-Rector in the University of the Andes, Bogotá, where he was also Dean of Aeronautical Sciences. Geographical and historical writer.

DR JOHN B O'DRISCOLL (b. 1952): Irish Rugby international, British Lions.

DR BARRY J O'DRISCOLL (b. 1941): Irish Rugby international.

RICHARD M O'FERRALL (1797–1880): Secretary to the Admiralty and the Treasury. Governor of Malta 1847–51.

BRENDAN O'FRIEL (b. 1941): Member of Prisons Service. He was Governor of Strangeways Gaol at the time of the 1990 riot. Chairman of the Prison Governors' Association.

DR GEORGE OLIVER (1781–1861): Historian and antiquary.

RAMON PAEZ: Son of the first President of Venezuela. Illustrator and travel writer. At Stonyhurst in 1840–1.

SIR BERNARD PARTRIDGE (1861–1945): *Punch* cartoonist.

AIR-CHIEF-MARSHAL HUBERT LEONARD PATCH (1904–87): Chief of RAF Fighter Command.

FR EDWARD PETRE SJ (1631–1699): Privy Councillor under James II.

FR CHARLES PLATER SJ (1875–1920): Founder of the Catholic Social Guild.

JONATHAN PLOWRIGHT (b. 1961): Concert pianist.

JOSEPH PLUNKETT (1888–1916): Irish rebel/patriot. Shot for his leading part in the Easter Rising.

SIR BERNARD PARTRIDGE

PAUL POTTS (1911–90): Bohemian poet and critic.

COL CHARLES REIDY (b. 1912): Soldier and sportsman, Irish Rugby international.

JOSEPH REIDY (1907–91): Plastic surgeon, specialist in treatments for the nose, palate and cleft lip. Played Rugby for the Barbarians against the All Blacks in 1935.

FR JOSEPH RICKABY, SJ (1845–1932): Philosopher and spiritual writer.

JAMES RODWAY (1914–98): President of the Rotary Club from 1947.

AMBROSE ROOKWOOD (c.1580–1606): Gunpowder plotter.

EDWARD L DE ROMANA at Stonyhurst 1899–1903: President of Peru.

MANUEL ROMERO DE TERREROS Y VINCENT, MARQUES DE SAN FRANCISCO: at Stonyhurst 1891–1900. Mexican author and scholar.

MERVYN F RYAN (1898–1952): Managing Director of the Buenos Aires and Pacific Railway 1945–8. Chairman of the Railway Executive in Buenos Aires on nationalisation in 1948. This meant that he was in charge of the entire Argentine railway network.

FR LOUIS SABRAN SJ (1652–1732): Chaplain to James III (the Old Pretender).

HERBERT SAYERS (1911–43): Irish Rugby international.

RICHARD LALOR SHEIL (1791–1851): Orator, playwright and politician. As Master of the Mint he issued the first florins without the legend 'Defensatrix Fidei, Dei Gloria'.

FR WALTER SIDGREAVES SJ, FRAS (1837–1919): Astronomer.

REAR-ADMIRAL SIR MATTHEW SLATTERY (1902–90): Chairman of Short Brothers, Bristol Aircraft and BOAC.

CHARLES STURRIDGE (b. 1951): Actor and Producer; best known for his TV production of *Brideshead Revisited*.

FRANCIS L SULLIVAN (1903–56): Actor; films included *Great Expectations*, where he played Mr Jaggers, and *Oliver Twist*, in which he was Mr Bumble.

SQUADRON-LEADER F R D SWAIN (OS 1919): Achieved the world altitude record of 49,967 ft. on 28 Sept 1936.

JOHN TALBOT, 16th Earl of Shrewsbury (1791–1852): Patron of the arts.

MARK THOMPSON (b. 1957): Controller of BBC2 (1996); Director or Regional and National Broadcasting (1999); Chief Executive at Channel 4 (2002): Director General of the BBC (2005).

SIR ROGER TICHBORNE (1829–54?): Central figure in the Tichborne Trial during which a 'claimant' from Wagga Wagga, Australia attempted to prove his right to the Tichborne inheritance.

MICHAEL TRAPPES LOMAX (1900–72) Novelist, historian and biographer. Somerset Herald.

WILLIAM TOBIN (1859–1904). Played Cricket for Australia in 1879 while still a pupil at Stonyhurst.

SIR FRANCIS ARTHUR TURNER (1912–91): First engineer to become a full Admiral in the Royal Navy. Specialist in aeronautical engineering pioneering the introduction of planned maintenance for naval aircraft.

SIR EDGAR UNSWORTH (b. 1906): Chief

Justice of Nyasaland, 1962–64, and of Gibraltar, 1965–76.

FRANCIS URQUHART (1868–1934): Dean of Balliol College, Oxford.

FR BERNARD VAUGHAN SJ (1832–1922): Preacher.

HERBERT CARDINAL VAUGHAN (1832–1903): Archbishop of Westminster.

HERBERT WALKER. Attended Stonyhurst in 1880–2: Golfer (the Walker Cup was established after him), grandfather of President George Bush.

SIR JOSEPH WALTON (1845–1910): Judge. Chairman of the General Council of the Bar.

GENERAL (retired) VERNON ANTHONY WALTERS (1917–2002): US Presidential advisor and diplomat. Held numerous positions including those of Deputy Director of the CIA (1972–6). Special Presidential Envoy and Ambassador-at-Large (1981–5). UN Ambassador for the USA (1985–9) and US Ambassador in Bonn (1989–91). His autobiography, *Silent Missions*, describes much of his fascinating career.

CHARLES WATERTON (1782–1865): Naturalist, eccentric and traveller.

SIR FREDERICK WELD (1823–1891): Prime Minister of New Zealand in 1864. Played a major part in calming the Maori disturbances there. Governor of Western Australia 1869–75 and Governor of Tasmania 1875.

GEORGE WELD SJ (1883–1959): Bishop, Vicar-Apostolic of British Guiana and Barbados 1932–54.

HERBERT WELD (1852–1935): Yachtsman.

SIR JOSEPH WELD (1909–1992): Public servant in the West Country. In his lifetime the head of the family which gave the Stonyhurst property to the College.

SIR JOHN WHYATT (1905–78): Chief Justice of Singapore.

PAUL WOODROFFE (1875–1954): book illustrator, stained glass artist and typographer. He designed the stained glass for the Lady Chapel at St Patrick's Cathedral in New York; at Stonyhurst his work can be seen in the Sodality Chapel.

STEPHEN WOULFE (1787–1840): Chief Baron of the Irish Court of Exchequer. He was the first Catholic raised to the Bench after the grant of emancipation.

JOHN G WYNNE-WILLIAMS (1912–77): Businessman. Managing Director of Pepsodent at the age of 24; manager of Mappins, a major department store in Sao Paolo, Brazil 1946–52; Chairman, Managing Director and majority shareholder of Masius Wynne-Williams advertising agency.

SIR THOMAS WYSE (1792–1862): Politician. Closely involved in the Don Pacifico affair and other aspects of Greek politics. Privy Councillor.

Appendix A: Rectors, Presidents and Headmasters of St Omers, Bruges, Liège and Stonyhurst College

St Omers

Superior

William Flack	1593

Rectors

Jean Foucart	1594
Gilles Schondonch	1600
Philippe Dennetiers	1617
William Baldwin	1621
Thomas Worsley	1632
Thomas Port	1636
Edward Courtenay	1646
Henry More	1649
Charles D'Arcy	1652
Thomas Babthorpe	1656
Henry More*	1657
Richard Barton	1660
Thomas Carey	1669
Richard Ashby	1672
Thomas Stapleton	1679
John Warner	1683
Michael Constable	1688
Edward Petre	1693
William Walton	1697
Henry Humberton	1701
Edward Slaughter	1705
Richard Plowden	1709
Lewis Sabran	1712
Francis Powell	1715
William Darell	1720
John Turbeville	1721
James Gooden	1722
Richard Plowden*	1725
Richard Hyde	1728
Thomas Eccleston	1731
Marmaduke Constable	1737
Percy Plowden	1739
Richard Hyde*	1742
Charles Wells	1745
Nathaniel Elliott	1748
John Darell	1752
Francis Scarisbrick	1759

Bruges

Nathaniel Elliott*	1762
Thomas Lawson (Jun.)	1766
Thomas Stanley	1769
Thomas Angier	1772

Liège

Director

John Howard	1773

Presidents

William Strickland	1783
Marmaduke Stone	1790

Stonyhurst

Presidents

Marmaduke Stone	1794
Nicholas Sewall	1808
John Weld	1813
Nicholas Sewall*	1816

Rectors

Charles Plowden	1817
Joseph Tristram	1819
Richard Norris	1827
Richard Parker	1832
James Brownbill	1836
Francis Daniel	1839
Andrew Barrow	1841
Richard Norris*	1845
Henry Walmesley	1846
Richard Sumner	1847
Francis Clough	1848
Joseph Johnson	1861
Charles Henry	1868
Edward Purbrick	1869
William Eyre	1879
Reginald Colley	1885
Herman Walmesley	1891
Joseph Browne	1898
Pedro Gordon	1906

William Bodkin	1907
Edward O'Connor	1916
Walter Weld	1924
Richard Worsley	1929
Edward O'Connor*	1932
Leo Belton	1938
Bernard Swindells	1945
Francis Vavasour	1952
Desmond Boyle	1958
David Hoy	1964
Thomas Dunphy	1971
William Broderick	1977
David Hoy*	1980
Michael O'Halloran	1984

Father Superiors

Michael O'Halloran	1988
Michael Bossy	1993
Michael Flannery	1998
Denis Blackledge	2004

Acting Superior

Adrian Howell	2003 and 2005

Jesuit Headmasters

Frederick Turner	1961
George Earle	1963
Michael Bossy	1972

Lay Headmasters

Giles Mercer	1985
Adrian Aylward	1996
Andrew Johnson	2006

* Second term as Rector.

Headmasters of Hodder and St Mary's Hall Preparatory Schools

Superiors		Ministers: SMH		Ministers: Hodder	
George Lambert	1856	Dermot Whyte	1946	Oswald Fishwick	1949
George Tickell	1857	Philip Prime	1948	John Firth	1959
John Laurenson	1858	William Maher	1954		
Francis Brownbill	1865	Anthony Powell	1959	*Lay Headmasters*	
Matthew Newsham	1869			Denis Unsworth	1965
Walter Bridge	1875			Rob. Sinclair	1969
Francis Cassidy	1876	*Lay Headmasters*		John Mallinson	1970
William Kerr	1878	R Vaughan Rigby OS	1965		
Francis Scoles	1880	Rae Carter	1968	Hodder thereafter integrated with	
William Burns	1882	Peter Anwyl	1978	SMH as a playroom with their	
Charles Clarke	1884	Rory O'Brien OS	1990	own Spiritual Father.	
Francis Cassidy	1885	Michael Higgins	1999		
Edward King	1916	Laurence Crouch OS	2004		
Walter Weld	1916				
Aloysius Parkinson	1925				
Leo Belton	1927				
Hubert McEvoy	1939				
Walter Weld	1942–9				

Appendix B: Chronology

The College Overseas

1582   Preparatory School at Eu founded as a feeder for the Rheims Seminary.

1593   Foundation.

1593   29 May 'Foundation Deed' of the College issued by Count Mansfeld granting the first Spanish Pension. Purchase of the Hôtel du Comte de Fressin.

1599   New Spanish Pension granted by Philip III of Spain. Constitutions drawn up.

1607   Chapel dedicated to St Thomas of Canterbury opened.

1608   St Omers Press started.
        First 'Great Academies' and prize-giving.

1609   Sodality founded.
        Opening of the new church built by Fr Schondonch.

1614   St Omers boys cease to be taught at the Walloon College.

1621   Fr Baldwin, the first English Rector, appointed.

1635   Outbreak of war with France. Boys requisitioned to repair St Omer town walls.

1638   French besiege St Omer.

1645   Number of boys falls to 24.

1677   French forces capture St Omer.

1678   St Omer ceded to France.
        Expulsion of Titus Oates.

1679   St Omers boys give testimony in the trials of Catholics and Jesuits accused by Oates.

1680   French Pension granted by Louis XIV to replace the Spanish Pension.

1684   St Omers boys testify in the trial of Oates for libel and perjury.
        First great fire.

1688   Bona Mors confraternity founded.

1711   Charles Dodd's *History of the College of Doway* published.

1714   Thomas Hunter's *Modest Defence of the Clergy and Religion* published.

1725   Second great fire.

1727   Rebuilding of the College completed.

1742   Preparatory school established outside Boulogne.

1748   Preparatory school moved to Watten outside St Omer.

1762   Migration to Bruges. St Omers buildings taken over by the English secular clergy.

1763   Preparatory school migrates to Bruges.

1768   New buildings erected for the Preparatory school or Little College at Bruges.

1773   Forcible shutdown of the Great College at Bruges. Remnants migrate to Liège.

1775   Closure of the Little College at Bruges.

1778   Pope Pius VI recognises the Liège Academy in the brief *Catholici Praesules*.

1782   Application by the Liège Academy to affiliate with the Russian Jesuits refused.

1792   French troops billeted in the Liège Academy during their temporary occupation of the town.

1794   Migration of the Liège Academy to Stonyhurst. Closure of the school run by Secular Priests at St Omer.

The College at Stonyhurst

1796	Playground laid out.
1799	Shirk built.
1800	Old North Wing built.
1803	Noviciate opened at Hodder.
1807	Preparatory school opened at Hodder.
1809	Thomas Weld gave the building and farm at Stonyhurst outright to the College.
1810	Old South Front built.
1811	Gas lighting installed.
1814	Society of Jesus restored by Pope Pius VII.
1821–27	Noviciate at Hodder suspended.
1827–29	Seminary built (St Mary's Hall).
1829	Society of Jesus recognised by the Papacy and bishops in England.
	Catholic Emancipation Act.
1832	Revision of the *Ratio Studiorum*.
1832–5	Construction of St Peter's Church.
1837	Donation of the Arundell library.
1838	Astronomical and meteorological Observatory built.
1840	Affiliation of Stonyhurst to the London Matriculation Examination system.
1842–3	Conversion of the coach-houses into Infirmary.
1843–4	Old North Wing on West Front demolished and new North Wing built.
1846	Gas plant transferred to Loach Field Wood.
1847	Gas plant installed at Hodder.
1850	Lady statue set up in (present) Pièta Gallery.
	First regular debating society established.
	Shrovetide plays begin.
	First Bathing Place constructed in the Park.
1851	New Washing Place below Refectory replaces stone troughs.
1851–2	Construction of Ambulacrum.
1854	First major Corpus Christi procession.
1855	Hodder formally opened as a preparatory school.
1853–6	Completion of the Front (Great) Quadrangle. Refectory extended and stone steps removed.
1853–7	New School Chapel opened (now the site of Rhetoric Common Room).
	New Community and Philosophers' Refectories opened.
	New Common Place constructed.
1857–9	Sodality Chapel built.
	Academic reforms of Fr Peter Gallwey.
1859	Bathing cots erected by Hodder Roughs.
1860	Stonyhurst Cricket Club founded.
	Tichborne Trial.
1861	Washing Place in Do Room extended.
1862	New kitchen block erected in Rear (Shireburn) Quadrangle.
	Refectory refloored with Sicilian marble.
	Iron railings replace high wall separating gardens from Playground.
1864–5	Cricket Oval laid out.
1866	Domed Observatory built. Magnetic chamber built below Old Observatory.
	New Kitchen block built.
1876	Playground levelled and enlarged.
1877–9	West Wing (of New South Front) built.
1879	The Stonyhurst Association founded.
1879–81	East Wing (of New South Front) built.
1880	Plunge opened.
1880–1	East and West Wings added to Seminary.
1881	*The Stonyhurst Magazine* founded.
	Stonyhurst Union Debating Society founded.
1882	Avenue Lady Statue erected.
1883	Central portion of the New South Front opened.
	Racquets courts built.
	Organ in St Peter's rebuilt.
1884	Association football introduced.
1885–9	Boys' Chapel built (although furnishing not completed till 1900).
	Old School Chapel converted into a museum.
1887	Lower Certificate exams introduced.
	Athletic sports introduced.
1888	Washing Place built.
1889	New Lady Statue set up on Chapel Landing.
1892	Tercentenary celebrations (actually a year early).
	Final disappearance of Stonyhurst Cricket.
1894	Centenary celebrations.
	Catholics allowed by the bishops to enter Oxbridge.
	Golf Links opened in the Park.
1894–5	New Higher Line Cricket Pavilion built.
1895	First football away match.
1896	Higher Certificate exams introduced.
1899	Sodality Chapel extended and Pièta removed to present site.
1900	Furnishing of the Boys' Chapel completed.
	Cadet Corps founded.
	Biology laboratory opened in Shirk.
1901	Stonyhurst football goalposts cut down.
1902	New Physics laboratory opened.
1906	Acetylene gas experimented with.
1908	Loco Vapour gas plant experimented with.
	Cadet Corps becomes OTC.
	Sanatorium established.
1911	Introduction of the 'Remove' system.
1914	Gym built.
1916	Last year of Philosophers.
1919	New style School Certificate introduced for Syntax.
1920	Catholic Evidence Guild founded.
1921	Rugby football replaces Association football.
	Committee established.
1920–2	Electricity plant built – replaces Gas lighting and heating.
1922	Miniature-rifle range built.
	War Memorial completed.
	Line system introduced.
1920–3	New Physics laboratories built above Gym.
1924	New laundry and servants' quarters introduced in Shireburn Quadrangle.
	Playroom membership based on age, rather than academic attainment.
1926	Seminary transferred to Heythrop. St Mary's Hall left empty.
1927	Organ in St Peter's replaced.
1933	More Library opened on the ground floor of the South Front.
	Racquets courts converted into squash courts.
1934	Plunge building extended.
1938	Prefects of Discipline renamed as Playroom Masters.
1940	OTC reorganised as the JTC (Junior Training Corps).
1940–6	English College at Rome migrates to St Mary's Hall.
1942	Iron railings removed from Playground as part of 'War effort'.
1946	St Mary's Hall opened as a preparatory school.
1948	Shireburn Almshouses re-erected in Hurst Green.

1955	Wrought Iron gates and oak doors installed in Gatehouse archway.
	Gym built in St Mary's Hall.
1957	Long Room becomes a Study Place; Waterton Collection transferred to Infirmary Gallery.
	500 boys at College, St Mary's Hall and Hodder.
1957–8	New Science laboratories built beyond the Gym.
1960	Sanatorium converted into a staff house.
1965	Closure of Beaumont announced.
1966	Opening of the Rhetoric Wing [building had begun in 1959].
	Study Place converted into the More Library.
	Advisory Council set up.
	Jesuit Community moved from West Wing to Shirk; Syntax moves to West Wing.
	First three-day Great Academies and first half-term holidays.
	First lay Director of Studies and Bursar.
	Lease of the College Farm.
1967	New classroom block completed (Chemistry and Biology on ground floor).
	Waterton Collection loaned to Wakefield Museum.
1969	Governing Body developed from Advisory Council.
1970	500 boys in the College.
	New self-service refectory built on ground floor below Arundell Library.
1971	Lescher tennis courts opened.
	First Girl pupil.
	Hodder boys absorbed into St Mary's Hall.
	HLHCT (now the SCHT) formed.
1973	Stonyhurst Charitable Fund established.
	Pièta classroom converted into Audio-Visual Room.
1974	Chapel Library and Museum converted into the present Rhetoric Common Room.
1979	Foundation of Stonyhurst Park Golf Club.
1980	Washing Place converted into the Campion Room.
1981	Grammar and Lower Grammar playrooms renovated.
1981–5	Rooms Master system tried out in Higher Line.
1983–4	New kitchens built. Old kitchen area converted into a staff Refectory.
1983	First overseas Rugby tour (to Canada).
1984	New Sports Hall built at St Mary's Hall.
1985	Dr Mercer – the first lay Headmaster – appointed.
1987	New swimming-pool built. Old Plunge converted into changing rooms.
	Foundation of Stonyhurst Sports Club (swimming and squash).
	Rooms for Poetry boys established in Shireburn Quadrangle.
1988	Opening of the Design and Technology Centre.
1989	Official announcement of Stonyhurst as a co-educational school. Girls admitted to Higher Line only.
	Conversion of Grammar Ia classroom into the first major IT centre.
1990	Queen Elizabeth II visits the College and presents new Guidon to the Duke of Lancaster's Own Yeomanry.
1991	Centenaries Appeal launched.
1992	Governing body reorganised with separate committees for Stonyhurst, St Mary's Hall and St John's Beaumont.
1993	Four-hundredth anniversary of the founding of St Omers celebrated.
	Renovation of the Ambulacrum and Common Place.
1993–4	Renovation of the Shireburn Quadrangle and Bread Room to accommodate separate subject teaching areas for English, Classics, Modern Languages and Geography.
	New specialised subject teaching areas created in various areas within the College.
1994	Two-hundredth anniversary of the migration to Stonyhurst celebrated.
	Opening of the Centenaries Theatre.
	'New Teaching Block' renovated and remodelled, renamed the Favretto Building, with Chemistry on the ground floor and Biology on the first floor.
	Renovation of the Art Department.
1996	Great Academies arrangements modified.
	Health Centre relocated to Shireburn Quadrangle.
	Former Health Centre (in Old Infirmary building) converted into Sixth Form Girls Wing.
1998	Archery attic in St Mary's Hall converted into Girls boarding accommodation.
1995–9	Renovation of the Top Refectory.
1998–9	Gerard Room (former Jesuit Refectory) converted into Higher Line IT workshop.
1999	Girls in Lower Grammar (with some others in remainder of Lower Line).
	Networking of Rhetoric and most academic departments.
	SMH Gym extended and new changing rooms added.
	Academy Room made available for concerts open to the general public following the insertion of a new (and very expensive) fire escape.
'99–2000	Top floor of the West Wing refurbished.
2000	Dormitories 5, 6, and Alaska (room between them and Poetry Common Room) opened for boarding girls.
2000–1	New all-weather pitch created on Harry Meadow.
'98–2001	New Eagles fitted to 'Eagle Towers'.
2002	Old Infirmary building converted for use by day pupils.
	SMH Library refurbished as The Tolkien Library.
	Stonyhurst Website set up.
2000–3	Improvements to Basement, including most music areas and the creation of showers and changing rooms for Lower Line girls.
	Old Plunge building converted into Lower Line and visitors' changing rooms, boarding accommodation for Lower Grammar boys with link corridor to Bottom Gallery (of South Front).
2003	Bicentenary of restoration of Society of Jesus at Stonyhurst.
	Access Appeal launched.
2003–4	Renovation and modernisation of The More Library.
2004	Opening of Hodder house at SMH (for pre-school age children).
2005	Visit by 37 Jesuit Provincials.
2006	Jesuit community moved from Shirk to the Old Infirmary building.
	Sixth Form Girls accommodation extended to the renovated Shirk building.
	Sodality Chapel renovated by The Stonyhurst Association.

Appendix C: Tables and Statistics

Table 1. Jesuit Organisation

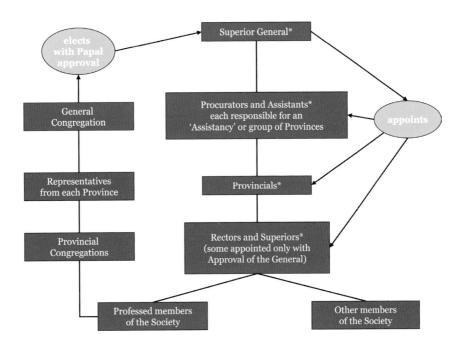

*Advised by Consultors (Socii) chosen from their Subordinates

Table 2. The St Omers Staff in 1618

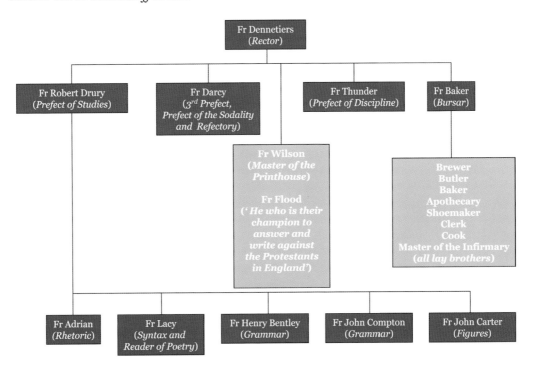

(Source: James Wadsworth, *The English Spanish Pilgrim* 1629.)

Table 3. Weekday Timetable from the Ratio Studiorum

		First hour	Second hour	Last half-hour
Morning	**Rhetoric**	1 – Recitals from memory. 2 – Decurians correct work while classes do exercises. 3 – Go over previous prelection.	Prelection concentrating on either the precepts or the working of the oration itself.	
	Poetry	1 – Cicero & art of versification recited by heart to the Decurians. 2 – Correct written work while students do exercises.	1– Brief examination of previous prelection. 2 – New prelection explained and then recited. 3 – Concertatio.	History and art of versification on alternate days.
	Grammar Classes	Correction of work while class does exercises.	1 – Revision of prelection. 2 – Do a new prelection. 3 – Theme dictated.	1 – New lesson started. 2 – Concertatio.

		First hour	Second hour	Last half-hour
Afternoon	**Rhetoric**	1 – Repetition of previous prelection. 2 – New prelection based on an oration. 3 – Repetition.	1 – Repeat previous lesson on a Greek author. 2 – New lesson began and recited. 3 – Either correction of work or a Greek Concertatio.	Greek syntax and versification.
	Poetry	1 – Poetry or Greek author recited from memory. 2 – Correction of written work assigned in the morning. 3 – Dictation of a theme.	1 – Review and explanation of some poet. 2 – Greek prelection and writing.	Same as 2nd hour.
	Grammar Classes	Correction of work while class does exercises.	1 – Revision of prelection. 2 – Do a new prelection. 3 – Theme dictated.	Same as morning.

Table 4. Saturday Timetable from the Ratio Studiorum

	Morning		Afternoon		
	First hour	**Second hour**			
Rhetoric	Explain a historian or poet.	*Either* Declamation or prelection by a student *or* Hear a lecture *or* Concertatio.	1 – Explain a poet. 2 – Review of Greek studies.		
			Half-hour	**Half-hour**	**Half-hour**
Poetry	1 – Recite prelections of the entire week from memory. 2 – Review prelections of the entire week from memory. 3 – *Either* Hold a declamation or a prelection *or* Listen to a lecture *or* Concertatio.		Poet and Catechism recited from memory while the master examines written studies and checks the marks sent in by the Decurians.	a) Review of any Latin poet. b) Review of any Greek poet.	Explanation of the Catechism.

Table 5. Curriculum specified by the Ratio Studiorum

Rhetoric	Precepts of Oratory, Style and Erudition taught from Cicero, Quintilian and Aristotle. Style to be taught only from Cicero: erudition to be taught from History, the custom of the Tribes (of Israel) and Spiritual Authority.
Poetry	Oratory – Cicero only. History – Caesar, Sallust, Livy, Curtius. Poets – Virgil, except the *Aeneid*, Bk. IV and the *Eclogues*.
Upper Grammar	Cicero – Letters, *De Amicitia*, *De Seneatute*, Paradoxes. Ovid – Elegies and letters. Selections from Catullus, Tibullus, Propertius, *Eclogues* of Virgil (4th *Georgic*), St Chrysostum, Aesop, Agapetus.
Middle Grammar	Epistle of Cicero, *Ad Familiares* only. Easter poems of Ovid. Greek Catechism. Tabula of Cubes.

Table 6. Grammar Teaching as specified by the Ratio Studiorum

Class	Greek		Latin: Grammar of Emmanuel Alvarez	
Upper Grammar (Syntax)	Remaining parts of speech and rest of rudiments.		Other appendices and 3rd Book dealing with the meaning of syllables.	
Middle Grammar	Contract verbs. Circumflex verbs. Verbs as μ.		Book 2 on the construction of eight parts of speech up to figured speech and easy appendices.	
Lower Grammar (Rudiments and Figures)	First elements – nouns, substantive verbs, simple verbs.		Book I and introduction to Syntax from Book II.	
	Upper Division	Simple Greek nouns. Substantive verb. Baritone verb.	Upper Division	See 1 (below).
	Lower Division	Learn to write Greek.	Lower Division	See 2 (below).

1. (a) Declensions of nouns without appendices: perits and supines from Book I.
   (b) Introduction to Book II on syntax up to impersonal verbs without appendices.
2. Nouns, verbs, rudiments and 14 rules of construction and kinds of nouns from the first book of grammar.

Table 7. Class Names in Jesuit Education

Ratio Studiorum	Walloon College Register 1612–14	St Omers in 1622	Douai College in the 18th Century (Lower Studies)	Stonyhurst in 1804	Stonyhurst and St Mary's Hall in 1991	Stonyhurst and St Mary's Hall in 2004
Rhetoric Humanities Upper Grammar Middle Grammar Lower Grammar	Rhetoric Poetry Syntax Grammar Figures	Rhetoric Humanities First Grammar Second Grammar Third Grammar	Rhetoric Poetry Syntax Grammar Higher Figures Lower Figures	Rhetoric Poetry Syntax Grammar Rudiments Figures Elements Preparatory (in Hodder)	Rhetoric Poetry Syntax Grammar Lower Grammar Rudiments Upper Figures Lower Figures Elements Preparatory	*College* Rhetoric Poetry Syntax Grammar Lower Grammar *St Mary's Hall* Rudiments Upper Figures Lower Figures Upper Elements Lower Elements Preparatory *Hodder House* Pre-prep 2 (KS1) Pre-prep 1 (KS1) Reception (Foundation Nursery)

Table 8. The St Omers Routine

5.00: Rise
5.30: Mass

6.00–7.00: Morning Studies

7.00–7.15: Breakfast

7.30–10.00: Schools:
One hour correcting themes
One hour devoted to Latin authors
Half-hour on a Concertatio

10.15–11.00: Studies

11.00–11.30: Lunch

11.30–12.30: Recreation
12.30–1.30: Studies
1.45–4.30: Schools
4.30–6.30: Night Studies

6.30–7.00: Supper

7.00–8.00: Recreation
8.00–8.30: Studies
8.30–8.45: Night Prayers
9.00: Lights Out

Half-holidays on Tuesdays and Thursdays
Sundays: Mass: 7.00
High Mass: 10.00
Vespers: Mid-afternoon
Litanies of Our Lady: 8.00 pm

Table 9. The Size of St Omers

	Boys	Community
1610	135	21
1615	about 130	27
1621	121	24
1635 beginning	200	25
1635 end	140	About 26
1636	140–150, falling to 115	29
1642	123	27
1645	24	12
1648	60	18
1649	90 (no Poetry class)	20
1651	109–110	22
1653	126	21
1655	140	22
1658	136	21
1670	140	?
1673	140	27
1674	120	27
1677	124	31
1684	78	28
1685	80	26
1690	134	32
1700	100	?
1705	80	26
1711	111	29
1714	123	27
1715	146	29
1723	113	?
1726	80	?
1727	96	27
1737	125	28
1740	105	28
1743	88	31

Sources:

H. Foley. *Records of the English Province* Vol. VII, Pt. 1 & 2, Burns & Oates, 1882–3. *Analytical Catalogue*, lxxi–cxxxv; *Temporal Returns*, cxxxix–clxviii and St Omers Annual Letters 1155–76. Note that in some cases there are discrepancies between these sources. The figures for 1642 are from H. Chadwick, *St Omers to Stonyhurst*, p. 164.

Table 10. St Omers' Income

	Scudi
1628	13,407
1636	17,884
1642	15,254
1645	6,040
1649	8,760
1651	10,560
1655	10,560
1658	11,670
1672	16,924
1685	9,072
1705	6,207
1711	8,795
1714	11,325
1727	6,968
1737	9,641
1740	5,328
1743	9,799

Sources: As for Table 9.

Table 11. The Ordination of English Priests

1558–1600	1600–1700	1701–1800
Secular Priests 613 Society of Jesus 166 Dominicans 9 Others 87	Secular Priests 1319 Society of Jesus 819 Dominicans 82 Benedictines 420 Franciscans 222	Secular Priests 766 Society of Jesus 536 Dominicans 82 Benedictines 269 Franciscans 154 Others 73
875	3056	1878

Source: Fr T. Clancy, 'Priestly Perseverance in the Old Society of Jesus', *Recusant History*, 19/3 (May 1989).

Select Bibliography

General Background

Basset, B, SJ: *The English Jesuits*, Burns & Oates, 1966.
Beales, A: *Education under Penalty*, Athlone Press, 1963.
Bossy, J: *The English Catholic Community 1570–1850*, Darton, Longman & Todd, 1975.
Caraman, P, SJ: *Ignatius Loyola*, Collins, 1990.
Edwards, F, SJ: *The Jesuits in England*, Burns & Oates, 1985.
Fitzgerald, E (ed.): *St Ignatius and the Ratio Studiorum* (containing a translation by A Ball of Part IV of the *Constitutions* and *Ratio Studiorum*), McGraw-Hill, 1933.
Graffius, J (ed): *The Rubens Engravings of the Life of St Ignatius* (containing a translation by W Yeoman SJ of the *Autobiography* of St Ignatius, introduction and prayers by W Hewett SJ, and article by J Graffius. St Omers Press, Stonyhurst, 2005.
Hastings, A: *A History of English Christianity 1920–85*, Collins, 1986.
Hicks, L, SJ (ed): *The Letters and Memorials of Fr Robert Persons SJ, Vol 1 1578–88*, Catholic Record Society, No. 39, 1942.
Mottola, A (trans): *The Spiritual Exercises of St Ignatius*, Doubleday, 1964.
Norman, E: *The English Catholic Church in the Nineteenth Century*, Clarendon Press, 1984.
Pollen, J. H, SJ: *The Memoirs of Fr Persons*, Catholic Record Society, No. 2, 1905.
Renold, P: *The Wisbech Stirs*, Catholic Record Society, No. 51, 1958.
Scott, G, OSB: *Gothic Rage Undone: The English Monks in the Age of Enlightenment.* Downside Abbey, 1992.

Stonyhurst and St Omers

Bence-Jones, M: *The Catholic Families*. London. Constable, 1992.
Berkeley, J: *Lulworth and the Welds*, Blackmore Press, 1971.
Chadwick, H, SJ: *St Omers to Stonyhurst*, Burns & Oates, 1962.
Gerard, J, SJ: *Stonyhurst Centenary Record*, Marcus Ward & Co. Ltd, 1894.
Graffius, J: *A Stonyhurst Museum Guide.* Stonyhurst. N.d.
Gruggen, G, SJ & Keating, J, SJ: *Stonyhurst: Its Past History and Life in the Present*, Kegan Paul, Trench, Trubner & Co., 1901.
Henderson, A: *The Stone Phoenix: Stonyhurst College 1794–1894*, Churchman Publishing, 1896.
Holt, TG, SJ: *The English Jesuits in the Age of Reason.* London. Burns and Oates. 1993.
——: *William Strickland and the Suppressed Jesuits*, British Province of the Society of Jesus, 1988.
Hoy, D, SJ: *The Story of St John's Beaumont 1888–1988*, St John's Beaumont, 1987.
Kirby, H, & Walsh, R: *The Seven VCs of Stonyhurst College*, THCL Books, 1987.
Muir, T: *Stonyhurst through Documents*, 4th edn., Stonyhurst College, 1988.
Sire, H J A: *Gentlemen Philosophers: Catholic Higher Education at Liège and Stonyhurst 1774–1916*, Churchman Publishing, 1988.

Technical Works

Bellenger, A, OSB: *English and Welsh Priests 1559–1800*, Downside Abbey, 1984.
Foley, H, SJ: *Records of the English Province*, Vols. 1–7, Burns & Oates, 1877–83.
Gillow, J (ed): *Records of the Abbey of Our Lady of Consolation at Cambrai 1620–1793*, Catholic Record Society, No. 13, ch 1, 1913.
Hanson, J (ed): *Register Book of the Professions of the English Nuns at Brussels and Winchester and now at East Bergholt 1598–1856*, Catholic Record Society, No. 14, ch. 3, 1914.
Holt, TG, SJ: *English Jesuits 1650–1829. A Biographical Dictionary*, Catholic Record Society, No. 70, 1984.
——: *St Omers and Bruges Lists 1593–1773. A Biographical Dictionary*, Catholic Record Society, No. 69, 1979.
Hunnybun, W, & Gillow, J (eds): *Registers of the Poor Clares at Gravelines etc. 1608–1837*, Catholic Record Society, No. 14, ch. 2, 1914.
Irwin, F, & Chichester-Constable, Capt: *Stonyhurst War Record*, Stonyhurst College, 1927.
Kenny, A (ed): *The Responsa Scholarum of the English College, Rome*, Pts. 1 and 2, Catholic Record Society, Nos. 54 and 55, 1962 and 1963.
McCoog, T, SJ: *English and Welsh Jesuits 1555–1650.* Catholic Record Society, Vols 74 (1994) and 75 (1995).
Trappes-Lomax, R: *Boys at Liège Academy 1773–91*, Catholic Record Society, No. 13, ch. 7, 1913.
Walsh, R: *Stonyhurst College War Record 1939–45*, THCL Books 1989 (supplement added in 1990).

Further References

Introduction

Wadsworth, J: *Memoirs*, 1679.

Chapter 1

Bossy, J: 'The Society of Jesus and the Wars of Religion', *Monastic Studies I*, Headstart History, 1990.
Dickens, AG: *The English Reformation*, Batsford, 1964.
More, H, SJ: *Historia Provinciae Anglicanae Soc. Jesu Anglia*, St Omers 1660; trans. By Edwards, Francis SJ under the title *The Elizabethan Jesuits*, Phillimore Publ, 1981.
Hicks, L, SJ: 'The Foundation of the College of St Omers', *AHSJ*, 19 (1950).
——: *The Letters and Despatches of Richard Verstegan 1550–1640*, Catholic Record Society, No. 52, 1959.

Jessopp, A (ed.): *The Letters of Henry Walpole SJ*, Norwich, 1873.

Jones, N L: 'Faith by Statute', *Royal Historical Studies in History*, 32 (1982).

Neale, J E: *Elizabeth and her Parliaments*, Vol. 2, Jonathan Cape, 1957.

Scott, W (ed.): *Somers Tracts*, Vol. 1, London, 1809.

Simon, J: *Education and Society in Tudor England*, Cambridge University Press, 1966.

Chapter 2

Johnson, P: 'Stonyhurst in the 1940s', *The Stonyhurst Magazine*, Vol. 45, No. 485, 198.

Chapter 3

Holt, TG, SJ (ed.): *The Sabran Letter Book 1713–15*, Catholic Record Society, No. 62, 1971.

Pollen, J H, SJ (ed.): *The Bedingfeld Papers*, Catholic Record Society, No. 7, 1909.

Warner, J, SJ: *The History of the English Persecution of Catholics and of the Presbyterian Plot* (ed Birrell, T), Catholic Record Society, Nos. 47 and 48, 1953 and 1954.

Chapter 4

Callow, J: 'The last of the Shireburns. "The art of death and life in recusant Lancashire", 1660–1754'. *Recusant History*. 26/4 (Oct 2003) 589–615.

Caraman, P, SJ (ed.): *Autobiography of John Gerard*, Longmans, 1951.

Clancy, T, SJ: 'Spiritual Publications of the Jesuits 1615–40', *Recusant History*, Vol. 19, No. 4 (Oct. 1981).

Chadwick, H, SJ: 'The Problem of Peregrine', *The Stonyhurst Magazine*, Vol. 29, No. 373.

Holt, TG, SJ: 'Free Places at the English College of St Omers and Bruges and at the Liège Academy', *AHSJ*, 53 (1983).

Hunter, T, SJ: *A Modest Defence of the Clergy and Religious etc.*, St Omer, 1714.

Tootell, H (under pseudonym Dodd, C): *A History of the College of Doway etc.*, 1713.

————: *The Secret Policy of the Jesuits*, 1716.

Chapter 5

Holt, TG, SJ: The Fatal Mortgage: The English Province and Père La Valette', *AHSJ*, No. 38 (1969).

Dolman, A H: *Much Love and Great Sadness: Memories of a Catholic Lady of Herefordshire 1810–51* (ed Reeves, N), 1988.

Trappes-Lomax, R: *The Expenses of Walter Tempest*, Catholic Record Society, No. 13, 1913.

Whitehead, M: 'In the sincerest intention of studying': The educational legacy of Thomas Weld (1756–1814). *Recusant History (Essays in honour of Geoffrey Holt)* 26/1 (May, 2002): 169–193.

Chapter 6

Waterton, C *Wanderings in South America* (ed Bellamy, D), Century Publishing, 1983.

Chadwick, H, SJ: 'The Paccanarists in England', *AHSJ*, Vol. 20 (1951).

Edwards, P, SJ: *Canute's Tower St Beuno's*, Gracewing Books, 1990 (for the quotation from Gerard Manley Hopkins).

Hewitson, A: *Stonyhurst College. Past and Present*, Preston, 1878.

Sire, H J A: 'The Collapse of Stonyhurst 1816–22', *The Stonyhurst Magazine*, Vol. 46, No. 486 (Autumn 1990).

Chapter 7

Fitzgerald, P: *Stonyhurst Memories*, Bentley & Son, 1895.

————: *Schooldays at Saxonhurst*, 1st edn., 1867 (also cited in Ch. 8).

Kenealy, E V (ed.): *The Tichborne Trial 1873–4*, 6 vols, The Englishman's Office, London, 1875.

Chapter 10

Rafferty, O P: 'The English Jesuit College, Manchester 1875', *Recusant History*, Vol. 20, No. 2 (1990), ch. 10.

Brigg, M (ed): *A Lancashire Weaver's Journal 1856–64, 1872–5* by John O'Neil, Record Society of Lancashire and Cheshire, Vol. 122 (1982).

Whitehead, M: 'Education and correct conduct': Randall Lythgoe and the work of the Society of Jesus in Early Victorian England and Wales' in S Gilley, ed.: *Victorian Churches and Churchmen. Essays presented to Vincent Alan McClelland*. Catholic Record Society/The Boydell Press. 2005: 75–93.

Chapter 11

Flory, H C, & Turner, F, SJ: 'Stonyhurst in the 1920s', *The Stonyhurst Magazine*, Vol. 45, No. 483 (Autumn 1987).

Hewett, W, SJ: 'Stonyhurst in the 1940s', *The Stonyhurst Magazine*, Vol. 45, No. 484 (Autumn 1988).

Holland, V (OS 1898–1904): *Son of Oscar Wilde*, London, 1954.

Macdonald Hastings, D: *Jesuit Child*, Readers' Union, Newton Abbot, 1972.

Chapter 12

Campbell-Johnson, M, SJ: 'The Preferential Option for the Poor', *The Stonyhurst Magazine*, Vol. 45, No. 484 (Autumn 1988).

Hardwick, P R, (ed.): 'The Characteristics of Jesuit Education': *The Stonyhurst Magazine*, Vol. 45, No. 483 (Autumn 1987).

Index

LDS